Law in a New Key

Essays on Law and Society

Amitai Etzioni

Contemporary Society Series

qp

Quid Pro Books

New Orleans, Louisiana

Law in a New Key

Essays on Law and Society

Published by Quid Pro Books. Printed in the United States of America.

ISBN: 1610270444
ISBN-13: 9781610270441

Quid Pro Books
Quid Pro, LLC
5860 Citrus Blvd., Suite D-101
New Orleans, Louisiana 70123
www.quidprobooks.com

qp

Publisher's Cataloging-in-Publication

Etzioni, Amitai.

   Law in a new key: essays on law and society / Amitai Etzioni.

   p.   cm.
   Includes index.
   Series: *Contemporary Society.*

ISBN: 1610270444 (pbk.)
ISBN: 1610270436 (Kindle)
ISBN: 1610270428 (ePub)

1. Law—United States—Public Policy. 2. Social Values—United States. 3. Social Problems—United States. 4. Sociological Jurisprudence. 5. National Security—United States. 6. Communitarianism. I. Title. II. Series.

K370.E225 2010   340'.129'07—dc22

Other Books by Amitai Etzioni

New Common Ground: A New America, A New World (Dulles, Va.: Potomac Books, 2009)

Security First: For a Muscular, Moral Foreign Policy (New Haven, Conn.: Yale University Press, 2008)

From Empire to Community: A New Approach to International Relations (New York: Palgrave Macmillan, 2004)

How Patriotic is the Patriot Act? (New York: Routledge, 2004)

The Common Good (Cambridge, Mass.: Polity Press, 2004)

My Brother's Keeper: A Memoir and a Message (Lanham, Md.: Rowman & Littlefield, 2003)

The Monochrome Society (Princeton, N.J.: Princeton University Press, 2001)

Political Unification Revisited: On Building Supranational Communities (Lanham, Md.: Lexington Books, 2001)

The Limits of Privacy (New York: Basic Books, 1999)

The New Golden Rule: Community and Morality in a Democratic Society (New York: Basic Books, 1997)

The Spirit of Community: The Reinvention of American Society (New York: Touchstone Books, 1993)

The Moral Dimension: Toward a New Economics (New York: The Free Press, 1988)

A Comparative Analysis of Complex Organizations (New York: The Free Press, revised edition, 1975)

The Active Society: A Theory of Societal and Political Processes (New York: The Free Press, 1968)

Winning Without War (Garden City, N.Y.: Doubleday, 1964)

Contents

For the youngest Etzioni,

Michael-Lo

Law in a New Key

Essays on Law and Society

Preface

The essays collected in this book all examine various facets of the relationship between law and society, including norms and values, institutions, and communities. The approach is communitarian. Hence, first, a few lines about this branch of social philosophy.

Communitarianism maintains that society's articulation of that which is good is both needed and legitimate. Communitarianism is often contrasted with classical liberalism, a philosophical position that holds each individual should formulate the good on his or her own. Communitarians examine the ways shared conceptions of the good (values) are formed, transmitted, justified, and enforced.

Ideas that are communitarian in nature are found in the Old and New Testaments, Catholic theology (for example, the emphasis on the Church as community), and more recently in socialist doctrine (for example, writings about the early commune and about workers' solidarity) and in subsidiarity—the principle that looks to the lowest level of authority capable of organization at the community level rather than leading from the higher governing bodies. The term *communitarian* itself was only introduced in the middle of the 19th century.

Communitarians stress the importance of the social realm, and in particular of community, as compared to the state. Hence their interest in informal social controls, norms, and social responsibilities. They differ in the extent to which their conceptions are attentive to liberty and individual rights. Early communitarians, such as Ferdinand Tönnies and Robert Nisbet, stressed the importance of closely knit social fabric and authority. Asian communitarians are especially concerned about the values of social order. They argue that to maintain social harmony, individual rights and political liberties must be curtailed. Some seek to rely heavily on the state to maintain social order (for instance, leaders and champions of the regime in Singapore and Malaysia), and some on strong social bonds and moral culture (as Japan does). East Asian communitarians also hold that the West's notion of liberty actually amounts to anarchy; that strong economic growth requires limiting freedoms; and that the West uses its idea of legal and political rights to chastise other cultures that have inherent values of their own.

In response to the breakdown in the moral fabric of society engendered by excessive individualism, I, with William A. Galston, began in 1990 to organize working meetings to think through communitarian approaches to key societal issues. We, along with Mary Ann Glendon, Jean Bethke Elshtain, and other figures from academia and politics, issued a platform endorsed by a wide range of leading Americans. Deeming ourselves "responsive communitarians," we were careful to distinguish the movement from East Asian, authoritarian communitarians.

Communitarians pay much attention to the relationship between the self and the community. Political theorists such as Michael Sandel and Charles Taylor depict the self as "embedded," which implies that the self is constrained by the community. Responsive communitarians stress that individuals who are well-integrated into communities are better able to reason and act in responsible ways than isolated individuals, but add that if social pressure to conform rises to high levels, it will undermine the individual self.

Communitarians pay special attention to social institutions, several of which form the moral infrastructure of society: families, schools, communities, and the community of the development of the moral self. Schools' role is to further develop the moral self and to remedy moral development if it was neglected or distorted by the family. Communitarians pay attention to the civil society and not just the prescriptive state (concepts explored in chapter 11).

In addition, communitarians have noted that communities need to be embedded socially and morally in more encompassing entities if violent conflict among them is to be avoided. Society should not be viewed as composed of millions of individuals, but as pluralism (of communities) within unity (the society). The existence of subcultures does not undermine societal unity as long as there is a core of shared values and institutions (as applied, for example, in chapter 15 to minority cultures and religions).

While liberals tend to privilege individual (and human) rights, and social conservatives, the norms set by society and obligations of the members to society, responsive communitarians take it as their starting point that we face two fundamental normative claims, those of *rights* and those of *responsibilities* (as applied, for example, to privacy concerns with airport scanners in chapter 5 and DNA banks in chapter 8). Neither interest is *a priori* privileged or trumped by the other. This core assumption underlines and is elaborated in the essays here collected.

Finally, a communitarian like myself considers the law an extension of social values and norms by other means (a theme explored in chapter 10). Norm enforcement relies mainly on informal social controls. The law relies on the powers of the state. Society, ample evidence shows, functions best when the gap between the prevailing norms and laws is small. When the gap is considerable, laws are likely to be considered illegitimate or coercive, and to be violated. However the gap can be narrowed not merely by revising laws to fit the changing norms (say, re gay marriages), but moral dialogues can lead to a change in norms to move closer to laws already enacted (say, re racial desegregation in the South).

Each of the following chapters seeks to illuminate one of these communitarian propositions.

— *Amitai Etzioni*

Washington, D.C.
October 2010

SECTION I

Security and Rights

Chapter 1

Terrorists: Neither Soldiers nor Criminals

In current hostilities in Iraq, Afghanistan, parts of Pakistan, and elsewhere from Colombia to the Horn of Africa, non-state actors—in particular, terrorists and insurgents who behave like terrorists—play a much greater role than they did during WWI, WWII, and the Korean War. In those wars between states, the accepted rules of war, embodied in documents such as the Geneva Conventions, applied much more readily than in contemporary conflicts. Currently, conventional armies that seek to adhere to the rules of war are disadvantaged when they confront terrorists, which suggests that the rules of war need to be updated.

Changes to the rules of war would hardly be unprecedented. The First Geneva Convention dealing with the treatment of battlefield casualties did not exist until 1864, and since then, additional conventions have been agreed upon and other rules of war have been modified. The same holds for "international law," which some people invoke as if it were cast in stone and unambiguous—though it is actually neither. Indeed, even in well-established democratic societies, laws are constantly recast; for instance, there was no constitutional "right to privacy" in the United States until 1965,[1] and the way we now understand the First Amendment and the right to free speech was formed in the 1920s.[2] In both cases, no changes were made in the text of the United States Constitution, but new interpretations were employed to bring the Constitution—as a living document—in line with the normative precepts of changing times. Hence, it stands to reason that the new threats to security now posed by non-state actors—several of whom have a global reach, are supported by massive religious radical movements, and have potential access to weapons of mass destruction—require modifications in the interpretations, if not the texts, of the rules of war.

NEW CONDITIONS

Advocates of two major approaches to counterterrorism present strong opposition to the needed adaptations. On the one side are those who speak of a "war on terror," which implies that terrorists ought to be treated like soldiers who, under the current rules of war, can be detained without being charged or tried until the end of the war. Such was the position of the Bush Administration. In the words of former Bush Administration Attorney General Michael Mukasey:

> The United States has every right to capture and detain enemy combatants in this conflict, and need not simply release them to return to the battlefield... And although wars traditionally have come to an end that is easy to identify, no one can predict when this one will end or even how we'll know it's over....those differences do not make it any less important, or any less fair, for us to detain those who take up arms against us.[3]

On the other side are those who favor treating terrorists like criminals, endowed with the rights and privileges accorded to citizens of democratic societies who have been accused but not yet convicted of having committed a crime. This view is held by prominent figures like Harvard professor and Obama advisor Samantha Power. She criticized the Bush Administration for "branding the cause a war and calling the enemy terror" and "[lumping] like with unlike foes and [elevating] hostile elements from the ranks of the criminal (stigmatized in all societies) to the ranks of soldiers of war (a status that carries connotations of sacrifice and courage)."[4] General Wesley Clark stated that terrorists "are merely criminals, albeit criminals of an especially heinous type, and that label suggests the appropriate venue for dealing with the threats they pose."[5] This position has also been held by United Kingdom Prime Minister Gordon Brown's administration. Brown's Home Secretary, Jacqui Smith, stated: "Let us be clear, terrorists are criminals, whose victims come from all walks of life, communities and religions."[6]

The difficulties in characterizing terrorists as criminals are highlighted by the difficulties in trying them. The few cases brought before American judges, even conservative ones, were decided against the government. As Benjamin Wittes and Zaahira Wyne of the Brookings Institution note, the U.S. District Court for the District of Columbia has thus far issued rulings in habeas corpus cases for 38 Guantánamo detainees—30 of which it held to be unlawfully detained.[7] Bring them to military tribunals? The evidence against them—often obtained on the battlefield—frequently does not satisfy even these less demanding tribunals. Benjamin Wittes reports that military prosecutors have estimated that even under the Military

Commissions Act they have enough evidence to be able to bring to trial at best only 80 Guantánamo detainees.[8]

TERRORISTS DO NOT FIT OLD CATEGORIES

Terrorists are defined as individuals who seek to drive fear into a population by acts of violence in order to advance their goals in a *sub rosa* manner.[9] Terrorists, as a rule, wear no insignia that identifies them as combatants, engage in a large variety of other means to make themselves indistinguishable from noncombatant civilians, and often use civilians' vehicles, homes, and public facilities, such as schools and places of worship, for their terrorist acts.

One aspect of this definition needs further elaboration. Several scholars hold that the individuals at issue qualify as terrorists only if they attack noncombatants;[10] if they limit themselves to openly attacking combatants, they do not qualify as terrorists. An open attack on combatants may qualify one as an enemy combatant (as in insurgency) but not as a terrorist. I suggest that one should rely much more on the observation that terrorists pass themselves off as noncombatant civilians, which is a cardinal factor affording them considerable advantages over conventional armies that turns confronting them into a highly asymmetric armed conflict and is a major reason for the collateral damage and the ethical and tactical difficulties they raise.

In contrast to terrorists, soldiers are agents of a state, which can be held responsible for their conduct; states can be deterred from violating the rules of war by cajoling, incentives, and threats of retaliation. In contrast, most terrorists and insurgents are not agents of a state, nor are they necessarily members of a group currently qualifying for POW status under international law. They often act in parts of the world that lack effective government, or are supported by foreign governments, but only indirectly, and hence one often cannot determine whether they fight for a government or on their own. Even when they are affiliated with a state or are part of a government, as Hezbollah is in Lebanon, the national government often is unable to control their actions.

That terrorists are typically not agents of an identifiable state is particularly an issue as we face what is widely considered the greatest threat to world security—the use of weapons of mass destruction (WMD) by terrorists.[11] Although nuclear forensics has made some progress, there is considerable likelihood that in the event of a terrorist nuclear attack, we would be unable to ascertain promptly and accurately from whom the terrorists acquired their weapons and how.[12] This absence of a "return address" and the resulting inability to deter nuclear attacks with the threat of retaliation alone ought to lead one to recognize that terrorists cannot be treated like soldiers.

Furthermore, the notion that terrorists are akin to soldiers wrongly presumes that there is a clear line that separates them from civilians who—it is widely agreed although not always honored—ought to be spared hostilities as much as possible. In WWII, it was considered highly troubling when civilians were deliberately targeted (as distinct from injured as "collateral damage"), for instance in London, Dresden, Tokyo, Hiroshima, and Nagasaki—given that here the difference between civilians and military targets was clear and well-understood, but ignored. In contemporary conflicts, in which non-state actors play a large and increasing role, such distinctions often cannot be readily made.

Terrorists capitalize on the blurring of the line between soldiers and civilians by acting like civilians as long as it suits their purpose, then deploying their arms and attacking before quickly slipping back into their civilian status. To the extent that state militaries adhere to the old rules, they are often expected to wait until the civilians reveal themselves as combatants before engaging them, and even then they cannot respond with full force because both terrorists and insurgents often hide in civilian homes and public facilities as they launch their attacks.[13]

The media reports with great regularity that American soldiers, bombers, or drones killed "X" number fighters and "Y" number civilians in Afghanistan, Pakistan, or in Iraq. One wonders how the media can determine who is who even after the fact. In any case, this clarity is often missing during the conflict. Ergo, such a line cannot serve as the basis for dealing with fighters who act like and locate themselves among civilians.

In short, characterizing terrorists as soldiers greatly hampers the security of those who abide by the rules of war, and casts doubt on the legitimacy of their actions if they do not.

As I showed in detail elsewhere,[14] without first establishing basic security, development cannot proceed. Regimes that do not provide for elementary safety lose not only their legitimacy but also their credibility. Second, there are strong limitations on what one can achieve through development.[15] To reduce corruption to tolerable levels, to elevate national commitments to a level in which they supersede tribal ones, to modernize an economy, and to build a civil society takes decades and a very large monetary investment, at best. Winning the hearts and minds of the population (to the extent that it can be achieved) supplements measures that enforce safety, but safety cannot be based on it alone in areas in which terrorists maintain a strong presence and in which significant elements of the civilian population are combatants.

Above all, to demand that civilians who raise their arms against us be treated like noncombatants until they choose to reveal themselves, and to allow them to slip back into this status whenever it helps advance their goals, imposes several costs. The most obvious one is casualties among the conventional force under attack. This approach also generates perverse incentives for nations with conventional armies, already explored above: to circumvent the rules, to find some *sub rosa* way to deal with combatant civilians. Redefining the rules of armed conflicts is not only a more effective but also a more legitimate method of dealing with violent non-state actors.

The reasons terrorists cannot be treated as criminals are equally strong. By far the most important of these is that security requires that the primary goal of counterterrorism be *preventing* attacks rather than prosecuting the perpetrators after the attack has occurred. This is particularly evident when we concern ourselves with terrorists who may acquire WMDs. It also holds for many terrorists who are willing to commit suicide during their attack and hence cannot be tried, and who are not going to pay mind to the personal consequences of their assault. Finally, even terrorists with no intention of committing suicide attacks are often "true believers" who are willing to proceed despite whatever punishment the legal system may prescribe. All these individuals—those who may use WMDs, the suicide bombers, and others who are merely fanatics—are best prevented from proceeding rather than vainly trying to prosecute them after the fact, and most cannot be effectively deterred by the criminal justice system.

In contrast to the need for prevention, law enforcement often takes action after a criminal has acted—when a body is found, a bank is robbed, or a child is kidnapped. Thus, while "criminal justice also has a preventive component...criminal law is generally retrospective in focus, in that it addresses past acts."[16] Law enforcement assumes that punishment after the fact serves to deter future crimes (not to eliminate them, but to keep them at a socially acceptable level). Furthermore, as Ruth Wedgwood writes, "The purpose of domestic criminal law is to inflict stigma and punishment, and so it must be applied cautiously. Such reticence is proper for civil government in peacetime, but it is not always appropriate in war."[17] True, to some extent law enforcement can be modified to adapt to the challenge of terrorism. For instance, greater use can be made of statutes already enacted against those who engage in conspiracy to commit a crime. However, significant kinds of preventive action cannot be accommodated within the law enforcement paradigm. For instance, as "criminal law is concerned with punishment, it sets a high bar for detention."[18] Acts that subject a considerable number of people to administrative detention, or even simply surveillance or interrogation—without any individualized suspicion—would not be allowed. The aim in such cases is to disrupt *possible* planning of attacks without necessarily charging anybody with anything, or to pry loose some information through what under criminal law would be considered fishing expeditions. For example, in 2002-2003, the FBI invited 10,000 Iraqi-Americans to be interviewed, without claiming that any of them were terrorists or supported terrorists.[19]

Following normal criminal procedures also makes the prevention of terrorist attacks and the prosecution of captured terrorists more difficult. First, collecting evidence that meets the standards of a criminal court while in the combat zones and ungoverned regions in which many terrorists are captured is often not practical. And, to quote Matthew Waxman, a professor of law at Columbia University, the criminal justice system "is deliberately tilted in favor of defendants so that few if any innocents will be punished, but the higher stakes of terrorism cannot allow the same likelihood that some guilty persons will go free."[20] In one 2009 case, Ali Saleh Kahlah al-Marri, who had admitted to being a sleeper agent for Al Qaeda, was granted a plea bargain which cut his maximum sentence in half, the Justice Department in effect acknowledging that it may have had a hard time prosecuting Mr. Marri in the criminal justice system.[21]

Additionally, most violent criminals act as individuals while most terrorists act in groups. Hence, the criminal procedures of open arrest records, charging suspects within 48 hours or so, and speedy trials in open court all undermine the fight against terrorism. Counterterrorism requires time to capture other members of the cell before they realize that one of their members has been apprehended, to decipher their records, and to prevent other attacks that might be under way. Also, security demands that authorities do not reveal their means and methods, and often it does not allow terrorists to face their accusers. As stated by Robert Chesney and Jack Goldsmith,

> Neither [the criminal justice or the military detention] model in its traditional guise can easily meet the central legal challenge of modern terrorism: the legitimate preventive incapacitation of uniformless terrorists who have the capacity to inflict mass casualties and enormous economic harms and who thus must be stopped before they act.[22]

In short, terrorists are a distinct breed that requires a distinct treatment.

A DISTINCT SPECIES

Distinct rules for engaging terrorists have not been developed, in part because the two camps are each locked into their soldiers/ civilians and criminal/innocent legal and normative precepts. We need a group of leading legal minds *combined with people who have extensive combat experience* to create these rules. This essay turns next to outline select preliminary guidelines concerning the ways to deal with terrorists during armed conflicts and in future counterterrorism campaigns, as well as with those individuals already detained. Important work on this issue has already been carried out by Matthew Waxman,[23] Tung Yin,[24] Jack Goldsmith[25] and Robert Chesney,[26] and Amos Guiora,[27] among others. In addition, Columbia University's Phillip Bobbitt makes such a case in his valuable *Terror and Consent: The Wars for the Twenty-First Century*, in which he implores policymakers to stop relying on outdated legal and strategic thinking in dealing with terrorism. Much more detailed work is carried out in *Law and the Long War* by Benjamin Wittes. Both agree that there is a need for distinct legal and normative precepts for dealing with terrorists.[28]

For each of the following suggested guidelines, much remains to be developed and surely additional criteria are called for. These guidelines principally serve to illustrate the third approach:

Terrorists Are Entitled To Select Basic Human Rights

Terrorists are entitled to select basic human rights by virtue of being human. Although terrorists should be treated as civilians who have forfeited much, certain basic rights should be considered inviolate. They should not be killed when they can be safely detained and held, nor should they be subjected to torture.[29] Other basic rights are implied in the examination that follows; for instance, concerning their rights not to be detained indefinitely and to an institutionalized review of their status. As Amos N. Guiora states, "The dilemma is in determining and implementing the appropriate balance between legitimate national security rights and equally legitimate rights of the individual. Democratic States cannot afford the luxury of refusing all rights for suspected terrorist detainees."[30]

Special Detention Authority

Terrorists cannot be held until the end of the war (as a POW may be) because the armed conflict with terrorists may continue indefinitely or fade without any clear endpoint. Furthermore, holding an individual without review for an indefinite period is a gross violation of basic human rights, and one that can be readily remedied. Detained terrorists should be subject to periodic review by a special authority (see below), to determine if they can be safely released or if their history warrants further detention. Note that while much attention has been paid by the media to the plight of those detained, little attention has been paid to those that have been released and proceeded to commit acts of terror, particularly killing civilians. For instance, Abdallah Saleh al-Ajmi, a former Guantánamo Bay detainee, was repatriated to Kuwait as per a prisoner transfer agreement with the U.S. In his trial in Kuwait, al-Ajmi was acquitted and then released. About two years after his release from Guantánamo, al-Ajmi killed 13 Iraqi soldiers in a suicide bombing.[31]

At the same time, terrorists should not be incarcerated for a set period of time depending on the gravity of their attack, the way criminals are. The main purpose of detention is to *prevent* them from attacking again rather than to punish them for their crime. Thus, if the conflict between Israel and Palestine is finally settled and the settlement is faithfully implemented, those terrorists jailed by Israel and by the Palestinian Authority can be released.

Additionally, holding terrorists merely for 48 hours or so before they must be charged, as criminals are in the United States, does not allow enough time for essential counterterrorism measures already listed. Various extended detainment periods, but not unlimited ones, that have been set in law in other democratic societies provide a precedent of sorts. For instance, in the UK, criminal suspects are usually held only 48 hours without being charged, but that can now be extended by a court to up to 28 days.[32]

Many related issues remain to be developed, including how to ensure that preventive detention is not used too widely and which procedures should be used to determine who can be released.[33]

A National Security Court

Neal Katyal, a highly respected legal scholar and the Principal Deputy Solicitor General of the United States, favors a separate judicial authority for dealing with terrorists: a congressionally created national security court.[34] Unlike a military commission, this court would be overseen by federal judges with life tenure, and detainees would have the right to appeal decisions—appeals which would then be reviewed by a second set of federal judges.[35] But unlike a civilian court, detainees would not receive the full plethora of criminal protections (for instance, they would not be allowed to face all their accusers, if these include, for example, CIA agents working covertly), and the national security court would also have different evidentiary standards from civilian courts[36] (such as allowing the introduction of certain kinds of hearsay as evidence).

Similarly, Wittes writes that, thus far, the main steps in the U.S. to develop a systematic position on the treatment of captured terrorists have been taken by the executive branch (various presidential declarations, orders, and "findings") and the courts (including decisions such as *Rasul v. Bush* and *Hamdan v. Rumsfeld*).[37] He criticizes this approach, and suggests that Congress should formulate a distinct legal architecture to deal with terrorists by authorizing the creation of a national security court, with rules and practices less exacting than those that govern domestic criminal courts, but in which terrorists are granted more legal rights and protections than in the current Combatant Status Review Tribunals (CSRT).[38]

Wittes also favors that the standards for admissible evidence be lower than for domestic criminal cases; the court should bar the admission of evidence gleaned from torture, but, aside from that, "probative material—even hearsay or physical evidence whose chain of custody or handling would not be adequate in a criminal trial—ought to be fair game."[39]

Terrorists cannot gain full access to all the evidence against them, which criminals are entitled to, without creating significant security risks. Even for the evidence that can be revealed, I favor allowing terrorists to choose only among lawyers who have security clearances. (This also greatly curtails the possibility that the lawyers will serve as go-betweens for terrorists and their compatriots, as was the case with lawyer Lynne Stewart.[40])

There is room for differences about the specific nature and workings of the national security court. For instance, it might be best called a national security review board to stress that it is not a typical court. However, the main point is that terrorists must be tried in different ways than criminals are.[41] Even "tried" may be the wrong term; granted a hearing might be more accurate.

Surveillance of Civilians

An essential element of counterterrorism is identifying the attackers before they strike. Surveillance has a key role to play in such efforts. This entails allowing computers (which do not "read" messages and hence cannot violate privacy) to screen the billions of messages transmitted through cyberspace as well as over phone lines. It is a highly obsolescent notion to suggest that in order to conduct this kind of surveillance the government must first submit evidence to a court that there is individualized probable cause for suspicion—as is typically done with criminals. All messages that pass through public spaces (as distinct from, for instance, within one's home) might be screened to identify likely terrorism suspects who then may be submitted to closer scrutiny.

Second, the notion that one can and should deal differently with Americans versus others is also highly anachronistic. Generally, there is no way of determining the nationality of those who communicate through modern technology. The rule of thumb used in the past by American authorities—that if the message originates in American territory or is sent to someone who is in American territory, it is presumed to involve an American—leads to results favorable to terrorists. For instance, numerous messages (such as emails, phone calls, or text messages) sent between those in foreign countries pass digitally through the United States; these messages cannot be legally scrutinized as long as said rule is followed. It is quite possible terrorists will be among the over 50 million visitors who come to the United States each year, and that before they strike, these terrorists will contact their superiors overseas, as the 9/11 attackers did, as well as did those who attacked other nations, such as the United Kingdom and Spain. Monitoring for this entails that all messages should be initially screened, in the limited sense that computers would determine whether they actually should be read or their patterns further examined.

One effective way to ensure that mass surveillance is not abused is to set up a review board that will examine regularly the ways in which data are collected and used, and that will issue annual reports to the public on its findings. That both the U.S. Department of Homeland Security and the Office of the Director of National Intelligence have privacy officers is also a step in the desired direction. This kind of oversight works largely after the fact, rather than slowing the collection of information to a crawl, which would be the case if each act of surveillance faced review by a special court before it was undertaken, and points to the right balance between allowing the government to advance security and subjecting these efforts to public scrutiny.[42]

TOMORROW'S FREEDOM FIGHTERS?

There are some who say that those we consider terrorists today will be considered freedom fighters tomorrow—and that some already view them in this way. As I see it, deliberately killing or terrorizing a human being is a morally flawed act. There are conditions under which this act is justified, as in self-defense, or legal, as when a court orders an execution or a head of state orders an army to defend the nation. However, this does not make killing and terror "good"; we are always commanded to see whether we can achieve the same purpose without killing or terror—for example, by taking the enemy soldiers as POWs rather than killing them once they no longer endanger us.

While killing and terrorism are always morally flawed means, there is no moral equivalency in terms of the purposes for which they are applied. Those who use these means to overthrow a tyrannical government (for instance, members of the underground in

France who fought the Nazis during WWII) may deserve support, while those who use them to undermine a democracy (for instance, those who attacked the United States on 9/11, and those who attacked Spain and Britain in the following years)—deserve special condemnation. *However, the fact that some purposes are noble and others foul does not make the means used good.* Hence, while combatant civilians are not all created equal, while some may indeed be today's or tomorrow's freedom fighters—none of them are engaged in regime change in ways that one should consider morally superior to non-lethal means.

IN CONCLUSION

Up to a point, these and other such counterterrorism measures might be viewed as merely modifications of the criminal justice system or as a hybrid of that system and the laws of war. However, given the scope and number of differences involved, together they amount to a distinct approach. This is most evident when one acknowledges that the prevention of terrorism requires questioning and even detaining some people who have not yet violated any law when there are reasons, insufficient to convince a criminal court, to fear that they may be mounting an attack.

The preceding suggestions are merely ways to launch and foster the explorations of the third approach. They do not constitute an elaborated model that could be implemented as public policy without considerable additional deliberations and modifications. Moreover, for the distinct treatment of terrorists to be fully embraced, it must gain acceptance by the American public, while also being viewed as legitimate by other people. It hence requires transnational dialogues and the development of new norms and agreements—for instance, a new Geneva Convention—which, to reiterate, would be hardly the first time these conventions have been significantly altered.

One might differ about the proper actions that may be taken to prevent terrorism and about how to best contend with terrorists, but still agree that it makes little sense to treat terrorists either as criminals or as soldiers. At issue is not a matter of neat classifications, but ways to maintain the institutions of a free society while also protecting it from devastating attacks.

Underlying many of the discussions of the issue at hand is a sub-text, a quest for a clean war, one in which no bystanders are hurt, collateral damage is minimized if not avoided all together, and in which strikes are "surgical." Thus, for instance, various observers objected to the use of airpower in Kosovo—and recently of bombers and drones in Afghanistan and Pakistan—and urged greater reliance on land troops, because they hoped that these troops might be able to better separate civilians from fighters.

As I see it, the same respect for human life and for human rights takes one elsewhere. One must recognize that, although some measures can be taken to protect noncombatant civilians, at the end of the day some such civilians are very likely to be hurt. Hence, the best way to minimize innocent civilian casualties is to exhaust all other means possible to manage conflict short of armed interventions—to go the extra mile, to ignore provocations, to invite intermediaries, to turn the other cheek, and to avoid, if at all possible, an armed clash. Combat is by nature bloody. Although it can be tidied up to some extent, at the end of the day it is tragic and best avoided if at all possible. However, when an armed conflict is forced on a people—for example, by those who bomb their heartland, killing thousands of innocent civilians working at their desks—an appropriate response requires dealing with the attackers as terrorists, and not being hobbled by precepts and rules concerning criminals and soldiers. The time has come to recognize that those who abuse their civilian status, by pretending to be civilians but acting like terrorists, forfeit many of the rights of true civilians without acquiring the privileges due to soldiers.[43]

Chapter 2

How Liberty is Lost

In the wake of numerous recent changes made in American law and that of numerous many countries following the September 11 terrorist attack, civil libertarians, libertarians, and many others have raised concerns that the nations involved are sacrificing their liberty to enhance their safety. Senator Patrick Leahy expressed concern that the United States was "shredding the Constitution." Civil libertarian organizations such as the American Civil Liberties Union (ACLU) have described the government's penchant toward obtaining new powers after September 11 as an "insatiable appetite," characterized by government secrecy, a lack of transparency, rejection of equality under the law, and "a disdain and outright removal of checks and balances."[44] Articles in the popular press express similar sentiments. Writing in the *American Prospect*, Wendy Kaminer expressed the fear that, "Give the FBI unchecked domestic spying powers and instead of focusing on preventing terrorism, it will revert to doing what is does best—monitoring, harassing, and intimidating political dissidents and thousands of harmless immigrants."[45] In short, it has been argued that in order to protect ourselves from terrorists, democracy may be endangered, if not lost.

The question, "Under what condition is democracy undermined?" has been the topic of considerable previous deliberations, especially by people who studied the fall of the Weimar Republic and the rise of the Nazis in Germany. However, for the last decades, much more focus has been on the question of how to help democracy grow in countries that have had little previous experience with this form of governance (for instance, some former communist nations and a fair number of developing nations), rather than on how democracy might be lost. Given the recent events and claims, the latter question deserves to be revisited. This question is particularly germane because if it were true that in order to survive future waves of terrorist attacks (including ones using weapons of mass destruction) we must turn our free societies into garrison states, many members of free societies might well be reluctant to accept such a trade-off.

Fortunately, the empirical basis for such a study of the conditions under which democracy is actually lost is very limited because democracy—once firmly established—has almost never been lost due to internal developments (as distinct from occupation by an invading force). Democracy seems to be an odd plant: it has been very difficult for it to take root, especially in parts of the world where it has not been "naturally" found, but where various efforts have been made to seed it. Once it buds, it often faces great difficulties and frequently dies on the vein, or at least suffers numerous setbacks before it grows properly. But after it firmly takes root, it tends to withstand numerous challenges well and is rarely lost. Indeed, one key example of democracy lost comes to mind—and that is the already mentioned Weimar Republic—and it is arguable whether democracy was even well-established there.

Before the discussion proceeds, a word on definition: if one defines "democracy" very lightly, such as a nation that holds regular elections, one finds that none of the preceding statements hold. Elections are held all over the world, including in nations in which there is only one political party, one candidate, a legislature which rubber stamps whatever the government proposes, a press controlled by the government, and individuals rights are not respected. Such "democracies" come and go, at the whim of the military or some other power elite. Democracy, here, is taken to mean a polity in which there are regular, institutionalized changes in power, in line with the preferences of the people, freely expressed. It entails a whole fabric of institutions: two or more political parties, some measure of checks and balances among the various branches of the government (although, of course, these may differ from the American setup), courts that effectively protect individual rights, and a free press. While some scholars draw important conceptual distinctions between liberal (rights-based) polities and democratic ones, and others focus on the definition of liberty, here we treat all of these as key elements of a democratic polity. To remind the reader of this fact, I will use the phrase "constitutional democracy"; our democracy is ensconced in a framework of rights that are not subject to majority rule.

THE SLIPPERY SLOPE HYPOTHESIS

The civil libertarian's narrative about how democracies are lost is basically as follows. First, the government, in the name of national security or some other such cause, trims some rights, which raises little alarm at the time (e.g., the massive detention of Japanese Americans during World War II). Then a few other rights are curtailed (e.g., the FBI spies on civil rights groups and peace activists during the Sixties). Soon more rights are lost and, gradually, the whole institutional structure on which democracy rests tumbles down the slope with nobody able to stop it.

If one fully embraces this argument, one cannot in good conscience support any significant adjustments in the ways we interpret the Constitution, its Bill of Rights, the powers allotted to public authorities, and other key features of a democratic polity. If one fears setting a foot on the slope because he may end up on his backside at the lower end of the slope, there is only one alternative—to remain frozen at the top, opposed to all changes. Indeed, during a debate about the USA Patriot Act (which includes numerous post-September 11 changes in U.S. laws to enhance the war against terrorism, including trimming some rights and redefining others [discussed in Chapter 3]), Nadine Strossen, president of the ACLU, was repeatedly asked whether there were any changes in public policies relevant to safety she would find acceptable. She refused to endorse any. (When Katie Corrigan, a legislative counsel with the ACLU's Washington office, testified before Congress she noted that the ACLU has supported some post-September 11 changes, including the fortification of cockpit doors, matching baggage with passengers, and limiting the number of carry-on bags passengers may bring on planes, a rather limited list.)

In contrast, I have argued that one should be able to make notches in the slope. In other words, before setting foot on it, one needs to and can clearly mark how far he is willing to go and what is unacceptable, to avoid slipping to a place one is not willing and ought not to go. A detailed examination of the changes introduced after September 11 in the United States find some of them very reasonable (e.g., roving wiretaps) and others quite unacceptable (e.g., the military tribunals as originally conceived). The distinction between these changes suggests that rather than refusing to adjust, we need to examine more closely the various new measures that are being advanced. Indeed, very few would seek to leave the Constitution as originally formulated, according to which non-Europeans do not count as full persons, there is no right to privacy, and free speech is much less protected than post-1920 interpretations (led by the ACLU, to its credit) made it. In short, changes in the ways we view individual rights do not signify the ending of a democratic form of government. Indeed, as I shall try to highlight in the next section, the relationship runs the other way around: when democratic institutions and policies do not provide an adequate response to new challenges, they are undermined.

THE WEIMAR HYPOTHESIS

There is an immense literature on the question of what led to the collapse of the Weimar Republic and the rise of Nazi Germany, containing numerous different interpretations of that piece of history. It is well beyond the scope of this essay to try to sort out these differences. For the purposes at hand, it suffices to cull out one hypothesis, which can be further examined in light of recent developments and data. The hypothesis is that the Weimar Republic lost its legitimacy and opened the door to a tyrannical government due to its woefully insufficient responses to major public needs.

Following the defeat of Germany in World War I, the people's pride was already shaken. People felt threatened when defeat in the war was followed by massive unemployment and runaway hyperinflation, leading to what historian Peter Fritzsche in *Germans Into Nazis* called "extraordinary hardship[s]" and "disastrous economic and political conditions."[46] The Weimar Republic's response was weakened by its difficulties in forming coalitions among what Theodore Abel described as its "superabundance of political parties," corruption, and scandals. For instance, the "growing number and severity of the problems confronting the German nation were largely due to the inefficiency of the government," Abel found in his *The Nazi Movement*,[47] as well as "discontent with the existing social order" which was the first factor contributing to the rise of the Nazi movement. Abel notes that discontent was expressed by people blaming the government for their problems. In their attempts collectively to act, they responded to perceived threats to their "personal and social values." Overall, "the Weimar system has enormous weaknesses," Kurt Sontheimer observed in 1967.[48]

Other scholars, for instance Sheri Berman, point to similar reasons the republic collapsed. She argues that although the Weimar Republic had an active civil society, its weak political institutions and structures sharpened divisions in German society and "obstructed meaningful participation in public life."[49] Likewise, Arthur van Riel and Arthur Schram note that the elected national assembly was unable to respond effectively to economic challenges and that "any struggle for political reform was viewed as a threat to the delicate equilibrium of political and economic interests."[50] Similar observations have been made by other historians as well. The inefficiency of democracy and the difficulty forming a coalition have been highlighted by Fritz Stern, who also argued that "as the economy faltered and the government was unable to react to the economic and political problems, voters turned their back on the Weimar Republic."[51] As a result of the lack of responsiveness, "too many Germans did not regard it as a legitimate regime," writes E. J. Feuchtwanger in his book *From Weimar to Hitler*[52] (though he notes the other numerous factors that contributed to the republic's demise). According to these as well as still other scholars, the Weimar Republic did not respond effectively—both economically and politically—to its citizens' major needs in the face of crises, and thus lost its legitimacy.

In short, inaction in the face of threats, not excessive action, killed the Weimar Republic. When democracies do not work, they open themselves to tyrannies.

POST-SEPTEMBER 11 LESSONS

Did our constitutional democracy lose support after September 11 and, if it did, under what factors? The data cited next suggest that during the immediate period after the attack, when the public was most concerned about its safety (fearing additional attacks from sleeper terrorist cells on short order), people were most willing to support a strong government, including one that would set aside many basic individual rights.

However, in the subsequent period, as the government did take numerous and varying measures to enhance public safety and no new attacks occurred, the public gradually restored its commitment to the rights-centered, democratic regime. What endangered it was not curtailment of rights—but fear that the public will not be protected. And as the government vigorously enacted measures to protect the public, the public's support for constitutional democracy was reaffirmed. That is, the U.S. experience in the months following September 11 helps support the suggested hypothesis by providing a case with a profile opposite of the Weimar one. When the government reacted firmly to a major challenge, support for constitutional democracy was sustained rather than undermined.

PUBLIC FEARS IN THE U.S.: 2001-2002

To put the hypothesis that is being explored here in semi-formal terms, it might be said that we seek to assess whether the size of a challenge (in this instance the September 11 attacks) minus the impact of new measures undertaken to enhance public safety will correlate with the extent to which the public will support a rights-based, constitutional democracy. (Correlate rather than equals because other factors will affect the dependent variable.) For the purposes at hand, no distinction is made as to whether the public's concerns are realistic, overblown, or underestimating the danger. (We know from crime studies that the public's fear of crime and the actual level of crimes do not necessarily go hand in hand.[53]) The reason for this approach is that democracy will be endangered if the public's fears rise above a certain level, regardless of whether these concerns are realistic or not. The same holds for safety measures. If putting armed guards in airports add little to public safety, but helps reassure the public, then armed guards will serve to reduce anxiety and help undergird the public support for our form of government.

A reasonable measure of the initial scope of the public's safety concerns and the extent to which it declined after September 11 is provided by statistics on domestic airline traffic within the United States, based on behavioral data which are considered more reliable than attitudinal data, to which I will have to turn shortly. Airline traffic fell precipitously in the period immediately following the attack, and gradually recovered, but it did not return to the pre-September 11 level by the end of the period for which information was available (through February 2002).[54]

Prior to September 11, airlines were experiencing a slight increase of a little less than one percent in enplanements over the year 2000; in August 2001, passengers boarding flights increased by 3.1 percent over the previous year (A year-high 56.1 million passengers boarded U.S. carriers for domestic flights in August 2001; 54.4 million did so in August 2000). In September 2001, (which includes the 10 days before the attack) enplanements dropped 34 percent from September 2000 (when 47.7 million total passengers boarded planes, compared to the 31.4 million who did so during the month of the attacks, when airports across the country were shut down).

Traffic began a slow but steady increase during the remainder of the year, though enplanements remained considerably less than what they were during the same months in the year 2000. In October, air carriers experienced 21.2 percent fewer enplanements over the previous year (a decrease from 50.5 million to 39.8 million). As the highly-traveled holiday months approached, the drop in enplanements continued to recede. In November, there were 18.5 percent fewer enplanements than the same month last year (a decrease from 50.9 million to 41.5 million) and December saw a 13.4 percent decrease over the 2000 holiday season (down from 46.7 million to 40.5 million).

The first two months of the year 2002 follow the same pattern, showing people slowly, but steadily returning to air travel. January 2002 enplanements were down 13.0 percent compared to 2001 (a decrease from 43.8 million to 38.1 million), and February saw 10.8 percent fewer enplanements compared to February 2001 (a decrease from 47.6 million to 42.4 million). In short, as numerous new airline safety measures were introduced, one new attack (by a so-called shoe-bomber) was successfully foiled, and no others took place, the public's confidence in airline travel was gradually being restored.

COMMITMENT TO CONSTITUTIONAL DEMOCRACY: ATTITUDES

We can see a base line of sort in the following data on perceptions about personal freedoms (Table 1). A year before the attacks, 54 percent of Americans were concerned that the government threatens their own personal rights and freedoms, while two months after the attacks the figure rose to 67 percent, encompassing two-thirds of all Americans. (By that time several measures to enhance safety had been introduced and public fears began to subside. Regrettably, no data is available for the same question immediately after the attack).

Table 1

GOVERNMENTAL THREATS TO PERSONAL RIGHTS AND FREEDOMS

Do you think the government threatens your own personal rights and freedoms, or not?			

	Yes	No	Don't Know
November 2001	30	67	3
June 2000a	46	54	b

Source: National Public Radio/Kaiser/Kennedy School Poll on Civil Liberties, October 31-November 12, 2001.

a National Public Radio/Kaiser/Kennedy School of Government
b Less than one percent

When people were asked explicitly, "Would you be willing to give up some of the liberties we have in this country in order for the government to crack down on terrorism, or not?" their responses tell the same story. Shortly after the bombing of the Murrah Federal Building in Oklahoma City in April 1995, a hefty majority (59 percent) favored giving up some liberties. Given a month, the numbers began to subside to 52 percent, only to zoom to about two-thirds (66 percent) of Americans on September 11.

The same sentiments are revealed in another poll that asked, "What concerns you most right now? That the government will fail to enact strong, new antiterrorism laws, or that the government will enact new antiterrorism laws which excessively restrict the average person's civil liberties?" While 44 percent were concerned that the government would enact laws that restrict civil liberties in 1995, about one-third (34 percent) expressed such reservations in September 2001.

The willingness of people to give up rights in order to fight terrorism, and their perception of whether or not they will need to give up some of their own rights, is also tied to their level of fear. As

Table 2 shows, a clear majority (59 percent) of Americans were willing to give up some liberties after what was, in retrospect, a small attack, the bombing of the federal building in Oklahoma City in April 1995. When the same question was asked a mere month later, people already had begun to calm down, and their willingness to support reductions of liberty declined to 52 percent. After the 2001 attacks on America, two-thirds of Americans were willing to sacrifice some liberty to fight terrorism. (When the question was worded differently, the percentage was even higher—78 percent).

Table 2

WILLINGNESS TO GIVE UP CIVIL LIBERTIES

Date	Question	Willing	Not Willing	Don't know/ No Opinion
April 1995	Would you be willing to give up some of the liberties we have in this country in order for the government to crack down on terrorism, or not?	59	24	10
May 1995a	Would you be willing to give up some of the liberties we have in this country in order for the government to crack down on terrorism, or not?	52	41	7
August 1996b	Would you be willing to give up some civil liberties if that were necessary to curb terrorism in this country, or not?	58	23	6
September 2001a	Would you be willing to give up some of the liberties we have in this country in order for the government to crack down on terrorism, or not?	66	24	7 cont.

January-March 2002c	You are now more willing to give up certain freedoms to improve safety and security than you were before September 11th.	78	22	

Source: a ABC News/*Washington Post* Poll, 11 September 2001.

b *Los Angeles Times* Poll, 3 August-6 August 1996. This poll was conducted a few weeks after the explosion of TWA flight 800 and the bombing at Centennial Olympic Park during the 1996 Summer Olympics in Atlanta. The poll also contained the response "it depends," chosen by 13 percent of respondents (which is not included in Table 2).

c Gallup Poll, 28 January-22 March 2002. Responses to the question included "strongly agree" (29.5 percent), "agree" (48.8 percent), "disagree" (13.6 percent), and "strongly disagree" (8.1 percent).

Questions about "necessity" instead of willingness to give up liberties (Table 3) reveal a similar pattern. More than six in ten Americans agreed that it was a necessary to give up some rights immediately after September 11. Two months later, the number fell to a bit to more than five out of ten Americans.

Table 3

NECESSITY TO GIVE UP LIBERTIES

Date	Question	Necessary	Not Necess.	Don't Know
September 2001[55]	In order to curb terrorism in this country, do you think it will be necessary for the average person to give up some liberties or not?	61	33	6
November 2001[56]	In order to curb terrorism in this country do you think it will be necessary for the average person to give up some rights and liberties, or do you think we can curb some terrorism without the average person giving up rights and liberties?	51	46	3
				cont.

November 2001[57]	Do you think you will have to give up some of your OWN rights and liberties in order to curb terrorism or not?	58	39	3

Notes: * Responses include "necessary for the average person to give up some rights and liberties" and "we can curb terrorism without the average person giving up rights and liberties."

** Responses include "yes" and "no."

Asked about specific measures, the picture is completely consistent: as fear subsides, support for safety, even at the cost of liberty, remained very high (as warnings about more attacks, including ones with dirty bombs and bioterror agents were standard diet), but declined over time with regard to all of the ten specific measures the public was asked about. Indeed, on seven out of the ten measures, more than two-thirds of Americans were initially willing to sacrifice the specific rights listed (Table 4, shown on next page).

When the same issue was raised in a different manner the results were similar. Table 5 (see page 29) shows that the percentage of Americans who held that the government went too far in restricting civil liberties to fight terrorism remained consistently small, but increased from eight percent to twelve percent as America experienced no new attacks and numerous new safety measures were introduced. The percentage of those who believed that the government did not go far enough declined somewhat.

In responses to overarching questions (such as, "Overall, how confident do you feel that U.S. law enforcement will use its expanded surveillance powers in what you would see as a proper way, under the circumstances of terrorist threats?"), we see the beginning of a shift, the decline in those who are very confident law enforcement will use such powers properly, which is less problematic than a significant increase in those who are not confident at all. While in March, the percent of people who felt "very confident" fell to almost one-third of what it was in September (from 34 percent to 12 percent), those who were "not confident at all" increased by a mere two percent (from four percent to six percent), well within the margin of error for such polls.

Table 4   LAW ENFORCEMENT AND CIVIL LIBERTIES

Here are some increased powers of investigation that law enforcement agencies might use when dealing with people suspected of terrorist activity, which would also affect our civil liberties.
For each, please say if you would favor or oppose it.

		Favor	Oppose	Not sure/ Decline to answer
Expanded under-cover activities to penetrate groups under suspicion	Sept. 2001	93	5	1
	March 2002	88	10	2
Stronger documents and physical security checks	Sept. 2001	93	6	1
	March 2002	89	9	2
Stronger documents and physical security checks for access to government and private buildings	Sept. 2001	92	7	1
	March 2002	89	10	1
Use facial recognition technology to scan for suspected terrorists at various locations and public events.	Sept. 2001	86	11	2
	March 2002	81	17	2
Issuance of a secure I.D. technique for persons to access government and business computer systems, to avoid disruptions.	Sept. 2001	84	11	4
	March 2002	78	16	6
Closer monitoring of banking and credit card transactions, to trace funding sources	Sept. 2001	81	17	2
	March 2002	72	25	2
Adoption of a national I.D. system for all U.S. citizens	Sept. 2001	68	28	4
	March 2002	59	37	5
Expanded camera surveillance on streets and in public places	Sept. 2001	63	35	2
	March 2002	58	40	2
Law enforcement monitoring of Internet discussions in chat rooms and other forums.	Sept. 2001	63	32	5
	March 2002	55	41	4

Source: Harris Poll, 13-19 March 2002 and Harris Poll, 19-24 September 2001.

Table 5   GOVERNMENT EXCESS IN RESTRICTING CIVIL LIBERTIES

	Too Far	Not far enough	Just about right	Don't Know
Based on what the Bush Administration has done so far and is proposing to do in response to terrorism, do you think they are going too far in restricting civil liberties in this country, not far enough, or are handling this situation just about right.				
September 2001	12	23	59	6
November 2001	11	14	72	3
February 2001	8	17	72	3

Source: Newsweek Poll, 31 January-1 February 2002.

As far as one can rely on attitudinal data that vary according to how the question is phrased, the data support the thesis that the higher the fear, the greater the willingness to curtail liberty to protect safety. And that as new safety measures are introduced, and no new attacks occur—when the government's response seems effective—fear subsides and support for democracy beings to re-increase. The fact that the support for strong anti-terrorist measures remains high reflects the fact that all of the data were collected within nine months of the attack and under frequent warnings about immanent attacks, new threats, and so on. The thesis would lead one to expect that if the panic subsides some more, the proportion of those supporting a curtailment of rights will further decline. This may seem obvious, but it surely is not so obvious to those who hold that democracy is lost by introducing new safety measures that entail some curtailment of rights. These are core elements of what protects the public and reassures it.

LOWER CRIME RATES—MORE SUPPORT FOR LIBERTY

Beyond the scope of this presentation is another relevant source of data: the correlation between the public support for "tough" elected officials and law enforcement personnel who favor restrictive and punitive policies that entail curbing individual liberties. Some informal evidence to this effect is available for the mid-1990s.

Following a series of high profile violent crimes, including a rampage killing five passengers on a Long Island railroad and several murders of European tourists in Florida, the public became highly fearful of violent crime and sought get-tough measures. In the mid-1990s the public cited crime as the biggest problem facing the country (19 percent) with an additional two percent identifying guns as the biggest problem, followed by the economy (14 percent) and unemployment and jobs (12 percent). In 1996, crime and drugs were identified as the biggest problem by nearly a quarter of respondents. In contrast, four years earlier, in January 1992, 54 percent of Americans cited economic issues as the most important issue facing the country, while only two percent cited guns or violence.[58]

In the mid-1990s, Americans overwhelmingly favored treating juveniles who commit violent crimes the same way as adults, as opposed to more leniently (by nearly a three to one margin).[59] They also supported more extreme measures such as caning, following American Michael Fay's such punishment in Singapore for vandalism.[60] A 1994 poll shows that less than half of Americans felt that caning is too harsh a punishment for assault (44 percent), robbery (48 percent) and drug dealing (36 percent). Nearly 60 percent of Americans favored the "surgical or chemical castration of men repeatedly convicted of rape or child molesting."[61]

During this same time period, demagogues advocated "street justice" and "shoot first, ask questions later." Former Los Angeles Police Chief Daryl Gates publicly made comments to this effect. For instance, at a news conference about the rioting that occurred after the beating of Rodney King by Los Angeles police officers, Gates was quoted on the front page of the *Los Angeles Times* as saying, "Clearly that night we should have gone down there and shot a few people. In retrospect that's what we should have done. We should have blown a few heads off. And maybe your television cameras would have seen that and maybe that would have been broadcast and maybe, just maybe, that would have stopped everything. I don't know. But certainly we had the legal right to do that."[62]

That wasn't the only time Gates made such comments. A few years later in *USA Today* (April 16, 1996), Gates stated, "No matter how use you that club, people are going to criticize." Law enforcement personnel were not alone in expressing their support of "street justice." Other public officials, including legislators, expressed similar views. For example, in 1995, a former member of the Georgia State Assembly introduced a bill (which garnered support, but failed to become law) dubbed "shoot first, ask questions later," which would have allowed homeowners to shoot intruders inside their homes.[63]

As the decade came to a close, these sentiments faded away to some degree. A poll conducted in 2000 shows the change in the public's perception of crime. The percentage of those who believed crime in the country was "very bad" or "bad" fell from 90 percent in 1996 to 80 percent in 2000. Even more to the point, among those who felt crime was a problem in the country, less than one-quarter (23 percent) characterized crime as "very bad or "bad" in their own community in 2000, as compared to the almost one-third (31 percent) who characterized crime as "bad" or "very bad" in 1996.[64]

Polls conducted in the late 1990s also showed that people believed there was less crime in their neighborhoods. (In 1998, 48 percent of Americans thought there was less crime in their area than a year ago.) Also, in the latter half of the decade, fewer people believed that crime in the country had increased over the previous year. (In 1998, 52 percent of Americans thought crime increased in the country over the previous year, as compared to 64 percent who thought crime increased in 1997, and 87 percent who thought crime increased in 1993.) [65]

By the end of the 1990s, as public authorities succeeded in curbing violent crime, fear of crime subsided and there was less talk of get-tough, extra-legal measures and less support for harsh but legal measures. By the end of the 1990s and in the year 2000, when polls showed that the public perceived crime as less of a problem, the statistics on violent crime corroborated their feelings. For instance, in 1998 there were 1.5 million violent crime offenses, and by the year 2000 offenses decreased even further to 1.4 million, a stark contrast with the much larger number of offenses in the mid-1990s (1.9 million violent crime offenses in 1994 and 1.8 million in 1995).[66]

To the extent that one can draw conclusions from the evidence at hand, some of it being historical, some behavioral, and some attitudinal, it seems to support the thesis that democracy is endangered not when strong measures are taken to enhance safety, to protect, and reassure the public, but when these measures are not taken. In short, the "correlation" between strong safety measures and demo-

cracy is just the opposite of what civil libertarians argue: it is positive rather than negative. This, of course, does not mean that any
and all new safety measures are needed, but that, in general, effective enhancement of safety (and more generally, those measures
which respond to public needs) is crucial for democracy to be sustained. Once safety is restored, the measures can be gradually rolled
back, without endangering public support for constitutional democracy.

Chapter 3

Privacy and Security in the Digital Age

This may be in sharp contrast with the conventional wisdom, but I have come to conclude that privacy is better protected now by technical means than it ever has been in human history. How could this be so?

If you think about how messages have been traditionally sent by messenger, by carrier pigeon, by phone or fax—all before encryption—they were easily intercepted. These messages could be read by a casual observer, a postmaster and, of course, the police. Strong encryption, however, typically used in day-to-day communication prevents routine violation of privacy. The capacity of strong encryption technologies to protect communication represents a significant factor of change—increasing the individual's power to protect privacy by a factor of a thousand, perhaps a million. This same principle applies as well to databases. Take health records, for example, databases often full of intimate details. Until rather recently, most patient medical records were kept on paper in file folders protected only by the lock on the file room door—a level of security easily overcome with a little effort. Now with the transfer to digital records, when encryption is engaged and the data is protected by access audit trails, the information is much more secure. The electronic audit trail provides an important level of security by identifying who entered the data as well as who accessed it and when it was accessed. It is not a matter of *technological determinism*, of course; it represents a technical affordance. In order to take advantage of the protective shield of encryption, one has to take the initiative to encrypt one's communication, whether routine or otherwise.

In the wake of 9/11, however, some of this new potential for privacy has been diluted. The reasons for this are complex and require us to carefully examine the trade-offs between privacy, clearly an important and fundamental right, and other important values and rights. I have argued elsewhere that the implicit assumption that personal privacy trumps all other claims needs to be carefully examined.[67] It may require a carefully crafted balance among core values. Perhaps it is best to understand this as a dynamic process akin to an arms race between technologies. Every year new technical means for invading privacy are invented as are new counter-measures. Government agencies such as the National Security Agency may become more intrusive, but private citizens have new and sophisticated security techniques available to them as well—it's a tug of war. The war has not been won or lost by either side; it is ongoing and that is the focus of this chapter. I will review the technical developments related to personal privacy in several technical domains—three that enhance personal privacy (I refer to them as liberalizing technologies): cellular phones, Internet communications, and strong encryption; and two developments that enhance surveillance (I label them public protective): technologies for intercepting digital communications, and technologies for intercepting actual computer keystrokes.

I argue that both individual rights and public safety must be protected. Given that on many occasions advancing one requires some curtailment of the other, the key question is what the proper balance between these two cardinal values should be. The concept of balance is found in the Fourth Amendment. It refers to the right not to be subjected to unreasonable search and seizure. Thus, it recognizes a category of searches that are fully compatible with the Constitution—those that are reasonable. Historically, courts have found searches to be reasonable when they serve a compelling public interest, such as public safety or public health.

The counterclaims of advocates on both sides are best understood within a historical context. Societies tend to lean excessively toward the public interest or toward liberty. Corrections to such imbalances then tend to lead to over-corrections. For example, following the civil rights abuses that occurred during the years J. Edgar Hoover was the director of the FBI, the attorney general imposed severe limitations on the agency in the 1970s. These limitations excessively curbed the agency's work in the following decades. The public safety measures enacted after September 11 removed many of these restrictions and granted law enforcement agencies and the military new powers. These changes arguably tilted excessively in the other direction. This over-correction was soon followed by an attempt to correct it (for example, by limiting the conditions under which military tribunals can be used and spelling out procedures not included in their preliminary authorization).

Historical conditions also change the point at which we find a proper balance. The 2001 assault on America and the threat of additional attacks have brought about such a change. This chapter argues that we should strive to achieve a balance by focusing on accountability.

LIBERALIZING TECHNOLOGIES

In 1980, communications surveillance could be carried out easily by attaching simple devices to a suspect's landline telephone. In the following decades, millions of people acquired several alternative modes of convenient, instantaneous communication, most significantly cellular telephones and e-mail. According to International Telecommunication Union estimates, by 2009 there were over 285 million cellular phone subscribers in the United States, a penetration of about 93 percent.[68] E-mail and Internet usage are similarly pervasive. According to June 2010 ITU estimates, 240 million people in the United States are online, representing a penetration of more than 77 percent of the population.[69] These technological developments greatly limited the ability of public authorities to conduct communications surveillance using traditional methods.

Attempts were made to apply the old laws to new technologies, but the old laws did not fit the new technologies well. The law governing full intercepts, contained in Title III of the Omnibus Crime Control and Safe Streets Act of 1969, originally required that court orders for intercepts specify the location of the communications device to be tapped and establish probable cause that evidence of criminal conduct could be collected by tapping that particular device. Hence, under this law, if a suspect shifted from one phone to another or used multiple phones, the government could not legally tap phones other than the one originally specified without obtaining a separate court order for each.[70] Once criminals were able to obtain and dispose of multiple cellular phones like "used tissues," investigations were greatly hindered by the lengthy process of obtaining numerous full intercept authorizations from the courts.

The rise of Internet-based communications further limited the ability of public authorities to conduct communications surveillance under the old laws. Title III did not originally mention electronic communications. Similarly, the language of the Electronic Communications Privacy Act of 1986 (ECPA) that governed pen/trap orders (recording the telephone numbers of the caller and called party but not the content of the call) was not clearly applicable to e-mail. To determine how to deal with this new technology, courts often attempted to draw analogies between e-mail and older forms of communication. Because electronic communication used to travel largely over phone lines, courts extended laws governing intercepts or traces for telephones to electronic messages as well. However, reliance by the police on such interpretations was risky because there was a possibility that a court would rule that e-mail did not fall under a pen/trap order.

Extending laws that were written with telephones in mind to e-mail was an imperfect solution because e-mail messages differ from phone conversations in important ways. Unlike phone conversations, e-mails do not travel in discrete units that can be plucked out. Each e-mail is broken up into digital packets, and the packets are mixed together with those of other users. This makes it difficult to intercept individual e-mails. Law enforcement agents attempting to intercept or trace the e-mail of just one user may violate the privacy of other users.

The decentralized nature of the Internet created additional complications in carrying out wiretap orders. When the old legislation was enacted, a unified phone network made it easy to identify the source of a call. E-mail, by contrast, may pass through multiple Internet service providers ("ISPs") in different locations throughout the nation on its way from sender to recipient. As a result, public authorities would have to compel information from a chain of service providers. Thus, until recently, if a message went through four providers, four court orders in four different jurisdictions would be needed to find out the origin of that message.[71]

Similarly, agents faced jurisdictional barriers when they tried to obtain search warrants for saved e-mail. Under old laws, a warrant had to be obtained from a judge in the jurisdiction where the search would take place. E-mail, however, is not always stored on a personal computer but often is stored remotely on an ISP's server. This means that if a suspect in New Jersey had e-mail stored on a server located in Silicon Valley, an agent would have to travel across the country to get a warrant to seize the e-mail.

In short, the introduction of both cellular phones and e-mail made it much more difficult to conduct communications surveillance, even in cases in which the court authorized such surveillance. The old laws and enforcement tools were not suited to deal with these new technologies.

Public authorities were also set back by the development of strong encryption. Although ciphers have existed for thousands of years, programmers have only recently developed 128-bit key length and higher levels of encryption that are extraordinarily difficult to break, even by the National Security Agency (NSA). Moreover, software that uses strong encryption is readily available to private parties at low cost. Today, manufacturers routinely prepackage such programs on computers.[72] Thus, encrypted messages are more private than any messages historically sent by mail, phone, messenger, or other means. Similarly, now data stored on one's own computer is protected much better than analogous data stored under lock and key. Despite court orders, strong encryption has frustrated the efforts of law enforcement in a growing number of cases.

The impact of the development of strong encryption is qualitatively different from the impact of the other privacy-enhancing technologies. The main factor that constrained public authorities in the area of new modes of communication was the obsolescence of laws. In the case of strong encryption, on the other hand, the technology imposes its own barrier. Updating the law was sufficient to enable law enforcement to handle the challenges posed by the other new technologies. By contrast, no court order can enable strong encryption to be broken.[73]

These technological developments have provided all people—law-abiding citizens and criminals, non-terrorists and terrorists—greater freedom to do as they choose. In this sense, these technologies are "liberalizing." At the same time, they have significantly hampered the ability of public authorities to conduct investigations. Some cyber-space enthusiasts welcomed these developments, hoping that cyber-space would be a self-regulating, government-free space. In contrast, public authorities clamored for the laws to be changed in order to enable officials to police the new "territory" as they do in the world of old-fashioned, landline telephones. Such pressures led to some modifications in the law before the 2001 attack on America, but the most relevant changes in the law have occurred since.

One provision of ECPA attempted to make the laws governing communications intercepts more effective by providing for "roving wiretaps" in criminal investigations. Roving wiretaps are full intercept orders that apply to a particular person rather than to a specific communications device. They allow law enforcement to intercept communications from any phone or computer used by a suspect without specifying in advance which facilities will be tapped.[74]

The process for obtaining a roving intercept order is more rigorous than the process for obtaining a traditional phone-specific order. The Office of the United States Attorney General must approve the application before it is even brought before a judge. Originally, the applicant had to show that the suspect named in the application was changing phones or modems frequently with the *purpose* of thwarting interception.[75] After the Intelligence Authorization Act for Fiscal Year 1999 changed the requirement, the applicant merely had to show that the suspect was changing phones or modems frequently and that this practice "could have the effect of thwarting" the investigation.[76] Although roving intercepts have not yet been tested in the Supreme Court, several federal courts have found them to be constitutional.[77]

Prior to September 11, the FBI could not gain authorization to use roving intercepts in gathering foreign intelligence or in investigations of terrorism. The Uniting and Strengthening America by Providing Appropriate Tools Required to Intercept and Obstruct Terrorism Act of 2001 (USA PATRIOT Act) amended the Foreign Intelligence Surveillance Act of 1978 (FISA) to allow roving intercept orders. FISA provides the guidelines under which a federal agent can obtain authorization to conduct surveillance for foreign intelligence purposes. Agents who wish to conduct surveillance under FISA submit an application first to the U.S. Attorney General's office, which must approve all requests (as with roving intercepts under ECPA). If the Attorney General's office finds the application valid, the application will be taken to one of seven federally appointed judges, who together make up the Federal Intelligence and Security Court (FISC), for approval. The FISC allows no spectators, keeps most proceedings secret, and hears only the government's side of a case.[78]

There has been some debate in the courts and among legal scholars about the application of the Fourth Amendment to the new technologies and to the new legislation governing these technologies. Before 1967, the Supreme Court interpreted the Fourth Amendment in a literal way to apply only to physical searches. In *Olmstead v. United States*, the Court had ruled that telephone wiretaps did not constitute a search unless public authorities entered a home to install the device. The Court held that the Fourth Amendment does not protect a person unless "there has been an official search and seizure of his person, or such a seizure of his papers or his tangible material effects, or an actual physical invasion of his house...."[79]

In 1967, the Court replaced this interpretation of the Fourth Amendment with the view that the amendment "protects people, not places." In *Katz v. United States*, the Court established that an individual's "reasonable expectation of privacy" would determine the scope of her Fourth Amendment protection.[80] Justice Harlan, in his concurring opinion, set out a two-part test: the individual must have shown a subjective expectation of privacy, and society must recognize that expectation as reasonable.[81]

Although legal scholars have criticized its test,[82] *Katz* still represents the state of the law. However, the emergence of new technologies requires a reexamination of what constitutes a reasonable expectation of privacy. In *United States v. Maxwell*, the military appeals court determined that there was a reasonable expectation of privacy for e-mail stored on America Online's "centralized and privately-owned computer bank."[83] However, a federal district court in *United States v. Charbonneau*, relying on *Maxwell*, held that an individual does not have a reasonable expectation in statements made in an Internet chat room.[84]

Additionally, there is some question as to whether roving intercepts are constitutional. The Fourth Amendment states, "No warrants shall issue, but upon probable cause, supported by oath or affirmation, and particularly describing the place to be searched, and the persons or things to be seized." Because roving intercepts cannot name the location to be tapped, they may violate the particularity requirement of the Fourth Amendment.

The argument in favor of their constitutionality is that the particularity of the person to be searched is substituted for the particularity of the place to be searched. In *United States v. Petti*, the Ninth Circuit Court of Appeals upheld the use of roving intercepts. It explained that the purpose of the "particularity requirement was to prevent general searches."[85] As long as a warrant or court order provides "sufficient particularity to enable the executing officer to locate and identify the premises with reasonable effort," and there is no "reasonable probability that another premise might be mistakenly searched," it does not violate the Fourth Amendment.[86] In other words, a court order to tap all phones used by a specific person does describe particular places but in an unconventional way. Public authorities cannot use the order to tap any location they wish. They can only tap a set of specific locations, namely those used by a specific person.[87]

Additional questions may arise regarding differential application of the laws to various classes of people. Should non-citizens be treated the same as citizens? Terrorists the same as other criminals? International terrorists the same as domestic terrorists? These are significant issues that go to the heart of the debate about the rights of non-citizens. These issues raise potential problems, such as how to define terrorism and whether that definition should extend to citizens, as well as the danger that a loose definition might allow ordinary criminals to be encompassed by terrorism laws.

PUBLIC PROTECTIVE TECHNOLOGIES

The liberalizing technologies already addressed enhance individuals' liberties but hinder public authorities. The following technologies are public protective technologies, which enhance the capabilities of government authorities and accordingly may curtail individual rights.

In July 2000, the FBI unveiled a new resource awkwardly labeled "Carnivore" to signal the breadth of its power to capture on-line communication. It was designed to capture a suspect's e-mail messages or trace messages sent to and from a suspect's account. To do so, it sorts through a stream of many millions of messages, including those of many other users. Carnivore has a filter that can be set to scan various digital packets for specific text strings or to target messages from a specific computer or e-mail address. The program can operate in two different modes: "pen" or "full." In pen mode, it will capture only the addressing information, which includes the e-mail addresses of the sender and recipient as well as the subject line. In full mode, it will capture the entire content of a message. Carnivore was designed to copy and store only information caught by the filter, thus keeping agents from looking at any information not covered by the court order. In response to ongoing negative press coverage the technology was renamed a more innocent "DCS1000" and the special purpose Carnivore package was shelved in 2002 in favor of commercial off-the-shelf products which function similarly and are known as "packet sniffers." The use of this digital traffic monitoring software generally requires the cooperation of ISPs or other third parties, which may be voluntary or by court order.[88]

Because packet sniffers still cannot overcome the protective power of strong encryption, security authorities sought means to track actual physical computer keystrokes to capture passwords and text before encryption. The FBI has developed two technologies, the Key Logger System (KLS), which requires physical installation on a computer, and the software-based Magic Lantern that can be surreptitiously downloaded and installed on a computer.[89]

Once agents discover that they have seized encrypted information, they can seek a warrant to install and retrieve KLS. In the case of Nicodemo Scarfo, a suspected racketeer, agents had to show before installing KLS both probable cause that Scarfo was involved in crime and probable cause that evidence of criminal activity was encrypted on his computer. As in other warrants, the FBI had to specify the exact location of the computer on which KLS would be installed.[90]

Once installed, KLS uses a "keystroke capture" device to record keystrokes as they are entered into a computer. It is not capable of searching or recording fixed data stored on the computer. Moreover, KLS is designed so that it is unable to record keystrokes while a computer's modem is in operation,[91] because intercepting electronic communications would require an intercept order that is more difficult to get than a warrant.

Because KLS must be manually installed on a suspect's computer, it requires breaking and entering into a suspect's home. In contrast, Magic Lantern allows the FBI to put software on a computer to record keystrokes without installing any physical device. Like KLS, Magic Lantern cannot decrypt e-mail by itself but can retrieve the suspect's password. The details of how it does this have not been released. It is said to install itself on the suspect's computer in a way similar to a Trojan horse computer virus. It disguises itself as an ordinary, harmless message, then inserts itself onto a computer. For example, when someone connects to the Internet, a pop-up box could appear, stating "Click here to win!" When the user clicks on the box, the virus will enter the computer.[92]

Groups like the Electronic Privacy Information Center (EPIC) and the Center for Democracy and Technology (CDT) have raised multiple arguments for why packet sniffers should not be used at all.

They are skeptical that these programs operate as the FBI claims and are troubled by the degree of secrecy the FBI maintains about the way it works. Furthermore, they argue that separating addressing information from content is more difficult for Internet communications than for phone calls. Therefore, Carnivore, they say, will not allow the FBI to do a pen/trap without seizing more information than authorized.[93] Privacy advocates also worry that packet sniffers violate the Fourth Amendment because they scan through "tens of millions of e-mails and other communications from innocent Internet users as well as the targeted suspect."[94] The ACLU compares a Carnivore search to the FBI sending agents into a post office to "rip open each and every mail bag and search for one person's letters."[95]

Officials at the FBI respond that when used properly, packet sniffers will capture only the targeted e-mails. Additionally, Carnivore's use is subject to strict internal review and requires the cooperation of technical specialists and ISP personnel, thus limiting the opportunities an unscrupulous agent might have to abuse it.[96]

A review of the original Carnivore program conducted by the Illinois Institute of Technology concluded that although it does not completely eliminate the risk of capturing unauthorized information, Carnivore is better than any existing alternatives because it can be configured to comply with the limitations of a court order. However, the report also determined that failure to include audit trails makes the FBI's internal review process deficient. Specifically, the operator implementing a Carnivore search selects either pen or full mode by clicking a box on a computer screen, and the program does not keep track of what kind of search has been run.[97]

Therefore, it is difficult, if not impossible, to determine whether an operator has used the program only as specified in the court order. Furthermore, it is impossible to trace actions to specific individuals because everyone uses the same user ID.[98] The head of the review panel commented, "Even if you conclude that the software is flawless and it will do what you set it to do and nothing more, you still have to make sure that the legal, human, and organizational controls are adequate."[99] This focus on accountability will be explored below.

The oversight of these surveillance activities has traditionally been conducted under the ground rules of the Foreign Intelligence Surveillance Act of 1978. The Act set up a special court to review wiretap or corresponding digital surveillance activities. The court routinely approved about 500 warrants a year, rising to 1,758 in 2004.[100] The court also oversees efforts to minimize the collection of information about American citizens given the focus on foreign agents. Since 2001 there has been an escalating controversy between the administration and the courts and Congress over the minimization procedures and the practice of issuing "national security letters" as an alternative to court-approved warrants. One estimate reports that the FBI may issue over 30,000 national security letters a year, indicating a high level of warrantless surveillance.[101] Further, the Bush Administration pressed for legislation that provides immunity from litigation for telephone and Internet companies that cooperate with authorities,[102] a proposal not well received by the Democratic Congress. As of mid-2008, the controversy continued without clear resolution and is likely to continue as an issue for the current administration.

ACCOUNTABILITY—A QUESTION OF BALANCE

When homeland protection is discussed, it is often framed in terms of finding a legitimate balance between two competing public goods—safety and liberty. As Senator Ron Wyden (D, OR), put it in a December 2007 *Washington Post* op-ed considering the reauthorization and updating of FISA: "For nearly 30 years, the Foreign Intelligence Surveillance Act of 1978 (FISA) has represented the ultimate balance between our needs to fight terrorism ferociously and to protect the constitutional rights of Americans."[103] Former Senator Russ Feingold (D-WI), speaking on the Senate floor explaining his "no" vote on the USA PATRIOT Act in 2001, framed his decision to do so in similar terms: "I have concluded that this bill still does not strike the right balance between empowering law enforcement and protecting civil liberties."[104] Back in 2004, the *Economist* framed the debate between Democrats and Republicans on homeland protection, again referring to this first balance:

> Since the terrorist attacks of September 11th 2001, the Bush administration has brought in a slew of law-enforcement and surveillance powers that critics fear is turning America into an Orwellian nightmare. The worriers are thinking of the all-seeing Big Brother of "1984", though so far the chaos of "Animal Farm" may be closer to it. Others—and they are still in a clear majority—feel that a few limits on their freedoms are a

small price to pay for fewer terrorist attacks. But even they agree that a balance has to be struck between civil liberties and security. The argument—between Republicans and Democrats, George Bush and John Kerry—is over where exactly this balance should lie.[105]

Moreover, courts regularly use the terminology of balance, weighing the public interest against individual rights, and allowing the latter to be curtailed when they undermine a "compelling public interest," for instance, allowing the violation of privacy of sex offenders in order to protect children from sex abuse, authorizing wiretaps for suspected killers, and to enhance security.

The next step is to recognize that the point of balance itself changes throughout history, as domestic and international conditions change. Thus, in the wake of Prohibition more power was given to national police forces—for example, to the FBI—after it was revealed that local law enforcement authorities were riddled with corruption. At that time, J. Edgar Hoover was a major positive force, bringing professionalism and integrity to police work. Over the decades that followed, the FBI accumulated more and more power and eventually itself became a major violator of individual rights and civil liberties, leading to the Church Committee reforms in the 1970s, which greatly curbed the bureau's powers—tilting the balance back toward stronger protections of individual rights. Following 9/11, the USA PATRIOT Act was introduced, followed by numerous other security-enhancing measures introduced by President Bush, which, as noted above, jerked the balance heavily in the opposite direction.

The question is, given the current conditions, which direction does the balance need to be pulled? Critics often argue that new security measures are excessive and demand that they be rolled back. But, it is necessary to proceed with some caution here. Although there have been no successful terrorist attacks on the U.S. homeland since 9/11, there is good reason to assume that continued attempts will be made to inflict harm on the United States. Moreover, old and new security measures are best treated not as one bundle, but reviewed one at a time. One should avoid both holistic positions—the ones that claim that we are at war and hence must pull out all the stops, or the position that all new security measures are suspect. An unbundled review finds the following:

1. *Some measures are fully justified, indeed overdue.* These often entail a mere adaptation of the law for technical developments. For example, FISA provided guidelines under which a federal agent could obtain authorization to conduct surveillance for "foreign intelligence purposes." Prior to 9/11, wiretap warrants were limited to a given phone. Because of the increasing use of multiple cell phones and e-mail accounts over the last decades noted earlier, federal officials engaged in surveillance under FISA found it much more difficult to conduct surveillance, as they could not follow suspects as they changed the instruments they were using unless they got a new court order for each communication device. As we saw, the USA PATRIOT Act, enacted in October 2001, overcame this difficulty by amending the existing FISA law to allow what is called "roving surveillance authority"—making it legal for agents to follow one suspect, once a warrant is granted, whatever instrument he or she uses. Unless one holds that terrorists are entitled to benefit from new technologies but law enforcement is not entitled to catch up, this is an overdue and reasonable measure.

Similarly, before 9/11, the regulations that allowed public authorities to record or trace e-mails were interpreted by Justice Department lawyers as requiring court orders from several jurisdictions through which e-mail messages travel.[106] This was the case because in the old days phone lines were local and hence to tap a phone, local authorization sufficed. In contrast, e-mail messages travel by a variety of routes. As of 2001, the USA PATRIOT Act permits national tracing and recording.

A third example of a measure that is overdue stems from another technological development. FISA warrants are not required for surveillance of foreign to foreign communications. Currently, however, many foreigner to foreigner communications (say, from Latin America to Europe) are routed through the United States. Still, the law is interpreted as requiring a warrant for tapping these communications, as if they were between U.S. persons. A progressive should not oppose updating this interpretation of the law to adapt to new technological realities.

2. *Some new security measures are reasonable.* One should note that although the PATRIOT Act has become a sort of symbol for great excesses in hasty pursuit of security, only a small fraction, about 15 of its more than 150 measures, have been seriously contested. (Indeed, one of them reduces the penalty on hackers!) That

is, most measures encompassed in the act are considered reasonable even by civil libertarians. Another example of a new security measure that seems reasonable is a tracking system of those who come to study, visit, or do business in the United States. Before 9/11, the United States did not check whether those who came into the country for a defined period of time, say on a student visa, left at the end of that period. Many did not leave, but there was no way of knowing how many there were, who they were, and above all what they were doing. The new Internet-based student tracking system requires colleges to alert authorities if a newly enrolled foreign student fails to show up for school or is otherwise unaccounted for. The system was initially plagued by a variety of problems (not the least of which was opposition by some college administrators, students, and others). One can argue whether or not such a measure is beneficial, but it is hard to see why it would be declared *prima facie* unreasonable, a system that is in place in practically all free societies.

3. *Some measures such as torture and mass detention of people based on their social status are beyond the pale.*

4. *Many measures are neither inherently justified because enhanced security requires them nor inappropriate because they wantonly violate rights.* Instead, their status is conditioned on their being subject to proper oversight. In other words, the legitimacy of such measures depends on their place in what I call the second balance.

THE SECOND BALANCE

Homeland protection requires drawing greatly on the second balance and not being limited to attempts to find the first one. The idea that underlies the second balance is that a measure that may seem tilted toward excessive attention to security may be tolerated if closely supervised by second-balance organs, while a measure that is judged as tilting toward excessive attention to individual rights may be tolerated if sufficient exceptions are provided that are backed up by second-balance organs. That is, new measures can either be excessively privileged (undermining either security or the regime of rights) or excessively discriminated against both (leading to inaction on behalf of either element of a sound balance). Such second-balance organs and mechanisms — layers of accountability, in essence — include limitations built into the law itself; supervision within executive agencies; the courts and judicial or administrative review; Congress, and even the public.[107]

The second balance sought here is not between the public interest and rights, but between the supervised and the supervisors. Deficient accountability opens the door to government abuses of power, and excessively tight controls make agents reluctant to act or incapable of doing so.

Although the two forms of balance have some similarities and at some points overlap, they are quite distinct. For instance, the argument that the government should not be able to decrypt encoded messages is different from recognizing that such powers are justified —as long as they are properly circumscribed and their use is duly supervised. The concern and focus of this second balance is not whether they government should be accorded new powers but rather how closely it is held accountable regarding the ways that it uses these powers.

A simple example of the idea at hand may serve to introduce this key point. On many highways drivers now have the option of using computerized toll-collection systems, such as the E-Z pass, whereby an electronic device deducts the toll from credit posted on a chip inside the person's car. The information gained by the computers of the toll booth—that a car owned by a given person passed a given point at a given time—can be treated in a variety of ways. At one extreme, it can be erased immediately after the computer deducts the proper amount from the credit stored in the car's chip. At the opposite extreme, such data can be kept on file for years, added to that person's dossier kept by a government agency or even private company, and made available for law enforcement, divorce lawyers and even the media (a far from hypothetical situation). One extreme maximizes individual rights, especially privacy, while the second excessively privileges security and arguably other common goods. And one can readily conceive of a variety of intermediary positions.

If one approaches this device only within a first-balance frame of mind, one will ask how long and for what usages one should allow the said information to be stored. One then judges the use of E-Z passes—or any other such measure—as proper or as illegitimate per se. The second balance adds another major consideration: it asks how the arrangements worked out in terms of the first balance are reviewed and enforced.

Different answers to this second question will lead one either to tolerate or reject a measure, whatever its standing according to the first-order balance. Thus, for instance, if we know that said information will be used only for curbing terrorism, and be available only if a proper search warrant has been issued by a court, one may find such storing of information more acceptable than if one learns that on many occasions the employees of toll agencies released the information to the likes of private investigators and the media. The same holds for all security measures except those that are tabooed.

The term *balance* is chosen because one can tilt excessively in either direction. Although most consideration is currently given to lack of adequate oversight, supervision or accountability (here, I use the term *oversight* to refer to all such second-order processes: those that examine, review, and correct first-order processes), the opposite can also take place. For instance, FBI and CIA agents may again become reluctant to act if they believe that the acts they were authorized—indeed ordered—to carry out in the past can be retroactively defined as illegal and they can be jailed for having performed their jobs, or at least be forced to assume large personal debts to pay for legal representation. (True, as the famous Eichmann case illustrated, from a moral standpoint there are some acts that "everyone" should know are beyond the pale regardless of what their orders are, and should hence refuse orders to carry them out. However, one cannot run a security system based on the notion that people will rebel routinely. Instead, one should seek to ensure that as a rule those involved will be able to assume that orders are legitimate, in part because they are subject to proper oversight.)

Oversight is already in place in several forms and modes. And it is without the desired effect. However, a progressive approach recognizes that in the current circumstances it is essential to make oversight much stronger—in order to allow enhanced security.

IN CONCLUSION

Determining whether a specific public policy measure is legitimate entails more than establishing whether it significantly enhances public safety and minimally intrudes on individual rights. It also requires assessing whether those granted new powers are sufficiently accountable to the various overseers—ultimately to the citizenry. Some powers are inappropriate no matter what oversight is provided. However, others are appropriate given sufficient accountability. If accountability is deficient, the remedy is to adjust accountability, not to deny the measure altogether.

Whether the specific powers given to the government sustain or undermine the balance between rights and safety depends on how strong each layer of accountability is, whether higher layers enforce lower ones, and whether there are enough layers of accountability. I suggest that we should ignore both the public authorities' claims that no strengthening of accountability is needed and the shrillest civil libertarian outcries that no one is to be trusted. Instead, we should promote reforms that will enhance accountability rather than deny public authorities the tools they need to do their work. This does not necessarily mean granting them all the powers they request. But in a world where new technologies have made the government's duties more difficult and in which the threat to public safety has vastly increased, we should focus more on accountability before denying powers to law enforcement.

Chapter 4

UAS: The Moral and Legal Case

In 1946, I was a member of the Palmach, a Jewish underground commando unit that pressured the British to allow Jews who escaped Nazi-ravaged Europe to settle into what would become Israel. I say "pressured" because unlike our competitor, the Irgun, we fought a largely public relations war. We did so by alerting the British military to leave before we blew up the buildings that housed them—to grab headlines not bodies.

One day we attacked a British radar station near Haifa. A girl and I, in civilian clothes and looking as if we were on a date, casually walked up to the radar station's fence, cut the fence, and placed a bomb. Before it exploded, we disappeared into the crowd milling around in an adjacent street. All the British could do was either indiscriminately machine gun the crowd—or let us get away. Indeed, their inability to cope with abusive civilians was one reason the British retreated from Palestine and scores of other colonial territories, the French ultimately lost the war in Algeria, the Soviet Union in Afghanistan, and the United States in Vietnam—although here the North Vietnamese regular forces also played a key role.

The substantial increase in the employment of Unmanned Aviation Systems (UAS) in Afghanistan, Pakistan, and other arenas has intensified the debate about the moral and legal nature of the targeted killing of people who are said to be civilians. As I see it, the United States and its allies can make a strong case that the main source of the problem are those who abuse their civilian status to attack truly innocent civilians and to prevent our military and other security forces from discharging their duties. In the longer run, we should work toward a new Geneva Convention, one that will define the status of those now called unlawful combatants. These people should be viewed as having forfeited most of their rights as civilians by acting in gross violation of the rights of others and of the rules of war.

51

To support my thesis, we must go back to the period in which the precept that currently still dominates much of the public discourse on the issue at hand was forged. For generations, growing efforts had been made to limit wars to confrontations among conventional armies, sparing civilians. That is, a sharp line was drawn between soldiers (who were considered fair targets during war) and civilians (whose killing was taboo). True, these shared understandings were not always observed. Thus during World War II, the Nazis tried to break Britain by blitzing London, and their dive bombers attacked many other civilian centers. The Allied Forces bombed Dresden, set a firestorm in Tokyo, and leveled Nagasaki and Hiroshima. However, these attacks were condemned, or at least ethically questioned, precisely on the grounds that they eroded the line that ought to separate armed forces from civilians and protect the latter.

Over the last decade, however, we have witnessed a rise in terrorism with a global reach and potential access to weapons of mass destruction—the gravest threat to our security, that of our allies, and of many others. These terrorists systematically and repeatedly use their civilian status to their advantage, both to enhance their operations and to mobilize public opinion. Thus, they have used ambulances to transport suicide bombers and their bombs—and have had their allies complain when security forces started checking ambulances, causing some delays in their services. Terrorists disguised themselves as civilian passengers in order to hijack airplanes full of innocent people, turning the planes into missiles in order to kill thousands working peacefully at their desks—and afterwards found people who complained vociferously about the security measures that were introduced to prevent such attacks. Terrorists stored their ammunition in mosques, mounted anti-aircraft guns on top of schools and hospitals, set their command-and-control centers in private homes and made them into bivouacs—and then screamed bloody murder when any of these installations were hit by our bombers, artillery, or drones. In short, we must make it much clearer that those who abuse their civilian status are the main reason for the use of UAS and targeted killing.

Another way to illustrate this key point is to conduct the following mental experiment. Take any fighting force, say the Japanese military in World War II. If that force is abiding by the rules of war—wearing clear insignia identifying the troops and their encampments, and thus the government that is accountable for their actions—they can be (and were) legitimately targeted, bombed, and killed. No one raises moral or legal issues—beyond a few pacifists who would rather surrender than fight at all—even if the particular unit is not engaged in battle: it might be resting in its camp, being resupplied, or in training somewhere in the hinterland. Now imagine the *same* troops take off their uniforms, put on civilians' clothing, and move into civilians' homes, community centers, and shrines. Now, are they no longer legitimate targets?

Unlike armchair ethicists—who write about this matter and never come closer to combat than watching a movie in a nearby theater—I have some firsthand experience in the matter, as illustrated by the personal account by which I introduced this chapter. Blending fighters with civilians has proved successful, and attempts to sift the two difficult and dangerous, as my experience demonstrated.

Does all this mean that we should attack masses of civilians, merely because some of them have—or may be about to—attack us? Certainly not. It does mean that in order to negate the tactical advantages abusive civilians have and to minimize our casualties, we must attack abusive civilians whenever we can find them, before they attack us. As we shall see shortly, UAS are a particularly well-suited means to serve this goal.

Hence instead of apologizing each time the wrong individual is targeted or collateral damage is caused, we should stress that the issue would be largely resolved in very short order if the abusive civilians would stop their abusive practices and fight—if they must—according to established rules of war. We should stress that they cannot have it both ways: violate these rules repeatedly and seek to be shielded by them. And while investigations after each incident have their place, to determine whether we received wrong intelligence or to further refine the decision-making matrix involved (more about this shortly), they should not be construed as an indication that the main source of the problem is our response to abusive civilians who attacked us.

To suggest that we need a new shared understanding, for which we must first make the moral case and then move to ensconce it in a new Geneva-like convention, is far from implausible. After all, the Geneva Conventions have been extended, revised, and augmented several times.

SMALLER PRINT

In examining the arguments about the moral and legal status of using UAS (and other forms of targeted killing), I am using as my text an October 2009 article by Jane Mayer in *The New Yorker*. The article touches on all the major issues involved, albeit with a dose of liberal coloring. (The article is called "Predator War,"[108] a name which is both accurate and revealing. Mayer has previously written critically about the treatment of terror suspects in her 2008 book, whose title again speaks volumes: *The Dark Side*.[109])

Mayer opens her reportage with a case in point: a man is lounging on the rooftop somewhere in Pakistan. He has a bunch of visitors. He is not well: he has diabetes and a kidney disease. We even can see—thanks to a drone that is hovering above—his IV drip. Suddenly, poof, two missiles strike, and all we have left is a torso. Several of the visitors are also dead.

The picture changes though, as Mayer reports that Baitullah Mesud was the man on the rooftop, a man responsible for the assassination of Benazir Bhutto, the September 2008 bombing of the Islamabad Marriott, and numerous attacks on American and coalition forces in Afghanistan. Another case Mayer points to is a 2002 killing by a UAV (unmanned aerial vehicle) of a few people driving in a car, somewhere on a road deep inside Yemen. This, Mayer tells us, was Qaed Salim Sinan al-Harethi, an Al Qaeda operative who is reported to have played a key role in the bombing of the U.S.S. *Cole*. It is helpful to keep such cases in mind when one faces the questions Mayer, speaking in effect for other skeptics of the program, raises about the use of UAS.

CAN ABUSIVE CIVILIANS BE TREATED LIKE CRIMINALS?

Some suggest that we would be better off if we with dealt with abusive civilians like criminals; that is—instead of killing them—haul them into a court of law. Of course in numerous situations, including the two Mayer describes, such capture could not be executed or only at very great risk to our forces and to the local civilian population.

Moreover, often—say, when dealing with Al Qaeda leaders and foot soldiers and others like them—security requires *preventing* attacks rather than prosecuting the perpetrators after the attack has occurred. This is particularly evident when we concern ourselves with terrorists who may acquire weapons of mass destruction. It also holds for terrorists who are willing to commit suicide during their attack and hence either cannot be tried, or will pay no mind to what might be done to them after their assault. Finally, even terrorists not bent on committing suicide attacks are often "true believers" who are willing to proceed despite whatever punishments the legal system may throw at them. As noted in Chapter 1, all these kinds of terrorists are best prevented from proceeding rather than vainly trying to prosecute them after the fact, and most cannot be effectively deterred by the criminal justice system.

In contrast to the need for prevention, law enforcement often springs into action after a criminal has acted: when a body is found, after bank is robbed, or a child is kidnapped. By and large, the criminal law approach is retrospective rather than prospective. Law enforcement assumes that punishment after the fact serves to deter future crimes (not to eliminate them, but to keep them at a socially acceptable level). This will not do for the likes of Osama bin Laden.

This is not to say that if captured, terrorists should not be grant-ed basic human rights. They should not be killed when they can be safely detained and held, nor should they be subjected to torture, or detained indefinitely without an institutionalized review of their status. However, they are not entitled to the full plethora of rights our citizens are entitled to because they choose to fight in a way that abuses the rules on which these rights are based.

I leave it for another day to examine the argument implied in the rules of war that both parties have the same basic moral status, and hence both must abide equally by the rules, and to examine the notion of fair play—which suggests that when we kill many of the enemy but have only few casualties of our own, that there "must be" something foul in the way we fight. Suffice it to say here, that those who attack us in the disguise of being civilians—and who act brutally, not only toward our civilians, but even toward their compatriots (e.g., if they heed a different version of the same religion, happen to be women, minors, or of a different color)—do not have the same moral standing as our troops.

IS THERE ENOUGH ACCOUNTABILITY?

The preceding analysis does not suggest that UAS should be used indiscriminately against anybody who may threaten our security or that of others. The statement Mayer quotes that "no tall man with a beard [i.e., similar to bin Laden] is safe anywhere in Southwest Asia"[110] is obviously false. Indeed, the use of UAS is subject to close review. The U.S. military developed a set of criteria that must be met before a strike is authorized. The details are not publicized, but during a visit with officers of a brigade before it shipped out to Afghanistan, I was told that they include the reliability of the intelligence that identified the target (in some cases, verification from two independent sources is required) and the number and status of other people in the area. The less reliable the information and the greater the potential collateral damage, the more people review the information and the higher the rank of those in the military who must approve the strike—all the way up to the Commander-in-Chief. Strikes also are reexamined after they occur in cases in which we erred. Thus, in effect, abusive civilians benefit from an extensive review before targeted killing takes place.

One should, though, note that just as the matrix (the decision-making apparatus used by the military) can be too accommodating, it can also be too restrictive. In several cases the delay in decision involved, or the strictness of the criteria employed, allowed abusive civilians of considerable rank and power to escape. (Bin Laden was given the time to escape to a new location in 2004 when the Pakistani government delayed giving permission for the attack on its soil.)

And at least according to one source, after General McChrystal decided to cut back on bombing and targeted killing, because of what was considered excessive collateral damage, our own casualties increased. The *Washington Post* reported on September 23, 2009 that there has been "a sharp increase in U.S. troop deaths in Afghanistan at a time when senior military officials acknowledge that American service members are facing greater risks under a new strategy that emphasizes protecting Afghan civilians."[111] The moral ground for this approach is far from self-evident. I turn below to the prudential argument that such sacrifices will win over the population, and hence will save lives—ours and theirs—in the longer run.

WHAT ABOUT COLLATERAL DAMAGE?

Even if one fully accepts that targeted killing of the leaders and maybe foot soldiers of groups like Al Qaeda is justified, one still must be concerned, for moral and prudential reasons, about collateral damage—which involves by definition innocent civilians.

Here, too, one must first of all reiterate that the main fault lies with the abusive citizens, who refuse to separate themselves from the local population.

Second, to some extent collateral damage can be reduced by enabling the general population to leave an area before an attack, as the Pakistani army did in Swat Valley. Or by encouraging the general population to separate itself from abusive citizens, as Israel did during the 2009 operation in Gaza.

Third, the extent of potential collateral damage is and should continue to be one criterion in the matrix of decision-making that is used by the U.S. military when UAS or drone strikes are authorized. That is, consideration is given not only to the "values" of the target and to the reliability of information about the target, but also the number and kind of innocent civilians surround the target (children in particular).

Additionally, one should note that some of the population acts like part-time spies, intelligence agents, lookouts, and providers of services like accommodations and medical care to the terrorists. To the extent that these services are provided voluntarily rather than coerced, the population must be warned that they will be treated the same ways as combat service support personnel that provide such services.

Last but not least, there is no reason to hold that UAS cause more collateral damage than bombing or even attacks with Special Forces or regular ones.

ARE UAS STRIKES LEGAL?

Are UAS strikes legal by our own laws? Congress has authorized the President "to use all necessary and appropriate force" against "persons he determines planned, authorized, committed, or aided" in 9/11 or who harbored such persons. Both the Obama and Bush Administrations have stated that this act of Congress grants them the legal power to authorize UAS strikes. And because the targets are engaged in combat against us, many legal experts state that the strikes are not in violation of Executive Order 12333's long-time prohibition on assassination.

Are strikes legal according to international law? Mayer reports that, "In order for the U.S. government to legally target civilian terror suspects abroad it has to define a terrorist group as one engaging in armed conflict, and the use of force must be a 'military necessity.' There must be no reasonable alternative to killing, such as capture, and to warrant death the target must be 'directly participating in hostilities.' The use of force has to be considered 'proportionate' to the threat. Finally, the foreign nation in which such targeted killing takes place has to give its permission."[112]

Without going here into a detailed analysis whether or not the United States strikes in all the cases, from Pakistan to Yemen, meet all these criteria, I should point out that international law (or for that matter domestic law) is rarely that unambiguous. Indeed, there is considerable literature on the subject, which reaches a wide range of conclusions.[113] Nor are the facts always as straightforward as one would need to meet the standards. For instance, the Pakistani government protests publicly the use of UAS, but privately provides bases for them and intelligence to identify targets. Does this mean that the foreign power did or did not give consent? And why should a government be expected to seek the consent of a nation that supports terrorism—say, if Israel targets a terrorist in Damascus, should it await the consent of Syria?

Most important, laws are not carved in stone. They are living documents. The Constitutional right to privacy did not exist until 1965. Our current understanding of the First Amendment's right to free speech, considered the most absolute right of them all, is an interpretation of the text fashioned in the 1920s. The Geneva Conventions were developed over decades—and thus can be further developed.[114]

DO UAS ALIENATE THE POPULATION?

Prudential arguments against the use of UAS are that they antagonize the population, create martyrs, invite retaliatory attacks, entail the loss of moral high ground, and undermine the legitimacy of the local government (for cooperating with Americans). All this may be true, but the same holds for other means of warfare. Using bombers often generates even more collateral damage and resentment. Attacks by Special Forces are considered more alienating than strikes by UAS because they entail a blatant violation of sovereignty. Nor are there necessarily fewer mistaken targets or less collateral damage when Special Forces or regular forces are used. Last but not least, important segments of the population resent the presence of foreign troops—and the governments they support—for a variety of sentimental, cultural, religious, and nationalistic reasons. No wonder that in areas and periods in which the use of UAS was scaled back, there was no noticeable change in the attitudes of the population.

Hence the main issues are how quickly we can turn over security to native forces and the extent to which we should interfere in the way the people govern themselves—not which means of warfare we use, as long as we stay engaged. Indeed, the reason UAS have recently gained special attention is largely because of their novelty and because their employment is rapidly growing. If they were replaced tomorrow with Autonomous Rotorcraft Sniper Systems, or some other new means of warfare, similar issues would be raised about these technologies.

Also, one should take into account the preferences of the American people and its allies. Using Special Forces or regular troops instead of UAS increases our casualties and tends to undermine the public support of the mission. UAS contribute to staying the course as long as this perseverance is called for.

In Cold Blood?

Finally, UAS are criticized on the grounds that they are manned by people sitting in air-conditioned offices, in Nevada or Florida, playing around with a joystick, before they go home for dinner and to coach little league. According to Mayer, ethicist Peter W. Singer believes that the drone technology is "'seductive,' because it creates the perception that war can be 'costless.'"[115] Moreover, the victims (Mayer's term) remain faceless. And the damage caused by the UAS remains unseen. Mary Dudziak of USC's law school opines, "Drones are a technological step that further isolates the American people from military action, undermining political checks on . . . endless war."[116]

This kind of cocktail-party sociology does not stand up to minimal critical examination. Would we or the people of Afghanistan and Pakistan—or, for that matter, the terrorists—be better off if they were killed in hot blood? Say, knifed by Special Forces, blood and brain matter splashing in their faces? If our troops, to reach the terrorists, had to go through IEDs blowing up their legs and arms, and through gauntlets of machine gun fire and RPGs, experiences that turn some of them into psychopath-like killers and return many home traumatized?

If all or most fighting were done in a cold-blooded, push-button way, it might well have the effects Mayer suggests. However, as long as what we are talking about are a few hundred drone drivers, what they do or do not feel has no discernable effects on the nation or the leaders who declare war. Indeed, there is no evidence that the introduction of UAS (and before that, high-level bombing and cruise missiles that were criticized on the same grounds) made going to war more likely or extending it more acceptable. Anybody who followed the history of our disengagement in Vietnam after the introduction of high-level bombing, or the difficulties President Obama faced in increasing troop levels in Afghanistan in the fall of 2009—despite the recent increased use in UAS—knows better.

THE MORAL TURNING POINT

As someone who lost many friends in combat and saw many other wounded, and who inflicted such losses on others—I strongly abhor violence. I have written books, essays, and op-eds, testified before Congress, consulted the White House, and demonstrated in the streets to promote peaceful solutions and urge the curbing of the use of arms, from handguns to nuclear bombs.

As I see it, however, the main point of moral judgment must be faced earlier in the chain of action, well before we come to the question of which means are to be used to kill the enemy. The main turning point concerns the question whether we should go to war at all. This is the crucial decision because once we engage in war, we must assume that there is going to be a large number of casualties on all sides and that these may well include many innocent civilians.

Often, discussions of targeted killings strike me as written by people who yearn for a nice clean war, one in which only bad people will be killed using "surgical" strikes that inflict no collateral damage. Very few armed confrontations unfold in this way. Hence when we deliberate whether or not to fight, we should assume that once we step on this escalator, it is very likely to carry us to places we would rather not go, but must. The UAS are a rather minor, albeit new, stepping stone on this woeful journey.

Chapter 5

Scanners: A Threat to Privacy?[117]

If you've passed through a major American airport in the past few months, you may have been subjected to a full-body scan. The new backscatter and millimeter-wave sensing devices that have been deployed across the country check whether people hide forbidden objects under their clothes. Privacy advocates refer to them as "virtual strip-searches." But how worried should one be about these scanners? Are they truly a grave threat to individual privacy, as civil libertarians contend?

I come at this issue as a communitarian. This philosophy holds that our public-policy decisions must balance two core values: our commitment to individual rights and our commitment to the common good.[118] Neither is *a priori* privileged. Thus, when threatened by the lethal SARS virus, we demanded that contagious people stay home—even though this limited their freedom to assemble and travel—because the contribution to the common good was high and the intrusion limited. Yet we banned the trading of medical records because these trades constituted a severe intrusion, but had no socially redeeming merit.[119] Viewed through this communitarian lens, I must say that the case against these scanners is deeply unconvincing.

The actual threat to privacy posed by these scanners has been inflated using sensationalistic imagery. In order to illustrate how intrusive this "strip-search" is, civil liberties advocates often display a rather graphic image obtained from a scanner.[120] Yet they neglect to mention that the image is not of an airline passenger but of a TSA employee who volunteered to test the machine. (After all, if someone is willing to expose themselves, especially for a good cause, we have little reason to object.) Moreover, as you can see, the images of passengers that actually appear on TSA screens are a far cry from the one circulated by civil liberties advocates, because the scanners are equipped with two kinds of privacy filters.[121] One conceals the genitals and the other the face. (What's more, new scanner software replaces the realistic images of the passengers who are being scanned with a cartoon of a generic, clothed body—an avatar for the subject—and marks areas that should be checked further.[122] This software is currently being tested.) Further preserving privacy, TSA

61

staffers who view the images are in a separate room and are un-aware of the identity of the passenger who is screened.

True, when we deal with millions of travelers, day in and day out, someone somewhere will cross the line. Thus, civil libertarians make much of the fact that a scanner in use in a Florida courthouse had stored over 35,000 images (although there is no evidence that any-body dispersed these images to people not authorized to review them). Yet efforts to flag such incidents should not distract us from the essential fact that these privacy violations are exceedingly rare and not necessarily damaging.

To wit, there is virtually no evidence that body scanners have ac-tually harmed Americans. Indeed, civil liberties advocates generally do a poor job of explaining precisely what kind of harm the scanners are supposed to cause. Libertarians may contend that the new secur-ity measures have a "chilling effect" on people beyond those directly affected. However, there is little evidence of this effect, and it is hard to explain what exactly it means in concrete terms. Do fewer people fly because of the scanners—even when dealing with short distances, where there are ready alternatives such as the Acela and rental cars?

The ACLU further asserts that the scanners amount to "a signif-icant assault on the essential dignity of passengers"[123] but provides no concrete evidence to this effect. On the contrary, the people whose dignity is supposedly being assaulted do not feel that way : a January 2010 CBS News poll found that roughly three out of four Americans (74 percent) think airports should use full-body x-ray scanners because "they provide a detailed check for hidden weapons and explosives and reduce the need for physical searches."[124] Who should we trust to judge what does or doesn't threaten a passenger's dignity? Civil liberties activists, or the passengers themselves? As the public is well aware, being unable to fly without fear of being bombed out of the sky assaults people, and not just their dignity.

Most important, civil liberties advocates also ignore the fact that people who subject themselves to body scans do it voluntarily. They are free to choose a pat-down rather than passing through the millimeter-wave machine, and even then about 70 percent of Amer-icans say they prefer to be scanned. (The option of choosing a pat-down should not be considered unduly coercive, since random pat-downs were mandatory even before the installation of body scanners—and civil libertarians cannot seriously argue that there should be no scrutiny at all.) Even a strong libertarian should agree that if one consents to a search, especially when there is a ready alternative, there is no room for challenges. All of these facts suggest that the main libertarian criticisms against body scanners are simply not credible.

Finally, there is the core question of proportionality and context. The real issue at hand is what experience scanners provide to most people, most of the time, how frequent exceptional violations of privacy are, and what remedies are in place. The Electronic Privacy Information Center (EPIC), in its critique of scanners, states that new security measures "present privacy and security risks to air travelers because they *might* create data files directly linked to the identity of air travelers. These files, *if* retained, could provide the basis for a database of air traveler profiles."[125] (Emphases mine.) Likewise, *The New Republic*'s Jeffrey Rosen argues that "the greatest privacy concern is that the images *may* later leak."[126] Other privacy advocates hold that the radiation involved *may* harm one's health. Yet these concerns—almost entirely hypothetical—pale in comparison to the possibility that terrorists might bring down more airplanes, or worse.

Moreover, in their core mission of deterring terrorists, the body scanners cannot help but work. The ACLU argues, "It is far from clear that body scanners would have detected the 'anatomically congruent' explosives [that Christmas Day bomber Umar Farouk Abdulmutallab] hid in his underwear." And, it says, "some experts have said explosives can be hidden by being molded against the human body, or in folds of skin, and British newspapers are reporting that government testing in the UK found that the technology comes up short in detecting plastic, chemicals and liquids."[127] But this type of argument—the same type that the ACLU applies to nearly every security measure—is a bait and switch. It does not answer the question of how much security the scanners add.

Simply put, security effectiveness does not require 100 percent success, just a significant increase in the detection capability of the measures in place. In this way, the millimeter-wave devices narrow the opportunities for terrorists, add ways in which they can be detected, increase the probability that they will make an error, and reduce their confidence—as well as the confidence of those who employ them.

When all is said and done, we must vigilantly protect our rights, but we must also be concerned about our security. The spirit of this approach is embodied in the Fourth Amendment, which does not ban all searches—only unreasonable ones.[128] And the searches that body scanners perform are reasonable, if we keep in mind the fact that terrorists are far from done, and that our nation has a vital interest in protecting not just rights but also lives.

SECTION II

Human Rights

Chapter 6

A Right Above All Others

The demise of democratization as a rationale for United States foreign policy is all too evident. One must now ask which *leitmotif* will replace it. I suggest the principle of primacy of life as the normative foundation for American foreign policy. At the core of this principle stands the recognition that all people have a right to life, generally understood as a right to be free from deadly violence, maiming, and torture.

The right not to be killed, maimed, or tortured is enumerated in the 1948 United Nations Universal Declaration of Human Rights and enshrined in the American Declaration of Independence, in which life precedes both liberty and the pursuit of happiness. It is reflected in such religious concepts as "we all are God's children" and in the Jewish notion that he who saves one soul, it is as if he has saved an entire world.

Many tend to view the improvement of security—or the protection of life—as antithetical to individual and civil rights. Critics warn that in the quest for security, a nation may inadvertently become a police state. These are indeed valid concerns; each nation must constantly wrestle with the extent to which the protection of life can be advanced without undermining legal and political rights.[129] Nonetheless, one should not overlook the primacy of the right to life.

Much of ethics deals with the *ranking* of two goods rather than with the determination of which is right versus which is wrong. Given that saving lives and protecting legal-political rights are, quite clearly, two very significant goods, people are naturally inclined to refuse to choose between them and to insist that both can be equally well served. But the question remains: what is it to be done if they cannot be simultaneously advanced?

The provision of basic security—ensuring the right to life—takes precedence precisely because all other rights are contingent on the right to life, while the right to life is not contingent on any other rights. It sounds all too simplistic to state that dead people cannot exercise their rights, while those living securely may invoke the full spectrum of rights. But it is still an essential truth that when the right to security is violated, all other rights are threatened as well.[130] (This of course refers to actual threats to life, not to attempts to invoke fear for political ends.)

Thus, primacy of life, the security first principle, does not favor curtailing basic freedoms for marginal, additional gains in security in such places as London, Madrid, or New York, where a basic level of security already exists. However, it *does* command first priority where basic security does not exist—for example, at least until recently perhaps, in the streets of Baghdad, and currently in many parts of Afghanistan.

The claim that we value the right to life over all others is also supported by the observation that in all criminal codes of free societies, the penalties for murder, maiming, and torture are much more severe than those for violating property rights, restricting speech, and discrimination. These codes reflect the ranking of moral values in a way that is much more reflective of societal preferences than philosophical deliberations. Indeed, these rankings reflect centuries of rulings by courts, deliberations by citizens and their elected representatives, social science findings, and general experience. The value we place on the right to life is also the reason torture is widely condemned, and why the prevention of genocide is considered a more legitimate reason for intervening in the internal affairs of another nation than, say, democratization.

In the earlier review of public opinion polls concerning attitudes toward civil liberties following September 11,[131] we found that shortly after these events, nearly 70 percent of Americans were strongly inclined to concede on various constitutionally protected rights in order to prevent more attacks. However, as no new attacks too place on American soil, and a sense of security returned—measured by the rates of return by passengers to air travel—support for rights was restored. By 2005, about 70 percent of Americans were more concerned with protecting civil rights than with enhancing security.

Along the same lines, several keen observers have already noted that if an American city were wiped out by a nuclear weapon activated by terrorists, rights would surely be suspended on a wide scale, just as habeas corpus was suspended in the United Kingdom at the height of the Nazi onslaught during World War II. In short, evidence shows that the better security is protected, the more weight is given to legal-political rights.

The same relationship between the right to life and all other rights was evident during a period of years in which violent crime rates were sky high in major American cities. For instance, when former Los Angeles police chief Daryl Gates suggested that riots following the Rodney King verdict in 1992 might have been stopped in their tracks had police officers "gone down there and shot a few people," many sympathized with his viewpoint. Other police chiefs also favored a "shoot first, ask questions later" attitude.[132] In recent years, however, as violent crime has considerably declined in many American cities, a police chief who favored a policy that disregarded rights in such a summary way would likely be dismissed before the day was out.

Another case in point is post-Soviet Russia. Although Russia has never met the standards of a liberal democracy, a good part of whatever it had achieved on this front was gradually lost as Russians began to experience alarmingly high levels of violent crime. Vladimir Putin, who has been moving the regime in an authoritarian direction, was until recently widely regarded in Russia as not being tough enough on crime, rather than being too tough, because too many felt that basic security was lacking.[133]

One may argue the necessity of effectively promoting both life and other rights overseas. As I see it, brutal international reality often requires following what might be called a "second-worst" course to avoid having to negotiate the worst one—a long way from the notion that our choices are between the best and the second best. The tragic fact is that often the ruling powers do not even deliver on protecting life, as is evident in Darfur, Congo, Iraq, Afghanistan, Burma, and many other places. Surely other moral goods deserve our support; however, to the extent that our ability to do good is gravely limited, the question of priority—"triage" might be a more suitable term—cannot be ignored. Protecting life must come first.

Chapter 7

The Normativity of Human Rights is Self-Evident[134]

Numerous attempts have been made to justify human rights in terms of other sources of normativity. This essay suggests that such attempts unwittingly weaken the case of human rights and that instead these rights should be treated as moral causes that speak to us directly, as one of those rare precepts that is self-evident.[135] Suggesting that human rights should be treated as self-evident does not deny the value of examining their historical sources, nor the need to spell out what they entail, merely that attempts to support human rights by inserting a foundation underneath them end up undermining their construction. Human rights stand tall on their own.

WEAKENING JUSTIFICATIONS

Michael Ignatieff complains that many in the West have conceded far too much ground to challenges of the universality of human rights (posed both from without and within), bemoaning what he sees as a "desire to water down the individualism of rights discourse." But, to strip rights of their individualism, he argues, is to strip them of their ultimate justification—namely the preservation of individual agency. He writes: "Rights are universal because they define the universal interests of the powerless—namely, that power be exercised over them in ways that respect their autonomy as agents."[136] This justification raises more questions than it answers. For instance, are those who are not powerless not entitled to have their rights respected? All such arguments do is to move that which needs to be justified over by one notch, relying for support on concepts (e.g., "agency") whose normativity is less compelling than that which they are supposed to support: human rights.

Several influential historical writings that prefigure contemporary human rights discourse sought to derive these rights from natural law. In his *Second Treatise on Government*, John Locke claimed:

> The state of nature has a law of nature to govern it, which obliges every one: and reason, which is that law,

teaches all mankind, who will but consult it, that being
all equal and independent, no one ought to harm another in his life, health, liberty, or possessions.[137]

But, natural law has been long recognized as a particularly
opaque concept. Oliver Wendell Holmes, Jr. characterized it dis-
paragingly as "a brooding omnipresence in the sky."[138] More recently, legal philosopher Michael S. Moore quipped that natural law
theories are "rather like the northern lights...but without the
lights."[139] In short, the concept of natural law calls for much more
explication, and, at this least in this day and age, is inherently much
less compelling than human rights.

Some have attempted to argue for human rights as a necessary
pre-condition for other values. Joel Feinberg, for instance, argues
that human rights must exist because they are a "necessary pre-
condition" for self-respect, respect for others, and for personal
dignity.[140] Similarly, a foundational United Nations human rights
document states that rights "derive from the inherent dignity of the
human person."[141] Like other attempts to base the normativity of a
given moral claim on its service to other causes, this endeavor ends
up making the moral claim contingent: human rights are justified
only as long as they serve. If one can show that they are not necessary for, say, respect for others, they lose their normative standing.

Furthermore, it is far from obvious that "self-respect" has a
higher, clearer or more compelling moral standing than human
rights. The claims entailed by the respect of human rights—that
human beings have a right not to be killed, maimed or tortured—
seem to be much more sharply etched than the respect of "human
dignity" and less open to subjective interpretation. Many devout
people hold that human dignity requires shrouding women, preventing them from being educated, condemning homosexuals,
avoiding critical thinking, and even "honor" killing. To use self-
respect to justify human rights is like arguing that we should look
after our children so that we shall sleep better at night. Once again,
the proposed foundation is weaker than the structure it is meant to
support.

Attempts to base human rights on rationality or the social contract or some kind of Kantian imperative are all precepts that invite
the often repeated criticisms of these approaches which need not be
repeated here.[142]

An especially weak justification of the universality of human rights seeks to rely on the fact that a global normative consensus exists which supports them. Actually, universal consensus on normative issues is extremely thin. According to one study, the scope of such a consensus does not extend far beyond the agreement that in revenge killing, slaying more than eight people is not acceptable.[143] Although consensus is politically beneficial, it is morally dubious; many people can and do agree on positions that are not morally justified. Thus, sixty years ago there was very broad based consensus across the world—especially in closed societies and among those of closed minds (more below on these concepts)—that women are at best a second class of citizens.

Moreover, predicating the legitimacy of human rights on a global consensus grants de facto veto power to outlier countries. If, say, Myanmar and North Korean do not share the global respect for human rights, this should hardly be taken as a challenge to the normativity of these rights.

In sum, attempts to undergird human rights with constructions that need more support than these rights themselves is not a constructive way to proceed.

HUMAN RIGHTS ARE SELF-EVIDENT

Instead, human rights are best recognized as one of the rare moral precepts whose normativity is self-evident, speaks to us directly, unmitigated by other causes, in a compelling manner.[144]

It should be noted that, while the Founding Fathers spoke of "self-evident truths," I deliberately avoid invoking the term "truth" here. The term implies, at least in contemporary context, a logical, empirical, objective and/or scientific validity, which is rather different from an axiomatic nature of self-evident precepts. It concerns "is" statements while I deal here with "ought" statements. I avoid the term moral truth because it evokes efforts, like those of David Hume, that seek to base morality on objective foundations. In contrast, my claim that the normativity of human rights is self-evident indicates that they are inherently morally compelling rather than based on some empirical or logical exterior judgments.

Self-evident moral precepts compose a small category of moral claims. Other than human rights, there are not many precepts for which one can credibly make such a claim. Another example of a moral claim that speaks for itself, effectively and directly, is the dictum that we have higher obligations to our own children than to the children of all others. When evaluating this claim, one does not sense that there is a need for a consequentialist explanation, a calculus of harm, or some other form of utilitarian analysis and justification. My observation is not based on the fact that there is very wide consensus on this point, but that when one evaluates this claim, the answer is "obvious"; one does not sense a need for an explanation.[145] To put it in more metaphorical terms, some lights shine so brightly one hardly needs to point them out—unless one's vision is blocked, a point explored below.

I conducted an informal study in several countries with audiences of more than four hundred groups of rather different social, intellectual, and political backgrounds and persuasions. In each case, I asked the group members to pretend that they were a public school committee that must decide which values to teach in the third grade next year. First, I pointed out that it is impossible to formulate a value-free or neutral curriculum about most matters. Whatever one teaches about slavery, the Holocaust, Washington's cherry tree, and so on will have implied moral judgments (including of course if one tries to present "both" sides objectively). Next, I asked the various audiences if one should teach that truth-telling is superior to lying or vice versa under all but limited conditions (such as when someone is dying from cancer and asks whether there is any hope left). Without exception the groups looked puzzled. They wondered: "Where was the question I said I would ask?"; "Was there something else I meant to ask and did not?" In sum, "Why, the answer to the question I did ask was self-evident!"

None of the members of the groups I queried engaged in any kind of philosophical argumentation, such as, "If one tells a lie, soon others will do the same, and then we shall find ourselves in a world of liars, a world we do not wish to live in, therefore, we must not lie": they did not require such a utilitarian, consequentialist explanation.[146] Instead, they found the answer staring them in the face, speaking directly to them. Similarly, when people are asked whether one should be free from the fear of death or torture, or have a right to meet with others or practice one's religion, they readily recognize the value of such rights—at least, where their vision is not obscured (more about this shortly).

That some regimes do not observe many human rights does not challenge their status as a self-evident moral claim.[147] To hold that the normativity of human rights is self-evident does not entail assuming that human rights are self-enforcing, self-implementing, or omnipotent. Rather, they constitute a claim that all regimes face—whether or not they have yet learned to abide by them.

The thesis that there are some select moral causes that present themselves to us as compelling points to something similar to what religious authorities speak of as *revelation*. Importantly, in both religious and secular realms, drawing on such a source does not entail adopting a blind faith in it. It does not mean that one cannot also *reason* about these matters. The fact that some cause appears to one as compelling does not prevent one from examining it. However, *here reason follows, buttresses, or challenges revelation, rather than being the source of judgment.*[148]

When one recites the dictum that "it is better to let a thousand guilty people walk free rather than hang one innocent person," this may at first seem self-evident. However, when one then notes that these freed criminals are sure to kill at least several innocent people, one finds that the certitude of the initial statement is no longer nearly as strong as it seemed at first blush. In contrast, when one learns that a person reacted to a crime by engaging in revenge, the dictum "two wrongs do not make a right" stands, even after being examined.

Charles Taylor writes about this dual nature of morality: "our moral reactions have two facets, as it were. On one side, they are almost like instincts; on the other, they seem to involve claims about the nature and status of human beings."[149] Naturalists and emotivists, Taylor argues, want to forget about the second part;[150] true enough, but it would be equally a mistake to forget about the first part. One must keep in mind that rational explanations of normativity are attempts to, as Taylor puts it, "articulate" the moral sense, but are not its essence.[151]

HUMAN RIGHTS AS A PRIMARY CONCEPT

All systems of thought, whether mathematical, scientific, religious, or moral, require at least one starting point, a primary or axiomatic concept or assumption that we must take for granted. Many a philosopher who is critical of the notion of self-evident moral claims may well agree that every moral argument ultimately draws on one or more *a priori* premises, that there are inevitably premises for which one cannot ask for further foundations[152]—what Alvin Plantinga calls "properly basic beliefs."[153]

In the Jewish tradition, this need to have such a moral anchoring point is expressed in the idea that "every tong is made by a prior tong." For many religions, God is this primary cause. For those who believe, God's commandments, as expressed in tablets or texts, or as interpreted, explained and specified by God's delegates, identify which acts are moral and which are not, but for those who do not recognize God as a compelling primary source of normativity, the rest does not follow. Other systems of thought employ nature or reason as their primary concept, fulfilling a role analogous to that played by God's commandments in religious systems.

Every sustainable moral construction builds upon a self-evident foundation.[154] Human rights are the primary normative concept for the construction of international law and norms.

MORAL DIALOGUES AND THE OPENING EFFECT

A critic may suggest that the concept of self-evident moral claims amounts to an assertion that my moral intuition is better than all others. As I see it, the opposite is the case. All will hear self-evident moral claims unless they have been severely distracted, and even these persons will hear these claims once they are engaged in open moral dialogue. By moral dialogues I mean, drawing on my teacher Martin Buber, conversations about values (as opposed to fact- and logic-driven deliberations) in which we truly open up to one another and, in the process, become open to self-evident moral precepts.[155]

German sociologist and social theorist Hans Joas criticized the concept of self-evident moral precepts by suggesting that if these claims were truly self-evident, the Founding Fathers—and all others who evoke this concept—would not have needed to proclaim it. The fact that they did, Joas says, constitutes *prima facie* evidence that these precepts are not self-evident.[156] Self-evident precepts may indeed elude people whose vision is obscured—either because they live in closed societies (fundamentalist theocracies or secular totalitarian states) or because, although they live in open societies, they have closed minds. In the first case, social pressure and cultural indoctrination have risen to a level that people are unable to hear the normative voice of the moral causes at issue. In the second case, people "under the influence" of one mind modifier or another, whether it is alcohol, drugs, or merely a high dose of mass culture (e.g., watching TV six hours on an average day), or who are mentally handicapped (e.g., psychopathic), are blind to even the most shining normative light. *However, even these people can be brought to see the compelling nature of self-evident normative precepts* when their societies are opened up, when they are freed to participate in unencumbered moral dialogues, or they learn to overcome their various mind- (and soul-) numbing addictions.

The preceding statement is supported by the observation that as totalitarian and authoritarian regimes such as Singapore and China open up, due to changes in their regime and technological developments in the realm of communication, they also move towards recognizing human rights — often in word, but also in deed. These regimes, which once dismissed human rights as particularistic, Western notions not applicable to their people, now increasingly pay homage to human rights (a) by abiding by some of them more than they did previously (e.g., allowing some free speech, and increasingly also due process); (b) by presenting various explanations for why their regimes cannot yet abide by the human rights but will do so in the future; or (c) by working to hide the violations of rights, for instance, those of inmates. Thus rather than maintain their original dismissive position, they increasingly accept the normativity of human rights.

Efforts to find texts and narratives in non-Western cultures in support of human rights — for instance, those enumerated by Amartya Sen[157] and Abdullah An-Na'im[158] — are also indications of a growing transcultural base of support. In contrast, in parts of the world where religious fundamentalism is gaining the upper hand— and is moving to close these societies and cut people off from dialogues with others—they lose sight of human rights.

I should note in passing that while open communications and dialogues with people in previously closed societies often moves them toward recognizing human rights, the opposite is not true: as champions of human rights hear from those that are dismissive, they are not won over. Belief systems that reject human rights rely on closed societies and closed minds to do so; all who are open find them compelling.

SOCIAL CONSEQUENCES OF TREATING
HUMAN RIGHTS AS SELF-EVIDENT

So far, my case against those who seek to provide extraneous foundations as justification for human rights has rested on the claim that human rights are self-evident. Oddly, the strongest support for treating them as one of those rare moral claims that are self-evident may well be a consequentialist argument. To argue that human rights are particular to a single culture and thus are, at best, self-evident to people from that culture, and to assert that hence one ought to refrain from rendering transnational moral judgments,[159] greatly weakens if not fully neutralizes the case for human rights and hinders their progress. In contrast, treating human rights as self-evident strengthens the case for human rights.

Social forces make people better or worse than they would be otherwise. A gang encourages its members to pursue anti-social behavior; a religious order to pursue charity work. *The same holds true across cultures.* Following reports by the global media that a state is violating the human rights of its people—especially if such disclosures are followed by considerable and lasting international criticism and protests—many a state will modify its behavior, at least somewhat. True, in such cases, the parties involved may act largely out of self-interest, seeking to maintain a positive public image for political, commercial, or some other self-serving purpose. However, what necessitated these actions, what made it in their self-interest to improve their human rights record, are the loud and clear moral voices carried across borders (as well as their own people, as already indicated, who come to see the normativity of human rights as they have access to open moral dialogues). If these voices are silenced or muted, the progress of human rights will be undermined.

While radical cultural relativism argues that we cannot and should not judge others, some moderate relativists hold that one is entitled to judge the policies of others, but not in universalistic terms; one must make it clear that one is merely expressing one's own culturally conditioned normative position and one should recognize that people of other cultures may well readily justify conflicting positions by drawing on their own respective cultures.[160]

Although this position is not as preemptive as radical relativism, it still greatly undermines the very essence of the moral claim: the call for others to heed a given value. In rejecting the transcultural standing of the moral claim, even such moderate relativists end up treating moral judgments like expressions of taste: "I like potatoes and recommend them to you, but you may well have strong reasons to prefer rice and I have no standing to complain about such a preference." Such a move undermines moral claims because one grants those subject to them a license to ignore them in the same breath they are made. Such hedged claims are like speeding tickets handed out to motorists together with the money to pay for them. One further notes that others, say religious fundamentalists, are not going to hedge their claims. Hence, by making our claims contingent and conditional, we yield a good part of the transcultural space for moral dialogues to those with unhedged voices. The world would be better off if our claims clashed with those of others in the agora of moral precepts, and let those that are truly self-evident stand out.

It is odd to read as major a philosopher as Richard Rorty argue that the claim that human rights are universal and self-evident cannot be sustained in part because Friedrich Nietzsche held that such claims "would only have crossed the mind of a slave" as a tool to enfeeble those in power.[161] The notion that the issues at hand could be settled by quoting an authority is surprising; if I come back and quote Locke, Mill, and maybe Kant, would the matter be settled by which philosopher ranks higher? By who garners more philosophical votes or citations? Note also that Nietzsche's claim is an empirical one; anyone who takes Nietzsche's notions to apply to the contemporary world must answer for the fact that many who are powerful do advocate human rights, and many who are weak (but live in closed societies) have yet to recognize them.

Rorty also argues for abandoning transcultural claims posed by human rights because racists and sexists find it easy to embrace these rights but simply deny that these rights apply to blacks, Jews, and women among others—because they consider them not human beings. It is not particularly difficult to show that the term *human*— those entitled to human rights—is easy to define (surely easier than to define a chair) as featherless bipeds. And that minorities and women clearly qualify.

The argument here advanced is not that one should claim a non-relativist status for human rights because such claims are beneficial, although those who subscribe to utilitarian, consequentialist doctrines might consider such a course.[162] Rather, given that human rights are a self-evident moral cause, giving it voice—allowing it to be carried across borders—would make for a better world, one that is more attentive to human rights and other moral causes.

Moreover, without cross-cultural moral judgments one cannot take the next step: asking what legitimate measures the inchoate global community ought to take to promote these judgments. Thus, key questions concerning the conditions under which it is appropriate to impose economic sanctions and, above all, to engage in armed humanitarian interventions (say, to stop genocides and ethnic cleansing) are all contingent on the recognition that there are actions that are taking place in another nation which violate human rights on a large scale. Only after such a conclusion is reached can one logically ask about the legitimate ways the global community ought to react to such findings.

SECTION III

Other Rights, Privacy, and the Unforgetting Internet

Chapter 8

DNA Tests: Protect Rights and the Common Good

This chapter seeks to outline a viewpoint on the study of the legal, ethical, and policy considerations raised by DNA tests and databases (from here on, DNA usages). It does not delve into the specifics involved. It outlines a way of thinking that has proven productive elsewhere[163] and seems promising in dealing with DNA usages in the United States, but little more. Given that this essay is about a communitarian approach that draws on specific communitarian values, I turn next to briefly present the approach here followed.[164]

COMMUNITARIANISM DEFINED AND DISAGGREGATED

Communitarianism is a social philosophy that maintains that society should articulate what is good, and asserts that such articulations are both necessary and legitimate. Communitarianism is often contrasted with classical liberalism, a philosophical position that holds that individuals would formulate their idea of good on their own. Communitarians examine the ways shared conceptions of the good (values) are formed, transmitted, justified, and enforced. Hence communitarians are interested in communities (and moral dialogues within them), historically transmitted values and mores, and the societal units that transmit and enforce group values such as families, schools, and voluntary associations (social clubs, churches, and so forth), which are all parts of communities.

Although all communitarians uphold the importance of the social realm and of community in particular, they differ in the extent to which their conceptions are attentive to liberty and individual rights. Early communitarians, such as Ferdinand Tönnies and Robert Nisbet, stressed the importance of closely knit social fabric and authority. Asian communitarians are especially concerned about the values of social order. They argue that to maintain social harmony, individual rights and political liberties must be curtailed. Some seek to rely heavily on the state to maintain social order (for instance, leaders and champions of the regime in Singapore and Malaysia), and some on strong social bonds and moral culture (as Japan does).

Asian communitarians also hold that the West's notion of liberty actually amounts to anarchy, that strong economic growth requires limiting freedoms, and that the West uses its idea of legal and political rights to chastise other cultures that have inherent values of their own.[165]

In 1996, Alan Ehrenhalt's book, *The Lost City: The Forgotten Virtues of Community in America*, questioned the value of enhancing choice achieved at the cost of maintaining community and authority.[166] In the 1980s before him, Charles Taylor, Michael Sandel, Michael Walzer, and Robert Bellah and associates criticized the excessive individualism of classical liberalism exemplified by the United States under President Reagan, and in Britain under Prime Minister Margaret Thatcher.[167]

My version of communitarianism, laid out in my book *The New Golden Rule*,[168] holds that the good communitarian society has two key elements: a carefully crafted balance between liberty and the common good as well as between individual rights and social responsibilities; and a social order based as much as possible on moral persuasion as opposed to coercion. Both point to the quest for common ground.

The second element is of special import for the issues at hand. It suggests an approach to policymaking and ethical deliberation that differs sharply from a notion that governs our legal system and often spills into our policy and ethical arenas—the notion that the best way to proceed is for two extreme advocates to present a case, one from each side. (The ultimate example of this approach was the CNN show, *Crossfire*.) Each side makes its case in the most extreme possible way, and from the clash of these polarized positions somehow justice, fairness, and an acceptable policy is to arise. This tendency has been evident in the debate about rights and national security in the age of terrorism: one side argues that our Constitution is being shredded, and the other argues that questioning new security measures aids and abets the enemy.[169]

Some signs of such polarization are found between those who view practically all new uses of DNA tests—especially DNA databases—as endangering individual rights, and those who view them as greatly advancing the common good. From my neo-communitarian viewpoint, the basis of all such legal, policy, and ethical deliberations should be that there is no one value that *a priori* trumps all others; that typically, a common ground needs to be and can be found most effectively through dialogue, not through confrontation.

THE FOURTH AMENDMENT AS A COMMUNITARIAN CONCEPT

The communitarian concept I just outlined is reflected in the legal concept outlined in the Fourth Amendment. The law distinguishes between reasonable searches, those in which there is a compelling public interest—and unreasonable ones, those in which the right to privacy prevails. To stress this point, one should contrast the texts of the First and Fourth Amendments. If the Fourth were to be written in the same strongly right-privileging language as the First, it might have read: "Congress shall make no law..." allowing searches and seizures. (Note that I am referring to the idea contained in the original text, and not to the numerous court cases that have taken place over the centuries and their accumulative—and modifying—effects on the way the Fourth Amendment has been viewed over the years.) The Fourth Amendment's further requirement that "no Warrants shall issue, but upon probable cause, supported by Oath of affirmation, and particularly describing the place to be searched, and the persons or things to be seized" provides a mechanism for sorting out when searches are unreasonable or reasonable.

Most importantly, that which is considered reasonable changes as the social climate changes. Thus, in response to the rise of radical individualism, the erosion of authority, and above all, new threats to the common good (especially to homeland protection), the courts have expanded the realm of reasonable search and seizure, specifically in the 2001 USA PATRIOT Act explored in Chapter 3. For instance, more legal searches have occurred for which neither warrants nor even specific suspicion is required. Examples include screening gates in airports (introduced in 1973) and searches of backpacks in New York City subways (in 2005), as well as gradually over the decades by one state at a time drug testing for specific professions such as train engineers or employing road-side sobriety checkpoints.[170] And the kind of DNA testing that involves a sweep of innocent people (a whole village, for example) in order to try to locate a criminal, the process of which has already taken place in the United Kingdom, but as far as I can establish not yet in the United States.

Indeed, much of what was considered unreasonable before the September 11, 2001 attacks has become reasonable during the past decade. But, as no attacks have since occurred, some of what had become reasonable was again considered unreasonable when the PATRIOT Act came up for renewal at the end of 2005.

DNA searches once considered matters of science fiction and entirely unreasonable are now becoming reasonable. As their service to the common good becomes better known, their intrusiveness declines (for example, the shift from blood tests to swabs to collect samples), and their usage becomes more widespread.

PREVENTIVE COLLECTIONS?

Even for those who view the recent trend in democratic societies to treat new security measures as reasonable, one measure is particularly difficult to consider as legitimate and particularly relevant to the application of DNA usages. Since September 11, 2001, the FBI has been explicitly instructed to shift its focus, when dealing with terrorism, from prosecution to prevention.[171] It is widely recognized that it makes little sense to try to prosecute suicide bombers after attacks such as those on the World Trade Center and that the threat of such prosecution is unlikely to deter them. In either case, an unacceptable level of damage will be done if one waits until a terrorist attack occurs before one acts.

At the same time, one must recognize that a shift from prosecution to prevention often entails harassing a large number of innocent people. To prevent attacks, one must question and search the property and communication of a large number of people (selected for example on the basis of their country of origin), most of whom have not committed any crimes, and show no sign of planning to do so. A typical example is the invitation issued to 5,000 Iraqi Americans in the Detroit area at the eve of the 2003 invasion of Iraq to come for an interview at FBI offices.[172] They were "invited" merely because of their country of origin and because they were males of a certain age, but not because of any specific suspicion. Such an invitation is a chilling experience for most people, especially as they realize that declining to interview will turn them into suspects.

Collecting DNA from people who have not committed a crime in order to have it on file for the future identification of a criminal is similarly preventive. Requiring innocent people to provide DNA samples—for example when applying for a passport or driver's license—when not provoked by a criminal search is an even more invasive situation than is testing an entire community in search of a specific criminal. In the latter case, testing may be justified as a crime has been committed by someone in the vicinity. In preventive collection, one assembles the DNA of a large number of people without the claim that any of them did anything illegal. In the case of a post-crime DNA sweep, DNA of all who are cleared can be destroyed; in preventive collections, DNA is stored for the foreseeable future.

An important lesson can be gleaned from the internment of Japanese people in America during World War II. One of the strongest legal criticisms of interning *all* Japanese-Americans was that the approach was both over-inclusive and under-inclusive. It was over-inclusive because it undoubtedly included Japanese-Americans who posed no threat to this country. It was under-inclusive because it did not include other possibly disloyal citizens of other ethnicities and national origins (for example, German-Americans). Obtaining DNA from those visiting the U.S. (some 300 million a year, not a mean task), and maybe even from all U.S. citizens, for storage in a databank bears the same problems. It will be over-inclusive because it will store DNA data of many scores of millions of innocent people. At the same time, the databank will be under-inclusive, because it will leave out many millions of illegal immigrants.

As of yet, the United States has no universal DNA database. Inclusion is mostly limited to convicted individuals, although some states (and possibly the federal government) are moving to take DNA samples from arrestees. The military also uses DNA samples to identify soldiers killed in action. Britain, however, *is* moving toward a universal bank. To the extent that the law and order system in America is shifting its focus from prosecution to prevention, we should expect to see America move closer toward the British approach. At the very least, we should expect to see databanks that include millions of innocent people, even if those databanks are not fully inclusive.

To conclude whether or not population-wide DNA databases are justified, we need to learn much more about the extent to which such databanks are truly useful in preventing terrorist attacks, and the extent to which their threat to privacy can be minimized. These questions largely remain to be explored and prevent a summary judgment here. Also important to keep in mind is that these banks may well cost so much that the same resources could be much more effectively employed elsewhere.

BALANCING INTRUSION AND SERVICE TO THE COMMON GOOD

In previous publications, I have tried to take the quest for the criteria of establishing the proper balance between individual rights and the common good in a different direction. In a study of privacy,[173] I suggest that there is no need to consider limiting privacy unless *not* doing so poses a serious threat to the common good. Other means of coping with a threat to the common good ought to be tried first, and, if some limits on privacy are nevertheless needed, they should be as minimally intrusive as possible. Following this analytic scheme, I found that judgments have come relatively readily. In some cases, a proposed course of action that requires little intrusion was highly necessary to safeguard the common good. Other situations had clearly the opposite profile: the intrusion they called for was immense while the contribution of the intervention to the common good was minimal.

For example, in the realm of medical privacy, if a person has a stroke, some banks that find out will call in their loans. There is little or no contribution to the common good in such interventions, but the intrusion is very high, indeed one of the highest intrusions one can imagine. An opposite example concerns surveillance cameras in public spaces on campuses where there have been several rapes. Assuming that notices are posted about the installation of the cameras and the use of the cameras is properly supervised, the cameras are minimally intrusive. To the extent that these cameras reduce rapes, and that no other even less intrusive but effective solutions are available, these cameras seem reasonable. (Note that closed-circuit television [CCTV] security cameras in the UK have been criticized as useless and intrusive,[174] but turned out to play a key role in identifying the 2005 subway bombers.) Whether or not one agrees with these assessments, they illustrate my suggestion that balancing the scope of an intrusion with its corresponding impact on the common good is *one* consideration that should be employed in determining reasonable limits on privacy.

DNA usages are more difficult to assess from the viewpoint of the criteria just outlined because they are often both highly intrusive and can contribute much to the common good. Whereas one of the examples cited above was highly intrusive and contributed little if anything to the common good (high/low), and the other example just the opposite (low/high), many DNA usages are often highly intrusive and highly desirable (high/high). As such, it is more difficult to read the scale and determine where a proper balance lies. We must take a closer look. Accordingly, I next examine the level of intrusion as well as the contribution to the common good of select DNA usages.

INTRUSION

The use of DNA is highly intrusive because DNA can reveal much more about a person than a picture of a face (as captured on surveillance camera), a license plate (as seen on a traffic camera), an identification card (as registered on traditional passports, distinct from those that use biometrics), and even a set of fingerprints. Moreover, DNA discloses information about our family members and ancestors. DNA is also highly accessible. We leave traces of our DNA in public all the time, whether it is in shed hair, skin, or saliva left on coffee cups, cigarettes, etc. DNA can be extracted and tested entirely unbeknownst to us. Authorities are also quite able to conceal that these tests have taken place. Not many intrusions are as invasive, and at the same time as easy to accomplish and conceal.

There are a number of factors that will work to mitigate the intrusiveness of DNA usages, at least in the near future. It is true that we can divine very specific information from DNA—for example the color of one's hair, or whether one is susceptible to certain diseases—but it will take a considerable number of years before authorities will be able to look at the genetic code and piece together a composite picture of a human being. Thus, whereas one's DNA has the *potential* to reveal an enormous amount of information regarding a person, at this stage authorities are unable to identify enough genes, their functions, or their expression patterns to *actually* reveal the information.

Additionally, proponents of DNA databases argue that the DNA profiles kept and stored by law enforcement—the thirteen STR loci—do not provide any meaningful information about individuals, aside from allowing us to determine whether two samples have come from the same person. STR is an abbreviation for short tandem repeat polymorphisms, which are distinctive parts or samples of a person's

DNA. The FBI has chosen a set of thirteen such samples (the thirteen STR loci) as a recording standard for its database. When a piece of DNA is found at a crime scene, it can be matched to a particular person's thirteen STR loci (if that person is in the database). Thirteen STR loci thus act a bit like fingerprints for identifying DNA. Indeed they are said to be no more intrusive than fingerprints. For by themselves, the thirteen STR loci cannot tell us what the person looks like or anything about their ancestry or susceptibility to disease. This point, however, should not be overestimated.

One may argue that once the DNA has been "fingerprinted" and the thirteen STR loci have been typed and entered into a database, presumably the DNA samples are no longer needed. The thirteen STR loci allow the police to match a sample, but they do not disclose much meaningful information about the individual. However, the DNA *samples* do contain *much* information about the individual—his family, history, predispositions, etc. Hence privacy advocates argue that even if there are safeguards regarding access to the DNA samples, keeping this potent information around is a risk that should not be taken. Temptation of authorities to misuse or abuse the information is too great. Hence the samples should be destroyed once the STR loci have been extracted.

The problem with this argument is that there *are* instances in which the entire DNA sample is needed, such as when settling claims that testing was inappropriately conducted. Also, DNA tests have become more discerning over the years, and are likely to become so in the future. That is, the authorities will be able to derive more information about the person whose DNA sample they found at the crime scene or elsewhere. Hence, being able to return to the samples for further testing is of clear value to the common good and to individual rights. At the same time, there is no denying that databases containing the original samples are potentially much more intrusive than limited DNA profiles.

In short, although the intrusiveness of DNA usages *can* be reduced, it is currently nevertheless substantial, and much of its intrusiveness is dependent on future developments in science and technology.

CONTRIBUTIONS TO THE COMMON GOOD

While banking DNA information entails a high level of intrusion, it also provides large contributions to the common good. For the last two decades, DNA tests and databanks have been the most powerful tool available to police and prosecutors investigating new crimes, solving old crimes, locating suspects, and indicating when authorities are on the wrong track. DNA tests are many thousand times more accurate than eyewitness testimony often relied upon to identify suspects and convict people. Walter Rowe, a leading academic forensic scientist, has gone even further, saying that DNA testing "may be the greatest advance in forensic science in history."[175] As tests and databanks are expanded, the benefits of DNA usages will be still greater.

There seems to be no data on the deterrence effect of DNA usages. However, as it becomes increasingly known to the public that a criminal can be identified if he or she leaves behind even one hair or drop of sweat, it would be surprising if this has no impact on deterrence. Indeed an early commentator on criminal punishment, Césare Beccaria, argued that deterrence varies more across the likelihood of detection and punishment than it does across the amount of punishment.[176] In plain English, it matters more how likely one is to be caught than how big the penalty is going to be. Following his argument, increased use of DNA in criminal justice would increase deterrence more than harsher sentencing would. It is hence likely that DNA usages will lead not only to more accurate convictions, but also to lower overall crime rates, which is of course a very desirable outcome. In short, benefits of DNA banking to public safety are substantial.

Further, DNA tests and databases help *protect* individual rights. One of the strongest, and indeed noblest, claims of free societies is that it is better to let a thousand guilty people go free rather than imprison just one innocent person. This is a very powerful conviction attesting to how abhorrent free societies hold the incarceration of the innocent. Extensive and accessible DNA testing and databases can be strongly justified on this ground alone: as of 2003, DNA tests had already exonerated 130 people falsely convicted and incarcerated. Twelve of these people walked off of death row. Unfortunately for some, the tests come too late. Frank Lee Smith, convicted in 1985, died of cancer on death row in 2000, waiting for

DNA testing that would exonerate him but was completed only eleven months later.[177]

Moreover, by making it possible to quickly identify the guilty person from among a group of suspects (a process to be much further accelerated if handheld, quick response DNA tests become available),[178] DNA usages greatly reduce the humiliation and costs entailed in being a suspect in a police investigation. (In one case in which data on this point is available, namely in Virginia, we find that DNA analysis routinely eliminates twenty-five to thirty percent of suspects in police investigations.[179]) Thus if one compares the use of DNA tests to identify a perpetrator relying on eyewitnesses and police line-ups, which are notoriously unreliable,[180] one sees the double virtue of DNA testing and databases: they vastly enhance the probability that those who are guilty will be convicted, and those who are innocent will be rapidly cleared.

Consider the following situation, based on an actual occurrence. A rape occurred in a hospital. Eleven people had ready access to the victim's room overnight. Before DNA tests were available, the police would have quite legitimately questioned all eleven people—asking them to provide alibis, checking their records for past offenses, and interviewing their supervisors, friends and family members. If the rapist was not identified, the case might go unsolved for years; none of the suspects would be cleared, and a cloud would hang over them at work and in their community despite the presumption of innocence guaranteed in trial court, but not in the court of public opinion. In the near future world of rapid DNA testing, the police could simply ask each of the eleven to provide a sample of saliva or a hair, and all but one suspect would be cleared in short order, without the undesirable effects of public speculation as to their guilt.

Some defense attorneys who recognize that DNA testing has the merit of quickly determining who is not a suspect nevertheless argue that this feature poses a problem. These attorneys agree that eyewitness identifications are notoriously unreliable, and point out that juries nonetheless give a disproportionate amount of weight to them, leading to numerous wrong convictions. They fear, however, that DNA evidence is becoming the new eyewitness evidence. If a biological sample has been found at the crime scene, and the DNA matches that of the defendant, juries may take that as a 100% reliable indicator of the defendant's guilt, even though the DNA evidence is only reliable in determining whether the defendant was present at the crime scene.

Take, for example, a rape prosecution. A semen sample was collected from the victim and the crime scene. The DNA matches that of the defendant. All that the DNA test proves is that the defendant and the victim engaged in sex.[181] The DNA test does not reveal guilt as to the rape charge, however, because the sex may have been consensual. Yet, defense attorneys worry that juries may take the DNA test results as conclusive proof that the defendant is guilty of rape.

As I see it, however, this confuses two issues here. DNA tests are many thousand times more reliable than eyewitness testimony. In *both* cases all that the evidence can claim to indicate is that the suspect was on location; the suspect is still subject to additional arguments and evidence. Like eyewitness testimony, DNA evidence can be misinterpreted. The claim, however, that extremely unreliable eyewitness testimony and extremely reliable DNA evidence *are* the same because they both can be misinterpreted is spurious.

More serious problems concern the possibility of carelessness or corruption of those who perform the tests. There have been a handful of cases in which mismatches occurred due to mishandling of the samples in labs, and other such errors. There have been a number of high profile cases in which crime labs have purposely falsified data in order to secure a conviction. Fred Zain, a serologist in a West Virginia crime lab, falsified DNA data over a number of years, throwing into question all the cases for which his data were used.[182] There were also serious problems found in FBI crime labs.[183] It follows that we must stress that although there is a great potential that DNA evidence will be used for "good," convicting the guilty and exonerating the innocent, there is also the potential that it can be used for "evil," falsifying evidence to secure convictions or to frame innocent people. The threat of negligent or incompetent lab work also cannot be overlooked.

In summary, like most other technologies, whether DNA usages are "good" or "bad" (in terms of serving the common good) depends upon the motives and actions of those in control of the tools. In this case, when the chain of evidence is carefully vetted, one at least knows that the tool itself is reliable. In the case of eyewitness testimony, often even if all the police and attorneys have conducted themselves in an exemplary manner, we still have unreliable information.

In short, DNA usages do make major contributions to the common good by facilitating crime solving, likely increasing deterrence, reducing the burden on suspects, and proving the innocence of the wrongly convicted.

Hi/Hi Profile and Accountability

To recap the argument thus far: in assessing DNA usages or any other such new measures or technologies, the communitarian approach here followed does not grant, *a priori*, the right of way to either the common good or to individual rights. Hence when a measure is highly intrusive and makes little contribution to the common good, it ought to be barred. And if a measure has the opposite profile, it should be embraced. Both statements are subject to many other considerations not explored here—for instance, relative costs, the extent to which the same results can be achieved by voluntary means, and so on. But how should one deal with measures (henceforth referred to as hi/hi measures) that are highly intrusive as well as make major contributions to the common good, including individual rights? One may of course seek to reduce intrusiveness, but judgment must still be made at a point in time in which the level of intrusiveness is given and considerable.

To make my next point, I return to the use of security cameras [CCTV] in London subway stations that helped to identify the London subway bombers in 2005. CCTV footage, which could have illuminated more facts regarding the shooting death of Brazilian man Jean Charles de Menezes at the hands of UK police in the London subway, has gone "missing." London tube workers claim that the CCTV cameras were working when Menezes was shot by police, yet the police claim the opposite. Many suspect a police cover-up regarding the killing of a man who turned out to be innocent.[184] This questions our trust in those conducting surveillance, not the reliability or reasonability of CCTV.

Placing a tool as powerful as DNA databases and testing in the hands of the police is clearly an effective crime-fighting tool, but it requires the introduction of stronger monitoring of the police, including a national civilian review board. Before further explaining this review board, however, it is necessary to discuss in more general terms how supervision and accountability are best ensured.

The discussion thus far, as often is the case in other such deliberations, has focused on determining what is reasonable and where the proper balance lies between individual rights and contributions to the common good. To complete the judgment as to whether or not a given new measure that enhances the powers of public authorities is called for, I have suggested that a second form of balancing needs to be considered which concerns not whether the government should be accorded new powers, but how closely it is held accountable regarding the ways it uses these powers.[185]

From this viewpoint, the key issue is not whether certain powers —for example, keeping DNA samples—should or should not be available to public authorities, but whether or not these powers are used legitimately, and whether mechanisms are in place to ensure such usage. The balance sought here is not of public interest and rights, but rather is of the supervised and the supervisors, and their superiors. Deficient accountability opens the door to government abuses of power. Excessively tight controls, however, can also cause harm. Thus, a case can be made that in the decades preceding the Church Committee, under most of Hoover's reign, the FBI was insufficiently accountable, but that after the Committee's rules were institutionalized, until 9/11, the FBI had excessive limits on its power. It follows that a carefully calibrated and judicious accountability system makes the introduction of hi/hi measures tolerable.

Some accountability is built into any organizational set of rules, regulations, and supervisory layers, as it is in various police departments and national security agencies such as the NSA, FBI, and the newer Department of Homeland Security. In addition, federal agencies have offices of Inspectors General which have in the past, in several cases, issued reports that were quite critical about the government's conduct and demanded corrections. The courts also provide a measure of accountability, with the U.S. Supreme Court acting as the ultimate arbitrator.

Under the American system of checks and balances, Congress is supposed to oversee the work of the executive branch, and has several instruments for doing so. These include requiring heads of agencies and other high ranking officials to respond to written questions, testify before congressional committees, and turn over documents; conducting hearings in which civil libertarians and others can make their case; ordering the General Accounting Office to conduct a study; and more. A survey of the extent to which Congress provides an effective layer of accountability regarding DNA usages is well beyond the scope of this chapter. However, given the fact that members of Congress are under constant pressure to raise funds, do the special bidding of their constituents, and vote on many hundreds of bills each year, and given the ease with which the Executive Branch in the past has often escaped proper scrutiny, I conclude that an additional source of accountability is needed for hi/hi measures like DNA testing.

The ultimate source of oversight is the citizenry, informed and alerted by a free press and civil liberties advocates, and briefed by public authorities about their needs. Both the press and various libertarian groups have been very active in alerting the public to the dangers of biological data banks and DNA testing and profiling, and arguing in favor of various limitations on DNA usages. To help focus and institutionalize public scrutiny, I favor an independent public accountability board, composed from public figures with known integrity and who command security clearance. (Lee Hamilton and Tom Kean, vice-chair and chair of the 9/11 Commission, and Paul Volcker, the former chair of the Federal Reserve, could so serve.) The board would act much like local civilian review boards that have formed in some sixty percent of our nation's largest cities where the public sought to keep an eye on the police after widespread corruption and abuse was revealed. The board would regularly visit different DNA testing facilities and issue an annual report stating the extent to which the board found that the various agencies complied with the various safeguards on the DNA usages passed by state and national legislatures, and whether such safeguards sufficed. For instance, are audit trails (which determine who accesses the databases) in place? Are those trails routinely reviewed to determine whether unauthorized people have queried the databases and used the information for illicit purposes? If such instances were found, were corrective measures taken?

Those who find such a board unlikely to be tolerated or able to do its job should look at the 9/11 Commission. Indeed, if the 9/11 Commission could be re-implemented it could serve as such an accountability board not only for DNA usages. It would likely be much more effective than the Civil Rights and Privacy Board included in the Department of Homeland Security. As with civilian review boards of local police, opposition to the formation of a national civilian review board to monitor hi/hi measures, of which DNA usages are only one example, may well be one indication that the system may be tilting too far toward concerns about the common good and may not be sufficiently concerned about individual rights.

Chapter 9

Second Chances and Social Forgiveness in the Digital Age[186]

We need the means, both technological and legal, to replace measures once woven into the fabric of communities.

A young man in upstate New York drinks too much and gets a little rowdy, picks a fight, smashes up the bar, and is arrested. When he gets into trouble again a short time later, the judge sends him to jail for a week. After his release, he gets fired and cannot find a new job because he has a record. The local newspaper carries a story about his misconduct. The merchants on Main Street refuse to sell him anything on credit. The young women gossip about him and refuse to date him. One day he has had enough. He packs his meager belongings, leaves without a good-bye, and moves to a small town in Oregon. Here, he gains a new start. Nobody knows about his rowdy past, and he has learned his lesson. He drinks less, avoids fights, works in a lumberyard, and soon marries a nice local woman, has three kids, and lives happily ever after. Cue the choir of angels singing in the background.

The idea that people deserve a second chance is an important American value. Perhaps it grows out of our history, in which those who got into trouble in Europe (whether it was their fault or not) moved to the United States to start a new life. And as the American West was settled, many easterners and midwesterners found a place there for a second beginning. More profoundly, the belief in a new beginning is a tenet of Christianity, which allows sinners to repent and be fully redeemed, to be reborn. In a similar vein, the secular, progressive, optimistic, therapeutic culture of today's America rejects the notion that there are inherently bad people. As individuals, we seek insights into our failings so we can learn to overcome them and achieve a new start. From a sociological perspective, people are thrown off course by their social conditions—because they are poor, for instance, and subject to discrimination. But these conditions can be altered, and then these people will be able to lead good lives. Under the right conditions, criminals can pay their debt to society and be rehabilitated, sex offenders can be reformed, and others who have flunked out can pass another test. Just give them a second chance.

The latest chapter of this deeply entrenched narrative introduces a big bad wolf, the Internet. It stands charged with killing the opportunity for people to have that much-deserved second chance. By computerizing local public records, the Internet casts the shadow of people's past far and fast; like a curse they cannot undo, their records now follow them wherever they go. True, even in the good old days, arrest records, criminal sentences, bankruptcy filings, and even divorce records were public. Some were listed in blotters kept in police stations, others in courthouses; anyone who wished to take the trouble could go there and read them. But most people did not. Above all, there was no way for people in distant communities to find these damning facts without going to inordinate lengths.

The first sign of trouble due to technological changes came about in the late 19th century when newspapers started publishing this sort of information. In 1890, after newspapers printed social gossip about the family of Boston lawyer Samuel D. Warren, he and his law partner, the future Supreme Court Justice Louis D. Brandeis, published in the nascent *Harvard Law Review* what is considered the most seminal law review article ever written, one that became the foundation of the American right to privacy. In "The Right to Privacy,"[187] they asserted that an individual has the right to keep certain information hidden from others.

Warren and Brandeis were not trying to stop gossip. (Although people often find gossip annoying, sociologists view it as an important part of the informal social controls that nudge people to be better than they would otherwise be, thus minimizing the role for policing. Hence the great concern with the breakdown of communities—where people know each other and gossip—and the quest for new soft tools to advance social order.) But Warren and Brandeis correctly saw that a major change takes place once gossip is spread to a large community, as it is via the print media, to people who do not personally know those who are being gossiped about, and who are therefore unaware of the special circumstances, of the "whole story."[188] This change was a harbinger of things to come.

In recent decades, online databases have dramatically increased the size of the audience that has access to public information and the ease with which it can be examined. Several companies have started compiling criminal records, making them available to everyone in the country and indeed the world. For instance, in 2008, PeopleFinders, a company based in Sacramento, introduced the site CriminalSearches.com. It offers a free service to access public criminal records and draws its data from local courthouses. A similar thing is happening to many other types of public records, ranging from birth records to divorces.

Such developments disturb privacy advocates and anyone who is keen on ensuring that people have the opportunity for a new start. Beth Givens, director of the Privacy Rights Clearinghouse, says that Internet databases cause a "loss of 'social forgiveness.'" For instance, a person's "conviction of graffiti vandalism at age 19 will still be there at age 29 when [he's] a solid citizen trying to get a job and raise a family"[189] —and the conviction will be there for anyone to see. Furthermore, as companies "rely on background checks to screen workers, [they] risk imposing unfair barriers to rehabilitated criminals," wrote reporters Ann Zimmerman and Kortney Stringer in *The Wall Street Journal*.[190] In short, as journalist Brad Stone wrote in *The New York Times*, by allowing the producers of databases to remove "the obstacles to getting criminal information," we are losing "a valuable, ignorance-fueled civil peace."[191]

But hold on for just a minute. Is the Internet age really destroying second chances, making us less forgiving and hindering the possibility for rehabilitation and even redemption? The sad fact is that most convicted criminals in the pre-digital age did not use the second chance that their obscurity gave them, nor did they use their third or fourth chances. Convincing data show that most criminal offenders—especially those involved in violent crimes—are not rehabilitated; they commit new crimes. And many commit numerous crimes before they are caught again. Thus, while obscurity may well help a small percentage of criminals get a second chance, it helps a large percentage of them strike again.

Take the case of James Webb (not the U.S. Senator from Virginia of the same name). He had served 20 years in prison for raping six women when, on August 16, 1995, he was released on parole. But rather than look for a new start, he raped another woman the day after he was released. Then he raped three more women in the next few months. He was re-arrested in December 1995, after he committed the fourth rape. Or consider the case of James Richardson, a New York resident who served 20 years of a life term for raping and murdering a 10-year-old girl. After he was paroled in 1992, he committed three bank robberies before being re-incarcerated. Both cases happened before the advent of databanks of criminal convictions.

These two are typical cases. In its most recent study on recidivism in the United States, the Justice Department's Bureau of Justice Statistics tracked two-thirds of the prisoners released in 15 states in 1994. It found that within three years of their release, 67.5 percent of them were re-arrested for a new offense.[192] In short, most people who commit crimes are more likely to commit crimes in the future than to make good use of a second chance. This was true long before the digitization of criminal data and the loss of obscurity.

Moreover, just because only two-thirds of the prisoners were re-arrested does not mean that the other third did not commit any crimes. Many crimes are never solved and their perpetrators never caught. Studies found that the majority of rapists and child molesters had been convicted more than once for a sexual assault—and committed numerous offenses before they were caught again. On average, these offenders admitted to having committed *two to five times* as many sex crimes as were officially documented.[193] That is, not only did they fail to use their second chances to start a new life, they used obscurity to their advantage.

In short, the image of a young person who goes astray, and who would return to the straight and narrow life if just given a second chance, does not fit most offenders. Indeed, prisons are considered colleges for crime; they harden those sentenced to spend time in them, making them *more* disposed to future criminal behavior upon release. Social scientists differ about whom to blame for the limited success of rehabilitation. Some fault "the system," or poor social conditions, or lack of job training. Others place more blame on the character of those involved. In any case, obscurity hardly serves to overcome strong factors that agitate against rehabilitation.

Online databases also display the records of physicians who do not live up to the Hippocratic oath; these doctors do harm, and plenty of it. The National Practitioner Data Bank allows state licensing boards, hospitals, and other health-care entities to find out whether the license of a doctor has been revoked recently in another state or if the doctor has been disciplined. Doctors' licenses are generally revoked only if they commit very serious offenses, such as repeated gross negligence, criminal felonies, or practicing while under the influence of drugs or alcohol.

If these databases had been used as intended in the late 1990s and early 2000s, they could have tracked Pamela L. Johnson, a physician who was forced to leave Duke University Medical Center after many of her patients suffered from unusual complications. In response, Johnson moved to New Mexico and lied about her professional history in order to obtain a medical license there and continue practicing. After three patients in New Mexico filed lawsuits alleging that she was negligent or had botched surgical procedures, she moved again and set up shop in Michigan.[194]

Similarly, Joseph S. Hayes, a medical doctor licensed in Tennessee, was convicted of drug abuse and assault, including choking a patient, actions which resulted in the revocation of his Tennessee license in 1991. But his license was reinstated in 1993. When he was charged with fondling a female patient in 1999, he simply moved to South Carolina to continue practicing medicine.[195]

Similar stories could be told about scores of other doctors. The exploits of one of the most notorious of these doctors are laid out by Pope Brock in his 2008 book, *Charlatan*. One odd footnote to John Brinkley's infamous efforts at sidestepping regulation and discipline for a time, and even a public campaign by the editor of *JAMA*, is the fact that Brinkley routinely transplanted goat testicles into men as some precursor to Viagra.[196]

Beyond assuming that Internet databases do little harm to those who are not likely to reform themselves, we can show real benefits from the widespread dissemination of information about wrongdoers—for their potential victims. Few doctors are hired by hospitals these days without first being checked through the digitized data sources. Before you hire an accountant, such data makes it possible to discover whether he or she has a record of embezzlement. A community can find out if a new school nurse is a sex offender. Employers may direct ex-offenders to other jobs, or they may still hire them but provide extra oversight, or just decide that they are willing to take the risk. But they do so well informed, and thus warned, rather than ignorant of the sad facts.

Registration and notification laws for sex offenders provide a good case in point. The Washington State Institute for Public Policy conducted a study in 2005 that evaluated the effectiveness of the state's community notification laws. In 1990, Washington passed the Community Protection Act, a law that requires sex offenders to register with their county sheriff and authorizes law enforcement to release information to the public. The study found that by 1999 the recidivism rate among felony sex offenders in the state had dropped 70 percent from the pre-1990 level, in part due to communities' awareness of the sex offenders in their neighborhoods.[197] In addition, it was previously established that offenders subject to community notification were arrested for new crimes much more quickly than offenders who were released without notification.[198]

True, online databases increase the size of the community that has access to information, but these technological developments merely help communities catch up with other social developments. People do business over greater distances and move around much more, and much farther, than they did in earlier eras. Our travel and transactions are no longer limited to the county store and local diner. Our access to data needs to expand to match the new scope of our lives.

All of this is not to deny that we face a moral dilemma. Although most offenders are not rehabilitated, some are. It is incorrect to assume that "once a criminal, always a criminal." Take the case of Mike Kolomichuk, who in 1979 pleaded guilty to two counts of battery after having an altercation with an undercover police officer in a bar in Florida. As punishment, he received unsupervised probation, during which he conducted himself well. Kolomichuk eventually moved to Ohio, where almost 30 years later he ran as a write-in candidate for mayor of the village of Lakemore and won. His criminal past was not an issue in the election because his record was unknown in the village of 2,500 people. When his criminal history came out a few months later, there was talk of the need for a new election,[199] but it soon subsided. Today, Kolomichuk remains mayor and is continuing his efforts to revitalize the community.[200] In this case, obscurity may well have helped.

The argument can be made, then, that just as we believe it is better to let a hundred guilty people walk free than to condemn one innocent person, we should let a hundred criminals benefit from obscurity in order to provide a chance at rehabilitation for the few who put obscurity to good use. But there are ways, although imperfect, for allowing second chances for offenders while still allowing a community to protect itself by using online databases.

What is needed is a mixture of technological and legal means to replace the measures that were once naturally woven into the fabric of communities with measures that can satisfy the needs of a large, complex, and mobile society.

For example, where the inefficiency of paper records once ensured that information would not travel far, we now must introduce into the digitized world barriers for information that should not be spread. Formerly, in smaller communities, if a person was arrested, his neighbors would learn whether he had been exonerated or convicted. The community might even have had a sense of whether a person who was released had in fact committed the crime, or whether the arrest was unjustified. These days, an arrest record may travel across the globe in nanoseconds, but it is difficult to find out whether it was justified. Either arrest records should not be made public (although they might be available to police in other jurisdictions) or they must be accompanied with information about the outcome of the case.

In addition, a criminal record could be sealed both locally and in online databases, say after seven years, if the person has not committed a new crime. There is considerable precedent for such a move. For instance, information about juvenile offenders and presentations to grand juries are often sealed.

Another measure could limit access to certain databanks to those who are trained to understand the limitations of these databanks. For instance, several states allow only police authorities and educational institutions to access databases on sex offenders.

One other major concern is that lawbreakers who have paid their debt to society will face discrimination in hiring and housing. Protections against such discrimination are already in place, but others might be added. For instance, employers cannot, as a general rule, legally maintain a policy of refusing to hire people merely because they are ex-cons, whether the employer gets this information from a police blotter or a computer.

Internet databases should be held accountable for the information they provide. If they rely on public records, then they should be required to keep up with the changes in these records. They should also provide mechanisms for filing complaints if the online data are erroneous. And they should make proper corrections in a timely fashion, the way those who keep tabs on credit records are expected to do.

These are a few examples of measures that provide obscurity equivalents in the digital age. Still, let's remember the importance of gossip fueled by public records. As a rule, we care deeply about the approval of others. In most communities, being arrested is a source of major humiliation, and people will go to great pains to avoid ending up in jail.[201] In such cases, the social system does not work if the information is not publicly available. This holds true for the digitized world, where the need for a much wider-ranging "informal social communication," as sociologists call gossip, applies not merely to criminals, sexual predators, and disgraced physicians. It holds for people who trade on eBay, sell used books on Amazon, or distribute loans from e-banks. These people are also eager to maintain their reputations—not just locally but globally. If we cannot find ways to deal in cyberspace with those who deceive and cheat, then our ability to use the internet for travel, trade, investment, and much else will be severely set back.

This need is served in part by user-generated feedback and ratings, which inform others who may do business via the Internet— much like traditional community gossip would. The ability of people to obscure their past in pre-Internet days made it all too easy for charlatans, quacks, and criminal offenders to hurt more people by simply switching locations. The new, digitized transparency is one major means of facilitating deals between people who do not know each other. With enough effort, its undesirable side effects can be curbed, and people can still gain a second chance.

SECTION IV

Norms

Chapter 10

Social Norms: The Ways They Are Formed, Transformed, and Affect the Social Order

Legal scholars have rediscovered social norms. For decades, the insights and findings of law and society[202] were largely ignored, and law and economics—which mostly ignores social norms—was all the rage. In the past several years, however, new powerful essays about social norms have begun appearing in law reviews.[203] As Richard Epstein wrote in 1997, "the subject of social norms is once again hot."[204]

Some of the scholars at the forefront of this revival attempt to integrate social norms into the law and economics paradigm,[205] while others may fit better under the emerging "law and socio-economics" model, which combines the law and economics and law and society perspectives into a single discipline.[206] Much more is at stake than the division of labor among academic disciplines; at issue are different conceptions of human nature and the social order, of the ways people behave, and of the ways laws can both modify and be modified by social conduct.

To highlight the alternative approaches to the study of social norms, I examine three pairs of opposing concepts central to a full exploration of the subject: (a) whether social norms affect individual behavior merely as environmental/external factors or whether they also shape people's intrinsic predispositions; (b) the specific processes by which norms influence people (i.e., whether preferences are considered predetermined or assumed to be modifiable as a result of internalization and persuasion); and (c) the ways social norms themselves are formed (whether merely via rational choice or also through historical transmissions). Law and economics scholars tend to use the first elements of each of these pairs (environmental factors, predetermination, and intentional choice) to integrate social norms into their models, to depict the actor as a free agent, and to portray the social order as based on aggregations of voluntary agreements. The law and society approach is based upon the opposite elements of the pairs: intrinsic predisposition, internalization and persuasion, and history. Law and socio-economics combines these two sets of elements in ways to be discussed.

All the legal scholars who study social norms stand out compared to the much larger number of colleagues who have yet to include this important concept in their scholarly paradigm. These same pioneering legal scholars differ, though, in terms of the concepts they draw on to conceptualize social norms. Only some deal with internalization, still fewer with persuasion, and next to none with the role of history. This essay argues that a full analysis of social norms requires the inclusion of all three conceptions. One can view the three concepts as the building blocks of a pyramid whose foundation is secure, while the other tiers are best shored up—or, in some cases, constructed.

After briefly highlighting the importance of social norms for legal scholarship, this chapter examines the core concepts of law and socio-economics and the importance of these for the understanding of social norms in legal studies in general.

SOCIAL NORMS: A MAJOR FOUNDATION OF SOCIAL ORDER

Social norms and laws both serve as foundations of social order, helping to ensure that people will act in ways considered pro-social by their society, from taking care of their children to paying their taxes. The relationship between social norms and laws is complex, and not the subject of this essay. It suffices to note for present purposes that it is widely held that strong social norms reduce the burden on law enforcement; that laws supported by social norms are likely to be significantly more enforceable; and that laws that are formulated in ways that are congruent with social norms are much more likely to be enacted than laws that offend such norms.

Robert Ellickson points out that social norms theory fills a significant lacuna in traditional law and economics models through its assertion that decentralized mechanisms also have an important role to play in maintaining social order:

> Oliver Williamson has used the phrase *legal centralism* to describe the belief that governments are the chief sources of rules and enforcement efforts. The quintessential legal centralist was Thomas Hobbes, who thought that in a society without a sovereign, all would be chaos.... Hobbes apparently saw no possibility that some nonlegal system of social control—such as the decentralized enforcement of norms—might bring at

least a modicum of order even under conditions of anarchy.... The seminal works in law and economics hew to the Hobbesian tradition of legal centralism.[207]

Richard Epstein captures the importance of social norms, in a few well chosen phrases:

> Even persons whose own world views are widely divergent often share one common belief about their preferred norms: they all believe the norms should be legally enforced. The set of purely social norms is often regarded as falling in an awkward no-man's land between the world of purely subjective preferences (vanilla against chocolate ice cream) and the law of fully enforceable legal norms. The older term, "imperfect obligation," refers to obligations enforced by conscience and social pressures but not law, and was thought in classical natural law theory to represent the *correct* way for society to implement norms of benevolence.[208]

Tracey Meares puts it succinctly: "It is time for us to take seriously the notion that social norms are better and more effective constraints on behavior than law could ever be. It is time to give norms a chance."[209]

In short, the study of social norms is of considerable importance for full study of the law.

A METHODOLOGICAL ASIDE

Recognizing the very existence and importance of social norms is, then, an important step in constructing a more encompassing and sounder analysis of the law than law and economics has traditionally provided. Seeking such a construction is clearly one goal that compels at least some members of the newer scholarship.[210]

There is no need to list again the various limitations of the law and economics model,[211] save for two because they are directly relevant to the steps next undertaken. Law and economics proponents argue that while their paradigm may be unrealistic, it is highly parsimonious (or "simple") and thus generates valid predictions even if based on false models.[212] Actually, while it is true that neoclassical economics[213] (the foundation of law and economics) starts from a few basic axioms, numerous ad hoc assumptions are added before most empirical observations can be made. For instance, in his attempt to explain addiction, Gary Becker uses 18 pages of ad hoc assumptions and mathematical equations.[214] The same holds true for many other economic theorists.[215] And neoclassical economics, unlike practically all other sciences, very often "fits" mathematical formulas or conceptual exercises to previously collected data, rather than first formulating hypotheses and then collecting new data to test them.[216] But the record of predictions made based on these models is far from compelling.[217] It hence seems reasonable to seek to establish whether a paradigm whose basic assumptions are somewhat less parsimonious, but use fewer ad hoc assumptions, might provide better understanding and predictions of economic and especially social behavior, including of course those generated by laws. Three elements of such a paradigm, that of law and socio-economics, are explored next.

SOCIAL NORMS: ENVIRONMENTAL AND INTRINSIC

A socio-economic paradigm draws on the observation that social norms are not merely a part of the actors' environment but also affect their intrinsic predispositions. "Intrinsic predispositions" refers to the directions in which an actor would channel her efforts if left to her own devices. They reflect a combination of biological urges and cultural imprinting. Such predispositions can be rather open-ended (for instance, the quest for food), somewhat specified (the quest for healthy food), or even highly so (the quest for a particular kind of healthy food). Specified predispositions often are referred to as preferences. That is, intrinsic predispositions include preferences but encompass other concepts as well.

Not all of the newer studies of social norms have incorporated into their paradigm the observation that social norms help shape intrinsic predispositions. Some legal scholars treat social norms basically as one more factor in the environment that the actor faces, an assumption that enables these scholars to incorporate social norms into law and economics without modifying the paradigm's neoclassical tenets. In such treatments, social norms are treated as one more source of costs the actor considers (e.g., would it annoy my neighbors if I were to operate my chain saw late at night, and would the gains from doing so exceed the costs of my neighbors' censure?), as one more constraint under which actors labor, or as one more resource the actor can draw on. Thus, Eric Posner writes that a "norm constrains attempts by people to satisfy their preferences."[218]

In the same vein, Lawrence Lessig notes that social norms do not merely impose a cost but also serve like economic resources—for instance, when norms motivate people to work—but he still treats norms basically as external, environmental factors. Lessig uses the term "social meanings" to describe the shared cultural understandings of concepts like right and wrong that norms rely upon. He then observes that "these social meanings impose costs, and supply benefits to, individuals and groups...."[219] In such a treatment norms are akin to droughts or rain, supply interruptions or new roads—that is, changes that take place outside the actor, which the actor includes in her calculations and choices.

Along the same line, Cass Sunstein writes that "we can understand a norm—with respect to choices—as a subsidy or a tax."[220] Sunstein elaborates:

> Hence the emphasis on social norms should not be seen as an attack on rational choice approaches to social and political problems. From the standpoint of an individual agent, norms provide a part of the background against which costs and benefits are assessed; more specifically, they help identify some of the costs and benefits of action. From the standpoint of the individual agent, this is hardly irrational, and it is hardly inconsistent with self-interest. (Whether certain norms are rational for society as a whole is a different question. Undoubtedly some of them are not.)[221]

I have no quarrel with these statements about the environmental roles of social norms, and the recognition of the importance of social norms in this external capacity clearly advances the study of law. However, these statements do not encompass a major way in which social norms affect behavior in general, and the law specifically.

An example might help introduce the point. I start by examining the environmental factors and move to the intrinsic ones: if a Jewish butcher in an Orthodox Jewish community is unwise enough to try to sell pork, he will soon learn the full constraining power of social norms. He will lose his customers overnight and be ostracized by members of his community. Moreover, the community is likely to draw on public authorities to prevent him from acting in a way that violates the community's very strongly held norm against consuming pork. Norms clearly *do* constrain behavior, externally.

However, social norms have yet another important effect on human behavior: they are a major factor among those that shape predispositions, the wants of people, and the bases of individual choices.[222] Beyond affecting the content and intensity of numerous particular predispositions, social norms help form (and re-form) the self, by profoundly influencing people's identities, their world views, their views of themselves, the projects they undertake, and thus the people they seek to become.[223]

To return for a moment to our butcher, the notion that he might sell pork would seem such a gross violation of his values and preferences that he would likely dismiss the notion without any serious consideration, were it to ever cross his mind in the first place. To sell pork would be profoundly incompatible with who he is, the way he perceives himself, and who he seeks to become. This aversion to pork reflects no constraint on his choices in the way this term is typically used, because the actor in this case never was inclined to act in this way in the first place. One cannot constrain or suppress (and hardly needs) a non-existent urge, want, or preference. In short, this example serves to illustrate that social norms, aside from their environmental role, also play a key role in ensuring that certain preferences will never be formed in the first place, while others will be strongly held.

The significance of the distinction between treating social norms as part of the actor's environment, affecting costs and constraints, and treating them as factors that shape the actor's predispositions, stands out in several important respects. First of all, the contrast is apparent in the levels of compliance with social norms achieved, the level of social order sustained, and the relative costs of enforcing norms. If people follow their community's social do's and don'ts because they see the social norms as costs or constraints, they will tend to violate the norms when the benefits of abiding by them are lower than the gains of violating them and the risks of detection are low (e.g., dumping garbage at the side of the road if the town dump has been moved to a far away place). If norms shape their preferences, people will tend to abide by these norms because such adherence is a source of intrinsic affirmation.[224] They will pray not out of fear that they will otherwise be beaten (as people are in some fundamentalist countries) or end up in hell, but rather because they find the activity itself to be an expression of their inner self.

A related systematic difference between the compliance of those adhering to norms because of environmental considerations versus intrinsic ones is noted by several of the social norms scholars, such as Richard McAdams and Robert Cooter, when discussing the difference between shame, which is externally generated, and guilt, which is internally generated.[225] Individuals motivated by the former will tend to resent the socially imposed costs of the norms, the "tax" they contain, and endeavor to evade or to change them. In contrast, if people accept the expected behavior as largely in line with their predispositions, they will be likely to blame themselves if they fail to live up to expectations and seek to change their behavior rather than the norms. As a result, compliance based on intrinsic forces such as guilt is less costly and more stable than that based on extrinsic forces such as shame.[226]

Neoclassical economists, law and economics scholars, and even some students of social norms try to obviate the need to modify their basic paradigms by arguing that when people abide by norms for what seems like intrinsic predispositions they actually have extrinsic motivations, such as aiming to please their friends or acquiring prestige. To the extent that this can actually be proven, rather than merely presumed, environmental explanations prevail. However, a socio-economic view suggests that there are numerous forms of behavior (such as work done out of enjoyment of one's scholarly, professional or artistic role, or voting) that cannot be empirically shown to be motivated by external considerations and do correlate with independent measurements of internal commitments.

Moreover, the different sources of compliance produce expected consequences: studies of taxpayers, for instance, show that they are much more compliant with the law and much less resentful when they feel that tax laws square with prevailing social norms of fairness (e.g., a fair sharing of the burden) and that the funds are being used for what they consider to be legitimate goals, than if taxpayers comply merely because they fear being caught if they cheat.[227]

The implications for the law of such findings are enormous. Given the billions of transactions people engage in each day, a social order based on laws can be maintained without massive coercion only if most people most of the time abide, as a result of supportive social norms, by the social tenets embedded in the law, and only if the majority of transactions are sufficiently undergirded by social norms, and thus do not require constant intervention by public authorities. Above all, laws work best and are needed least when social norms are intrinsically followed. For example, the failure of prohibition is often attributed to the populace's unwillingness to accept temperance as a norm. Finally, those social norms that shape actors' intrinsic predispositions are less likely to be subjected to attempts by members of the community to change them (e.g., not only was prohibition not abided by, but lacking political support, it was repealed) or weaken their force (e.g., calling for decriminalizing rather than repealing laws prohibiting the use of marijuana).[228]

A reviewer of a previous draft of this essay argued at this point that the distinction here made may be of interest to those concerned about the "truth," but that "a pragmatic law and norms scholar might not much care" because whether or not norms are driven by the environment or internalized, they will still serve to curb criminal behavior. As I see it, not only would there be significant differences in the costs and stability of law enforcement backed by the two different sources of social norms, but understanding the different sources (or causes) leads to rather different pragmatic public policies. For instance, the more one is blind to the importance of internalization, the more one would be inclined to increase fines and jail sentences to curtail crime. But if one understands internalization and the ways it can be enhanced, one would rely more on character education, peer groups, and shaming (a subject explored more fully in chapter 13). Moreover, to rely on enhanced internalization, one must have an understanding of the ways it works. To put it in more general terms, the quest for truth and pragmatic measures, while far from identical, tend to enrich one another.

ADHERENCE TO SOCIAL NORMS: FIXED VERSUS SHAPED BY INTERNALIZATION AND PERSUASION

Given the importance of intrinsic adherence to social norms, the question arises whether one can convert compliance that relies largely on environmental factors into compliance that relies mainly on intrinsic forces. Such a change would be reflected in a change of preferences to modify either what the actor actually prefers (e.g., increasing desire to attend church rather than play golf) or the intensity with which the actor prefers one activity or object over others (e.g., engendering support for the purchase of recycled paper).

Most neoclassicists tend to assume that preferences are given and fixed.[229] Ellickson notes, "One of the [rational actor] model's most serious limitations is its failure to explain how people come to hold particular preferences."[230] As Cooter observes, "[i]nternalization of norms changes preferences and decisively affects behavior. However, economic theory cannot explain internalization or predict its occurrence. Filling this gap requires a theory of endogenous preferences linking economics and developmental psychology."[231]

Assuming that people's inner predispositions and selves are immutable allowed law and economics scholars to focus on environmental factors. Indeed, the assumption of predetermined preferences is crucial for the neoclassical paradigm. It is profoundly related to the core assumption that people are free and rational agents. These assumptions can be sustained only if the actor's preferences are given and he or she selects the most suitable means for realizetion of these goals. If the preferences themselves are changeable by social and historical factors and processes the actor is neither aware of nor controls, the actor's behavior may be non-rational and is not free.[232] To some extent this is true by definition: without drawing on information and deliberation, the actor is not acting rationally. (The possibility that the norms themselves will lead to rational behavior, even without deliberations by the actor, is discussed below.) And to the extent that the actor's choices are set by others, he or she is not a free agent.

Socio-economics, in contrast, assumes that people's predispositions (including preferences) are formed in part by social norms, and thus can change over time as social norms are changed, as well as that these changes can take place through non-rational processes. (The differences between non-rational and irrational are discussed below.) The newer field of socio-economics and the older one of law and society have paid much attention to the processes involved in numerous studies of value socialization, character education, and, above all, internalization.[233]

Internalization is an element of socialization whereby the actor learns to follow rules of behavior in situations that arouse impulses to transgress and there is no external surveillance or sanctions.[234] This is accomplished through such non-rational processes as identification with authority figures and affective attachments.[235]

Several of the legal scholars who study social norms have recognized the importance of socialization. Robert Cooter, for instance, observes that "[i]nternalization of obligations is pivotal in a theory of decentralized law: after internalizing an obligation, the net benefit from cheating becomes a new cost to the actor. This sign reversal dramatically lowers the costs of enforcing norms."[236] One should disregard Cooter's economist-like wording and focus on the pivotal observation: internalization is a remarkable process through which imposed obligations (compliance with which must be forced or paid for) become desires. Sign reversal is not a phenomenon that is often observed in the social sciences; the mathematical metaphor effectively captures the magnitude and importance of the difference between externally enforced norms and norms that have been internalized.

Similarly, Richard McAdams notes that internalization of norms refers to the process by which "an individual acquires a preference for conformity to a behavioral standard and suffers some psychological cost—guilt is an appropriate term—when she fails to conform, whether or not others are aware of her violation."[237]

McAdams points out that although norms initially elicit compliance through external reinforcement, they often are subsequently internalized by individuals:

> Without internalization, one obeys the norm to avoid external sanctions made possible by the desire for esteem, though the sanctions may in fact include material punishments. After internalization, there is yet another cost to violating a norm: guilt. The individual feels psychological discomfort whether or not others detect her violation.[238]

Lawrence Lessig also agrees that internalization plays a key role in generating compliance with norms.[239] Cooter suggests that preferences can be changed not only through non-rational internalization but also through another process, which he also calls internalization, and which is compatible with the rational assumptions of law and economics. He describes this process as the "acceptance of a new reason."[240] According to this view, which Cooter associates with Jean Piaget and Lawrence Kohlberg, "a child perfects the ability to internalize norms as he or she acquires a capacity for general reasoning."[241] Writes Cooter:

> Piaget's and Kohlberg's research, like my characterization of internalization as acceptance of a new reason

for acting, makes the process sound cool and rational. In contrast, "depth psychology" often traces the internalization of morality to processes that are hot and inchoate. According to these theories, internalization of morality ingrains new impulses in a child through emotional experiences. An example is Freud's theory that morality is the "ghost in the nursery," meaning the repressed memory of parental punishments. Repression transmutes fear into guilt, which changes behavior.[242]

Upon closer examination, however, one notes that Piaget's and Kohlberg's research actually deals with cognitive development and not with changes of preferences. Kohlberg posits that all human beings pass through several stages of development of their moral judgment as they mature intellectually. There are, he says, six stages, grouped into three major levels. In the preconventional level (Stages 1 and 2), individuals obey rules out of fear of punishment or some similar self-interest. In the conventional level (Stages 3 and 4), individuals are able to grasp basic ethical concepts like the Golden Rule. In the postconventional level (Stages 5 and 6), individuals reason in terms of abstract notions like individual rights, utilitarianism, and the social contract.[243]

Thus, while individuals who have progressed through Kohlberg's stages may well be capable of complex ethical reasoning, this does not necessarily mean that they will have stronger moral commitments or act more virtuously.[244] Kohlberg himself is quite explicit in his belief that it is possible to "reason in terms of such [high level] principles and not live up to them."[245] Unfortunately, to know the good cannot be equated with doing the good; one can be rather conversant with Kant and Rawls and still act immorally. To put it in the terminology followed here, knowledge affects behavior by affecting considerations of costs and benefits but, as a rule, does not shape preferences. Internalization clearly does.

A major goal of education (as distinct from teaching) is to foster internalization of social norms by children and thus to affect their preferences. Children are born with broad, vague predispositions. For instance, they are predisposed to food over hunger, but these general predispositions are translated into specific preferences in line with the particular social norms they internalize. Thus, while children have an inborn need for food and perhaps even for variation in food and combinations (e.g., proteins and carbo-hydrates), the specific foods they consider desirable—Kosher, soul, those their parental or peer sub-cultures cherish—are a function of acquired tastes. Moreover, the acquisition is often not the result of any conscious reasoning. Teenagers do not prefer Cokes and french fries because they have calculated that such consumption will en-hance their peer standing; they *feel* that these are the right foods to consume and typically are unaware how they gained such tastes.

Once children become adults, their preferences do not suddenly become immutable (like the "Rocky Mountains," as George J. Stigler and Gary S. Becker put it),[246] independent, or hermetically sealed. Non-rational processes continue to affect them. *Persuasion* is the term often used to refer to the non-rational processes through which adult preferences are changed.[247] Persuasion works by non-rational means, such as identification with authority figures (like Minister Louis Farrakhan); group enthusiasm generated through rituals and appeals (e.g., KKK leaders' calls for a cross burning); and relating new forms of behavior to values that the person already holds in high regard (e.g., convincing a non-activist to join a political demon-stration on the grounds that the person already believes in the ideals of political activism and in the cause the demonstration seeks to advance). Persuasion is also part of processes such as acculturation (especially of immigrants from other countries or of people moving within the same society from one area to another where the sub-culture is different[248]), religious conversions, joining social move-ments, or joining a cult. Leadership, mass hysteria, mob rule, and propaganda are all forms of persuasion.

The issue at hand is highlighted by the debate over the role of ad-vertising. Neoclassical economists tend to insist that advertising is strictly informational rather than a means of subconsciously affect-ing people's preferences, and thus a form of persuasion.[249] Stigler and Becker write of their disagreement with thinkers like John Kenneth Galbraith, who claim that

> the advertising "persuades" the consumer to prefer his product, and often a distinction is drawn between "persuasive" and "informative" advertising....We shall argue in direct opposition to this view, that it is neither necessary nor useful to attribute to advertising the function of changing tastes.[250]

The underlying reason that neoclassicists must deny the existence of manipulative ads is that if people purchase an item which does not serve their preferences, but rather those that some Madison Avenue firm has implanted in them without their knowledge, people could no longer be considered logical-empirical (rational) actors. Furthermore, they could not be the free agents the neoclassical paradigm assumes them to be.

In contrast, a socio-economic paradigm has no reason to deny that many ads contain information about changes in costs and constraints (e.g., flight schedules and fares) but also pays attention to the persuasive element of much advertising; for example, ads that appeal to people's subconscious motives ranging from guilt to sexual desire.

It should be noted in passing that to argue that preferences are initially set by internalization and thereafter subject to persuasion is not to deny that the actors have several degrees of freedom. They can become more aware of the forces that shape them, including social norms, and they can work with others to change these forces. There are, though, considerable limits to their ability to liberate themselves from the constitutive influence of social norms. And the extent of freedom they possess is significantly less than the neoclassical paradigm posits, although smaller than some law and society paradigms assume, the Marxist's for instance. A wit expressed the difference by suggesting that in economics everything has a price; in sociology—nothing. Socio-economics builds on the notion that some transactions are highly affected by prices, while other relations are not transactions at all, and not affected by prices except under unrealistic, limited conditions. (One might note in addition that the desire to gain insight into self and enhance one's independence, for instance through psychoanalysis, is itself, in part, a reflection of social norms. A comparison of the relevant social norms of Westerners to those of Asians, of this generation's to those of earlier ones, and of people on liberal campuses to those in traditional small towns, further highlights this point.)

Recognizing that social norms can affect compliance with mores and laws by forming preferences and by changing those that have been formed, through internalization and persuasion, is an important element of the law and socio-economics paradigm. Several legal scholars have adopted these elements. Others have kept one foot in the law and economics camp and planted the other in law and society, while still others have yet to add these core conceptions to their evolving paradigm.

SOURCES OF SOCIAL NORMS:
RATIONAL CHOICE VERSUS HISTORY

The more one recognizes the importance of social norms, the more one is drawn to the question of where these norms come from, and what forces influence their development. The social norms scholarship has yet to reach definitive conclusions on this subject. Some of the discussion reflects law and economics responses; some, law and society; and some, a synthesis of the two much like the socio-economic approach.

The law and economics position is that norms themselves are "rational" and thus can make actors act rationally, without having to deliberate before each action—or even at all. Norms are said to either reflect previous deliberations or, while not traceable to any actual deliberations, seem "as if" they were the outcome of rational choice. That is, the specific norms adopted "fit" the assumption of rationality as if rationality was some kind of a mathematical formula that best fits the patterns of the evidence at hand.

A simple example of a rational rule is that of an actor who follows a rule of carrying an umbrella everyday, rain or shine. His rule is considered to be rational because he is portrayed as having assumed to have calculated that the costs of checking weather forecasts every day (and their reliability) are higher than those of carrying the umbrella on rain-free days. No evidence is provided that anyone ever made such calculations; however, such assumptions allow law and economics to reconcile certain seemingly irrational behaviors with the presumption of rationality.[251]

McAdams provides one of the many highly theoretical models of how norms may arise rationally:

> Under the right conditions, the desire for esteem pro-
> duces a norm. For some behavior X in some population
> of individuals, a norm may arise if (1) there is a con-
> sensus about the positive or negative esteem worthi-
> ness of engaging in X (that is, either most individuals
> in the relevant population grant, or most withhold,
> esteem from those who engage in X); (2) there is some
> risk that others will detect whether one engages in X;

and (3) the existence of this consensus and risk of detection is well-known within the relevant population. When these conditions exist, the desire for esteem necessarily creates costs of or benefits from engaging in X. If the consensus is that X deserves esteem, a norm will arise if the esteem benefits exceed, for most people, the costs of engaging in X. Conversely, if the consensus condemns X, a norm will arise if, for most people, the esteem costs exceed the benefits of engaging in X.[252]

Ellickson's pioneering study of the matter stands out precisely because he examined the matter empirically. He concludes:

In uncovering the various Shasta County norms, I was struck that they seemed consistently utilitarian. Each appeared likely to enhance the aggregate welfare of rural residents. This inductive observation, coupled with supportive data from elsewhere, inspired the hypothesis that *members of a close-knit group develop and maintain norms whose content serves to maximize the aggregate welfare that members obtain in their workaday affairs with one another....* Stated more simply, the hypothesis predicts that members of tight social groups will informally encourage each other to engage in cooperative behavior. It should be stressed that this proposition was *induced*, rather than deduced from an explicit model of social interactions.[253]

Others, following Robert Axelrod's work,[254] have argued that rational norms arise out of experience. Cooter writes:

The economic analysis of social norms draws upon a fundamental result in game theory: One shot games with inefficient solutions...often have efficient solutions when repeated between the same players. This generalization grounds the "utilitarianism of small groups," by which I mean the tendency of small groups to develop efficient rules for cooperation among members.

The utilitarianism of small groups has been demonstrated for cattle ranchers, Chinese traders, medieval merchants, and modern merchant associations. Research on property rights has revealed variety and detail in the political arrangements by which small groups manage their assets. Utilitarianism applies to social groups whose members repeatedly interact with each other, such as the Berkeley Chess Club, but not to social categories of people who seldom interact, such as chess players in California.[255]

Other mechanisms that lead to rational norms are said to include rational elites who cause rational selection of rules even if most people do not deliberate.[256] Still others assume that history is rational, as if God were a utility maximizer who guided history through all its gruesome developments, an assumption initially embraced (though later abandoned) by Nobel laureate Douglas North.[257]

The newer scholars of social norms have increasingly recognized that while some social norms are certainly rational, others are clearly affected by the kind of forces law and society focuses on: history, broadly understood, including tradition, institutions,[258] customs, and habits. ("History" refers here not merely to past events but also to the narratives about such events, which are interpreted in ways that help transmit social norms.) According to this approach, the sources of norms are remote in time (e.g., Moses brought the Ten Commandments down Mt. Sinai); they are passed from one generation to the next; and they derive authority by virtue of their being a part of tradition rather than reflecting deliberations.

To return to the umbrella example for a moment, law and society students would argue that taking an umbrella on sunny days in the dry season is irrational (say, obsessive) or non-rational, or that if a person does so, somebody must have persuaded him that carrying it is the right thing to do, say because it is a status symbol. (British citizens used Bowler hats and rolled up umbrellas in this way.) Cooter makes this point as follows:

> Someone subsequently convinces me, contrary to my previous beliefs, that smoking is morally wrong ("God forbids us to harm ourselves for pleasure's sake," "You risk orphaning your child," etc.). After my conversation, I have an additional reason for not smoking; smoking violates a moral rule I now hold.[259]

Some of these norms are irrational; many others, non-rational. For example, most people who pay their brokers for stock selection act irrationally, and so do most of those millions who put money into their IRA accounts toward the end rather than beginning of the year.

Much more often, social norms are non-rational as they govern behavior dealing with matters that Talcott Parsons called "other worldly" and hence do not implicate empirical-logical matters.[260] These include whether or not one believes in God, spirituality, the idea of progress, and many other such beliefs. Each of these are not merely abstract values but also the source of numerous norms.

Many of these values, and the norms that govern the behavior associated with them, are transmitted from generation to generation, through communal processes such as rituals, holidays, and identification with older authority figures. These norms are commonly legitimated on such grounds as tradition, superstition, nationalism, or some other such cultural factors. While people often also offer valid consequentialist-utilitarian instrumental arguments to explain why they heed the norms under discussion, these explanations are secondary to ritualistic invocations of the past.[261] Thus, many New Age gurus recommend meditation as a way to reduce stress. However, should social science tests show that meditation has no such effects, most followers of these gurus would probably not stop meditating. Religious people speak of the benefits to mental hygiene of being devout, but this obviously is not the leading reason they are religious.

Socio-economics can accommodate both cultural and cost considerations. Social norms are often heeded because they are viewed as "how things are done here." Norms, however, are more likely to be modified when costs they inflict are high than when they are low.

Dennis Chong recognizes this dual position of norms, although at times he slips into a law and economics line of thinking:

> Although some group norms appear calculated to further the interests of group members, many group norms seem to be adopted without reflection and appear instead to be driven mainly by imitation and group identification....
>
> Although much cultural transmission has this inertial quality, it does not always violate the process of rational decision making. No individual has the resources to evaluate thoroughly all of the choices he must make, so

by conforming to the status quo he takes advantage of the cumulative wisdom of the community. In effect, he operates on the assumption that existing practices have survived the trial and error test.[262]

Chong adds: "even if people act primarily in response to the advantages and disadvantages of the options presented to them, they still economize in their decisions by developing and relying on rules and information embodied in their attitudes, beliefs, and values."[263] At another point he concludes:

> The economic model...underestimates the extent to which motivation from enduring group loyalties and values can override changes in the opportunity costs of available choices. People sometimes resist cultural changes even when environmental changes undermine the original rationale for their values and actions. Also, much value formation and transmission occurs through limitation and conformity without involving explicit instrumental calculation.[264]

This point is also recognized by Lawrence Lessig, who writes:

> For even if an institution arises in response to demands of efficiency, it does not follow that the institution survives if and only if it continues to advance efficiency. "[A]t a particular time in a particular economy, there may exist lots of institutions which serve no social purpose and which though once valuable to society, may now actually be harmful."[265]

THE SOCIO-ECONOMICS OF SOCIAL NORMS: THE ART OF COMBINATIONS

Once one fully accepts that human behavior is deeply affected both by social norms imbedded in the actor's environment and by their embodiment in the self, that the actor's predispositions are formed and modified in part by processes of internalization and persuasion, and that social norms themselves are in part the fruits of rational choice and in part reflect historical processes, one can explore the ways in which the factors modeled by law and economics and law and society may be effectively combined into a socio-economic perspective. This is a huge, complex, and developing subject that is only briefly illustrated here.

Social factors often play a larger role in setting "priors" than in determining the considerations that follow. Thus, social factors (especially psychological and cultural ones) may largely determine the extent to which a given actor (or actors in a given culture) is risk-averse. Economic factors may play a larger role in determining which specific low-risk investment an actor will choose, given his or her particular predispositions.

Another form of combination of the two kinds of considerations can be observed in well-functioning economies, where social factors play a significant role in setting the limits on the reign of market forces, but leave it largely to economic forces to form the processes that take place within the market.[266] For instance, the government sets the limits of acceptable pollution but leaves it to the industry to choose the most efficient way to reduce pollution rather than requiring that smoke stacks be equipped with government-approved scrubbers.

Another way to think about socio-economic combinations is to view them as defining a two dimensional space. Behavior that is both endorsed by social norms and also rewarding in narrow economic terms is likely to be the most stable. Conversely, behavior that is censured by social norms and economically unrewarding is most likely to be abandoned. The differences between the stability of behavior that is highly normative but not rewarding, and behavior that is considered a violation of norms but still rewarding, remains to be studied. The particular response is, of course, affected by the respective magnitude of the two key factors. For instance, acts that are considered minor violations of norms but are highly rewarding are much more likely to occur than acts that are considered serious violations of norms and are not highly rewarding.

To reiterate, these very preliminary illustrations are intended solely to call attention to work that largely remains to be done.

In Conclusion

The implication of the preceding discussion, that human nature allows elders and peers to constitute and reconstitute our preferences, is a much less sanguine view of the individual and society than the image of a group of free and rational citizens, of people who convene to deliberately, voluntarily, and reasonably form (or reform) the social norms they seek to live by. However, socioeconomics does not assume that people are fully determined. It builds on the observation that we are both persuadable and deliberative creatures, that social norms both affect our predispositions and reflect our choices.

It encompasses both facets of the self, recognizing our more vulnerable side. While not ignoring our deliberative capacity, it takes into account that we are susceptible to persuasion. Indeed, it suggests that such an understanding of the self will enhance the reach of our choice and reduce the scope of those forces we neither understand nor control.

The focus of this chapter's discussion was establishing the concepts needed for a fuller understanding of the role of social norms. The complex relations between social norms and the law have not been explored, other than to briefly note that strong social norms allow for less reliance on the coercive power of the state, make for better law enforcement of enacted laws, and make it less likely that laws will be repealed, and hence are more compatible with liberty.

Chapter 11

Law in Civil Society, Good Society, and the Prescriptive State

Two reports call attention to the fact that the American society faces two "crises" rather than one. These studies are the National Commission on Civic Renewal's *A Nation of Spectators: How Civic Disengagement Weakens America and What We Can Do About It* (from here on, *A Nation of Spectators*), and the Institute for American Values' *A Call to Civil Society: Why Democracy Needs Moral Truths* (from here on, *A Call to Civil Society*).[267] The first malaise results from the deterioration of the civil society reflected in declines in voter turnout, people interested in public affairs, and participation in voluntary associations, among other developments. The second results from the deterioration of society's moral fiber reflected in and further fueled by a decline in focus on the family, high rates of teen pregnancy and out of wedlock births, and a rise in the vile and violent elements of the mass culture, among other developments.

To highlight that these reports go beyond the topics encompassed in numerous previous examinations of the civil society, *A Nation of Spectators* repeatedly refers to the "civic moral conditions" of our country, and to the "moral and civil ills," to indicate that much more than civility is at stake. The second report, *A Call to Civil Society* (which in many ways parallels the Communitarian Platform)[268] states from the outset that a "democracy needs moral truths," and dedicates a good part of the discussion to the symptoms of the "moral crisis" and what might be done to overcome it. "Moral truths" is a phrase that up to now has been avoided by much of the literature on civil society for profound reasons explored below.

The author very much shares the basic diagnosis and prognosis of these two reports and has written two books in support of the same basic thesis.[269] This chapter will argue that, in order to gain a more complete understanding of the two challenges, the deterioration of civil society and of society's moral fiber, and the ways they are to be faced, we had best treat them as distinct notions rather than try to pack both into the notion of a civil society. This is suggested for both sociological and intellectual reasons.

Sociologically speaking, the term *civil society* has a rather deep ensconced meaning in both academic and public discourse. It is deeply associated with the Toquevillean notion of a society whose citizens' liberty is protected by a rich fabric of intermediary bodies that stand between them and the state, and that themselves are shored up by citizens able and inclined to participate in these bodies, termed voluntary associations. The enemy of the civil society thus is the overbearing state.

A typical definition of the civil society is "[t]hat area of social life that is neither familial and intimate on the one hand, nor state-directed on the other. It includes voluntary organizations of various kinds, ranging from private economic enterprises, to farmers' granges, to the Little Leagues." [270] Similarly, another source describes it this way: "Civil society is a particular form of society, appreciating social diversity and able to limit the depredations of political power."[271] A third:

> The institutional core consists of the following combination of political and socioeconomic arrangements: a government which is limited and accountable and operates under a rule of law; a market economy (implying a regime of private property); an array of free, voluntary associations (political, economic, social and cultural); and a sphere of free public debate.[272]

Yet another scholar states that

> [t]he values of civil society are those of political participation, state accountability, and publicity of politics.... The institutions of civil society are associational and representative forums, a free press and social associations. The inhabitant of this sphere is the rights bearing and juridically-defined individual, i.e., the citizen. And the protection of the members of civil society is encapsuled in the vocabulary and the institution of rights.[273]

Literally hundreds of books and articles, if not thousands, use the term in this way. While it is true that one can find rather different definitions, especially in the original use of the term,[274] there seems to me little doubt that currently the term is strongly established and hence resists being subsumed into other meanings, such as arguing that a civil society entails equal command of economic and social assets by citizens (equality), accepts the feminist orientation,[275] or is moral. This takes nothing away from the power of the moral renewal argument other than it needs, as the two reports strongly imply, an added and distinct concept from that of the civil society. I shall refer to this as the good society.[276]

Intellectual analysis points in the same direction. It is the thesis of this article that the crisis of the good society, the means to revive it (to use Jean Elshtain's fine term),[277] and the role of law within it, are all conceptually significantly different from, although not necessarily incompatible with, the same factors of the civil society.

After a brief discussion of the basic terms I delineate the difference in the following realms: basic philosophical anchoring; the basic role of law; differences between citizenship and membership; the kinds of virtues the two societies uphold; their rather divergent views of voluntary associations; their distinct relations to achieved vs. ascribed status; and perspectives on individual rights and social responsibilities. One reason one might be tempted to speak about the civil society even when one deals with issues of the good society (especially the moral crisis and how it might be overcome) is that the second concept is much more contested. People from a very wide ideological and political spectrum favor a civil society. A call supporting the renewal of a good society per se (without civil society overtones) is likely to garner much less support because what is entailed in social definitions of the good, those who are liberal fear would turn into an intolerant state which would impose that which it considers virtuous. I hence must introduce a third concept, that of the prescriptive state, to show that a good society can be intellectually distinct and sociologically viable without becoming such an entity.

THREE IDEAL TYPES

Following a very long tradition which has generated thousands of books and articles, the term "civil society" is best used to refer to societies that have a rich fabric of voluntary associations and other intermediary bodies that stand between the individual and the state, and whose citizens have the wherewithal required to sustain such a society (e.g., are able to think critically). In a book often cited in this context, Peter Berger and Richard Neuhaus define the civil society as

> ...those institutions that stand between the private world of individuals and the large impersonal structures of modern society. They "mediated" by constituting a vehicle by which personal beliefs and values could be transmitted into the mega-institutions. They were thus "Janus-faced" institutions, facing both "upward" and "downward."[278]

Among the many others who define or treat the civil society in same manner are Robert Fine and Shirin Rai, Benjamin Barber, E.J. Dionne, and Robert Putnam.[279] Putnam in particular relies on a Toquevillean perspective:

> When Alexis de Toqueville visited the United States in the 1830s it was the Americans' propensity for civic association that most impressed him as the key to their unprecedented ability to make democracy work. Recently, social scientists of a neo-Toquevillean bent have unearthed a wide range of empirical evidence that the theoretical premise of his argument is no less accurate today—that the quality of public life and the performance of social institutions (not only in the United States) are powerfully influenced by norms and networks of civic engagement.[280]

The term "good society" might be used to refer to societies that rely mainly on their moral infrastructure (families, schools, communities) and informal social controls to foster a core of substantive (as distinct from merely procedural) moral values. (For an outstanding treatment of these, see the 1998 discussion of "everyday democracy" by Nancy Rosenblum.[281]) And the term "prescriptive state" might be used to refer to states that to a considerable extent rely on their means of coercion to enforce such values and that have an extensive list of values they seek to impose rather than a limited core.

I cannot stress enough that these are three abstractions or ideal types. Actual societies mix various elements of these categories, although some are much more of one kind than others. I return to the question of combinations after the ideal types are further discussed. This is a particularly important issue given that there are those who argue that ultimately a civil society rests on the moral foundations provided by the good society, a position explicitly embraced by *A Call to Civil Society*.

To illustrate the differences among the three basic concepts: no society has ever truly approximated the civil society, but Britain and the United States are often said to have approximated such a social order. A relatively pure case of a good society in the terms defined here was found in the early kibbutzim because these communities have strong shared definitions of the good but foster it with next to no reliance on coercion. Examples of strongly prescriptive states have been seen in theocracies such as contemporary Iran and Taliban-controlled Afghanistan, and nationalistic or socialist tyrannies such as the Nazi regime, the USSR, and North Korea. Comparatively very mild and moderate versions of the prescriptive state are advanced by American social conservatives who wish to outlaw abortion, ban divorce, require prayer in public schools, ban homosexual activities, vastly increase the kind of actions for which criminal punishment is meted out as well as sharply increase the severity of these punishments, all of which are measures that seek to control behavior through the force of the state.[282]

Philosophical Foundations

The three concepts are anchored in three social philosophies. The civil society rests on classical liberalism and its contemporary offshoots. Given that this philosophy seeks to rely on each person to define the good rather than the society, liberalism seeks to leave value decisions as much as possible in the private realm, keeping the public realm thin and procedural and hence of very limited substantive normative moral content.[283]

John Rawls seems to go a step further, not only implying that the various mediating institutions are morally equivalent, but also suggesting that the entirety of civil society—not merely the liberal state!—is little more than a neutral zone in which various virtues compete, and in which none is prescribed or even preferred as a matter of societal policy. (I write "seems" to indicate that I do not join here the very elaborate debate concerning what Rawls says, really meant to say, and how he changed his mind from one volume to the next.) The following quote seems to me to speak quite directly to the issue at hand, and it is this Rawls I address here:

...[A]ll discussions are from the point of view of citizens in the culture of civil society, which Habermas calls the *public sphere*. There, we as citizens discuss how justice as fairness is to be formulated, and whether this or that aspect of it seems acceptable.... In the same way, the claims of the ideal of discourse and of its procedural conception of democratic institutions are considered. Keep in mind that this background culture contains comprehensive doctrines of all kinds that are taught, explained, debated against one another, and argued about—indefinitely without end as long as society has vitality and spirit. It is the culture of daily life with its many associations: its universities and churches, learned and scientific societies; endless political discussions of ideas and doctrines are commonplace everywhere.[284]

This text is compatible with the notion that a civil society is not a good society because it does not promote one "comprehensive doctrine," but rather simply provides the forum in which a plurality of such doctrines can be debated "indefinitely without end," within the numerous voluntary associations. Civil society is thus desirable because it affords and sustains endless debate, thereby precluding any general consensus on the good to which society at large can subscribe and attempt to foster in its members. In that sense, the "endless" element is not merely dismissive but actually essential.

Michael Walzer, often considered a communitarian, espouses the same basic viewpoint very clearly:

I would rather say that the civil society argument is a corrective to the four ideological accounts of the good life than a fifth to stand alongside them. It challenges their singularity but it has no singularity of its own. The phrase "social being" describes men and women who are citizens, producers, consumers, members of the nation, and much else besides—and none of these by nature or because it is the best thing to be. The associational life of civil society is the actual ground where all versions of the good are worked out and tested...and proved to be partial, incomplete, ultimately unsatisfying.... Ideally, civil society is a setting of settings: all are included, none is preferred.[285]

The good society builds on communitarian philosophy. It assumes social definitions of the good, and that a well functioning society, let alone a good one, requires a core of substantive (rather than merely procedural) shared values which in part define not only public but also private proper behavior. To transmit these values from generation to generation, the good society heavily relies on the family, schools, and the community (including its places of worship and civic associations). It also draws on moral dialogues[286] to recast values bequeathed by earlier generations. And a good society relies first and largely on informal social controls (or the moral voice)[287] rather than on coercion to undergird shared values.

The prescriptive state relies on socially conservative conceptions. Of these, the most commonly observed are religious, in those instances where religious groups sanction the use of the state to enforce their very extensive (as distinct from "core") list of values, reflected in the dictates, duties and obligations imposed by the state. Secular tyrannies have a similar pattern, although the values they promote are often national, social, or both, rather than religious. Prescriptive states of both kinds often seek to control most of what a person does, consumes, reads, hears, and even thinks.

THE BASIC ROLE OF THE LAW

The three approaches define the basic role of law in society rather differently. Much more will be said about this subject below, but as an early observation, the civil society seeks to minimize reliance on the law because it sees it as a tool of the state that such an approach seeks to countervail. In addition, this philosophy views the law as largely instrumental, facilitating voluntary arrangements among parties, especially contracts.

Most important, in civil society law is designed to be evenhanded, fair, and largely procedural. The law is "blind"; all citizens are to be treated equally. Indeed, one of the main objections liberal advocates of the civil society raise to conceptions of the good society is that on the face of it they are discriminatory because some people are viewed as more moral than others. This possibility disappears when the society per se has no shared definition of the good and this matter is left to each individual. As Will Kymlicka states,

> Some communitarians argue that the liberal preference
> for the cultural marketplace over the state as the

appropriate arena for evaluating different ways of life stems from an atomistic belief that judgements about the good are only autonomous when they are made by isolated individuals who are protected from social pressure.[288]

The good society seeks to minimize reliance on the law not because the law often preempts private decisions but because it often undermines (although it does sometimes serve to reinforce) informal social controls by replacing them. Also, while the good society recognizes the instrumental role of the law, it also draws on its expressive role, to state and underscore the values the society cherishes. Thus, when the law in such a society enforces parents' duties to their children, its primary purpose is not to facilitate familial arrangements but to communicate the high value this kind of society puts on parenting. And laws that "require" people to be Good Samaritans serve more to define such a moral expectation than to make people Good Samaritans by the small fines imposed if and when a person is charged and convicted of not being a Good Samaritan.

Most important, the good society is willing to rely on the law to promote a limited but important list of substantive social values, even if this means treating citizens unequally.[289] Such measures include environmental protection, reverse discrimination, and limited reallocation of wealth. (An argument can be made that all such laws are meant to ensure that all citizens will become equal, but one can show quite readily that actually these laws reflect substantive concepts of what is considered good by the societies that enacted these laws.)

While prescriptive states too might prefer not to resort to the law, given the strong and wide disaffection of their members, and the very extensive and comprehensive list of values to which they demand compliance, these states end up making law and law enforcement the mainstay of their regimes.

CITIZENS THIN AND THICK VERSUS MEMBERS

The three approaches differ fundamentally in their view of the place of the person within the social order, which is highlighted in their legal treatment of citizenship. The civil society draws a sharp line between the citizen and the person. The citizen is the role the person has in the public realm (paying taxes, voting, serving in the military and on juries, obeying the law), while most of life takes place (or ought to take place) in the separate private realm of the individual. While the thin realm of citizenship is governed by various laws, the thick private realm is subject to individual choices. While there is some role for laws in the private realm, for instance those concerning private property, basically the civil society is not merely incompatible with a thin layer of laws in the private realm, but also with a thin public realm, and hence with relatively few laws governing public roles. (Feminist[290] and communitarian[291] criticism of this sharp distinction between the public and the private realm seems to me well taken.)

While the ideal citizen's role in the civil society is limited, proper citizens of the civil society are expected to be active, follow public affairs, participate in local decision making, and so on, rather than act like passive consumers, a point often stressed by Benjamin Barber[292] as well as Henry Boyte and Nancy Kari.[293]

The good society's main concern is with membership, not citizenship—that is, with the roles a person plays in various social bodies, largely governed by mores rather than by laws, although obviously these have a role. Most of the responsibilities of the good person are neither political nor personal but social: to one's children, parents, spouse, friends, neighbors, or other members of his or her immediate community and more encompassing social entities. While in actual societies various laws help to define some of these membership roles (e.g., child support), in the ideal good society, people fulfill their social roles most often because they believe that this is the right thing to do rather than because they fear the law. To repeat, the early kibbutzim approximated this ideal type.

A core concept of the prescriptive state is thick citizenship and thin membership, as it in principle recognizes little of the personal sphere. Citizenship is typically involuntary (as highlighted by sealed borders). Citizens' duties are very numerous, reflecting a vast list of values which are ensconced in numerous laws and adherence to which is enforced by law. These concern practically every aspect of personal life, including what people wear (e.g., veils), eat (no pork), drink (no Coca-Cola), listen to (no jazz nor BBC), the number of children permitted, and so on. Moderate versions of such states are found in authoritarian communities in the USA in the '50s, for instance, those in which hanging a UN flag, frequenting a gay bar, or introducing a black person into a public school led to violence supported by the state.

A closely related and very telling difference among the three types of societies concerns their view of human nature. As I have spelled out this point elsewhere,[294] I note here merely that the civil society views people as essentially good in nature, but corruptible by the state. The prescriptive state views people as highly impulsive, rather irrational, and in need of restraint by the state. The good society views people as initially, in childhood, as rather impulsive and irrational but open to socialization capable of developing them into good persons, allowing for an intact moral infrastructure. Given that unlike the civil society this concept does not view people as good by nature, it recognizes that even if socialization is highly successful people will be considerably tempted by the lower angels of their nature and require a continual exercise of informal social controls if they are to be as good as they can be. Accordingly, while both the state and the society can corrupt people, the society is often a major source which introduces and sustains their virtues.

WHICH VIRTUES?

While analysts of all three kinds of societies refer to virtues, the list of virtues they extol and are needed to sustain each kind of society are far from identical, a point all too often disregarded. The typical virtue list of the civil society consists of moderation, tolerance, self control, critical thinking, following news about public affairs, participating in public affairs (democratic process), and volunteering. Others claim that

> [b]eing honest, kind, dependable, fair, and respecting others' rights are some of the character traits most highly valued in our society. Initiative, organization, decision skills, and readiness to apply all the above traits to betterment of the community (citizenship), are also highly regarded....[295]

These civil virtues have two important attributes: they concern individuals (unlike, say, the virtues incorporated into public policies and laws, for instance those mandating national service in Germany) and they are by and large procedural rather than substantive.

Take, for instance, staying informed about public affairs (rather than merely sports and consumer goods), as an attribute of individual citizens. It is basically content free: there is no particular kind of the very large world of public affairs of which staying informed is considered, in principle, as more virtuous than any others. Tolerance is another personal attribute, closely related to self control. Both of these are content free: the virtuous citizen of the civil society is not more tolerant of, say, Jews than blacks and blacks than homosexuals, and so on. The same of course holds for religious tolerance that encompasses all religions as well as atheism.

The essential virtues the civil society requires are personal rather than social ones (those which the society considers good). This point is illustrated by laws concerning marriage. Advocates of the civil society have difficulty explaining why they refuse (when they do refuse) to recognize gay marriages, polygamy, and many other "alternate lifestyle" arrangements as equally legal as traditional marriages as long as these arrangements are between (or among) consenting adults, who wish to encode their relationship in a legal form.

In the same vein, public education, an essential feature of the civil society, is focused on building up personal virtues and capabilities, critical thinking for instance,[296] rather than social ones, such as dedication to preserve the environment for future generations. During a panel discussion on the subject during the 1999 meeting of the American Political Science Association a line repeated was that civic education should entail "transmission of knowledge and skills but be character neutral." When one of the participants suggested that children should be taught reverence for the Constitution, Amy Gutmann argued that there was no reason to exempt the Constitution from critical examination. The well known debate on whether Amish children should be exempted from attending required secondary education concerns the question of whether they can be citizens of a civil society without learning to think critically.[297]

In contrast, members of the good society are expected to have not only merely personal, but also relational and social, virtues. In addition to being reliable citizens, they are also supposed to be good parents, friends, neighbors and community members. That is, particularistic loyalties (rather than merely reciprocity) are an earmark of members of the good society.

Above all, members of good societies are expected to contribute to select causes the good society seeks to foster, rather then merely choose their own causes. The good society, for instance, holds in higher regard working in soup kitchens and clinics for the poor, volunteering to serve in the Peace Corps or AmeriCorps, and helping AIDS victims, more than donating to the opera or serving on a country club board. Many continental societies value the welfare state, lower inequality, and social amenities even if these social virtues entail sacrificing some measure of economic growth. (They advance these social virtues as good in their own right rather than as instrumental values that help people become equal and effective members of the civil society.)

Education for membership in the good society includes developing commitments to substantive values and a shared definition of the good. Commitments to the protection of the environment are a case in point as are various notions about the virtue of diversity and social justice.

The prescriptive state's list of virtues is still different. The good citizen is one who first of all complies with the law and discharges diligently and in good faith the numerous state defined duties. Better yet, the virtuous citizen voluntarily makes contributions to the state, above and beyond those demanded by it, for instance donating time or resources to causes the state specifies. And, the good citizen helps law enforcement by checking on neighbors, friends and kin, to ensure that they also conduct themselves as virtuous citizens.

The differences among the three kinds of societies are highlighted by their tax laws. Civil societies seek tax neutrality; they prefer to avoid favoring one behavior over another. Proportional taxes are compatible with the civil society; progressive taxes only to the extent that they can be shown as promoting the ability of citizens to partake in the civil society, but not to the extent that they promote a particular conception of social justice in its own right.

In contrast, a good society might well provide special tax privileges to behavior it considers socially virtuous, for instance, being married or having children. (Many societies provide subsidies to those who have children.)

The same issue arises with regards to public support of the arts and other cultural projects. Champions of the civil society objected strenuously when federal agencies such as the National Endowment for the Arts and the National Endowment for the Humanities sought not to fund projects that offended some core social values, for instance photos that showed Christ on a cross dipped in urine. A good society would take it for granted that it will provide public funds only to projects that enhance, or at least do not undermine, that which it considers virtuous.

The prescriptive state tends to require people to follow its various dictates and punishes them when they do not, rather than rewarding them when they do. For instance, divorce is banned rather than marriage rewarded; abortions are banned rather than adoptions provided for children not wanted by their parents; community service is required rather than extolled to the point people volunteer; the armed forces rely on the draft rather than on pay and patriotic persuasion.

THREE VIEWS OF VOLUNTARY ASSOCIATIONS

From the viewpoint of the discussion at hand, the most important characteristic of civil society is that it draws *no difference among voluntary associations with regard to the substantive values* that are fostered by these associations. I am not suggesting that these associations are without specific normative dispositions. Little Leagues, for instance, may cherish a healthy body and sporting behavior (or—winning at all costs); book clubs foster respect for learning and culture, and so on. But from the viewpoint of their contribution to civil society, they all are treated by champions of civil society as basically equivalent; none is, normatively speaking, inherently morally superior to the other.

Certainly champions of civil society do recognize some differences among voluntary associations, but these are limited to their functions as elements of the civil society rather than to their normative content. For instance, voluntary associations that are more effective in developing citizenship skills are preferred over those that are less so. But the actual values to which people involved in these groups apply their skills is not under review, nor are other substantive values such associations embody.

For the civil society, an association that facilitates playing bridge has the same basic standing as the Red Cross; members of the Elks command the same status as those of the Promise Keepers; and bowling leagues are indistinguishable from the North American Man/Boy Love Association (which advocates removing the age of consent for sex), whose members meet to exchange tips on how to seduce boys younger than eight. Beyond league bowling (and bridge playing), other mainstays of "social capital" that Robert Putnam found in his studies of civic society in Italy as more soundly civil and democratic than others were bird-watching groups and choral societies.[298] Bird-watching groups may enhance respect for nature and choirs may cherish culture (or certain kinds of culture over others), but this is not the reason Robert Putnam praises them. As Putnam puts it, he extols them because "[t]aking part in a choral society or a bird-watching club can teach self-discipline and an appreciation for the joys of successful collaboration."[299] So could most, if not all, other types of voluntary associations.

While from the basic standpoint of the civil society, one voluntary association is basically as good as any other,[300] they differ greatly from the perspective of the good society, precisely because they embody different values. Thus, to the extent that American society cherishes the notion of interracial integration, it views the Urban League and the NAACP as much more in line with its values than the Nation of Islam; and the Ripon Society more so than the Aryan groups—all voluntary associations.[301] Berger and Neuhaus concede this point in a revised edition of their book:

> Possibly, though, we were a bit carried away in our enthusiasm for these institutions, overlooking the fact that some of them definitely play nefarious roles in society. Thus, strictly speaking in terms of our definition, the Mafia, the Ku Klux Klan, and the social branch of an organization seeking to get the government to negotiate with visiting aliens in UFOs could also be described as mediating structures. They do, indeed, mediate between individuals and the larger society. It just happens that the beliefs and values thus mediated are criminal, immoral, or just plain crazy. We would suggest now that there are (to put it plainly) both good and bad mediating structures and that social policy will have to make this differentiation in terms of the values being mediated.[302]

Michael Walzer clearly distinguishes the civil society from the good society. Indeed, at one point he makes mocking reference to a potential slogan for civil society, "join the associations of your choice,"[303] arguing that it entails a less than morally-compelling and mobilizing vision. Walzer regrets that the anti-ideological nature of the civil society makes it unable to inspire citizens, but implies that this feature is necessary to prevent the idealization of the state. I will return to the importance of this point, which reflects a fear, implicit in Walzer's remarks, that the social formation of the good will lead to authoritarianism, if not totalitarianism.[304]

I digress to note that no society is "good" in some ultimate sense; they are societies that aspire to promote specific substantive social virtues, and in this sense aspire to be good societies. The extent to which they are successful, and the normative evaluation of the specific virtues one society promotes as compared to others, are subjects not studied here because this would require an extensive treatment that I have provided elsewhere.[305] All that I argue here is that good societies promote particularistic, substantive formations of the good; that these are limited sets of core values that are promoted largely by the moral voice and not by state coercion. The conditions under which the particular values fostered earn our acclaim are not studied here.[306]

The difference between the two ways of treating voluntary associations is reflected in tax and other laws. A civil society grants all voluntary associations a tax exempt status, whatever the social virtues it promotes or undermines. A good society would deny such exceptions to all associations that offend any of its core values, for instance discrimination against minorities and women.

While both the civil and the good society draw on voluntary associations, these play rather different roles within the two systems. In civil societies, voluntary associations serve as mediating institutions between the citizen and the state, and help cultivate citizenship skills (ways to gain knowledge about public affairs, form associations, gain a political voice, and so on); they develop and exercise the democratic muscles, so to speak. In the good society, select voluntary associations also serve to introduce members to particularistic values, as well as to reinforce individuals' normative commitments. Thus, attending and actively participating in a meeting of the Moral Majority, the National Rifle Association, the AFL-CIO, and Mothers Against Drunk Driving serves not merely to develop civic skills but also to enforce a whole slew of substantive values, although of course rather different ones.

The prescriptive state's views on voluntary associations is well known and hence requires no discussion. It tends to consider them as a threat to its general regime and to specific laws. Prescriptive states tend to enact laws banning voluntary associations or seek to ensure that they serve the state by maintaining a voluntary appearance while actually serving as arms of the government.

ACHIEVED VERSUS ASCRIBED RELATIONS

It is far from accidental that while hardcore advocates of the civil society invariably view voluntary associations as the pillars of the civil society, families and communities are often not cited at all, or added as an afterthought. For instance, David Boaz writes that "civil society is all the rage these days. The term refers to the complex network of voluntary organizations in society—churches, schools, clubs, associations, business, labor unions and so on."[307] In a special issue of the *Brookings Review* dedicated to the civil society, editor E. J. Dionne, Jr. characterizes the civil society as (a) "a society where people treat each other with kindness and respect, avoiding the nastiness we have come to associate with 30-second political ads and a certain kind of televised brawl." And (b) "a collection of voluntary associations that includes Boy and Girl Scouts, Little League, veterans groups, book clubs, Lions and Elks Associations, churches, and neighborhood crime watch groups."[308] Most discussions stress the second feature. "Bowling alone" has become somewhat of a symbol for this line of thinking. Robert Putnam argues that bowling with one's friends (which he terms alone) is less sustaining for civil society than bowling as members of a bowling league because such leagues are part and parcel of the voluntary associations that civil society requires.[309]

In effect, one of the best indicators of the underlying position of various advocates is to note the place of families and communities in their analysis. While civil society purists do not list them at all, those who combine the advocacy of a civil and good society list both voluntary associations and families and communities as "intermediary" bodies. For instance, Jean Bethke Elshtain describes the civil society as such:

> By civil society, I mean the many forms of community and association that dot the landscape of a democratic culture, from families to churches to neighborhood groups to trade unions to self-help movements to volunteer assistance to the needy.[310]

And those who are strong advocates of the good society but prefer the language of the civil society for various reasons list families and communities first and all other bodies as secondary.[311]

The underlying reason for this position is that families and communities are often much less voluntary and provide much fewer opportunities for civil education and practice than voluntary associations. This is especially true of ascribed membership, the kind one acquires by birth rather than fashions, i.e., the kind of membership one has in one's family, one's initial membership in an ethnic or racial group, and "birth" residential and other communities (e.g., religious). Even those families and communities one joins cannot be as readily changed as membership, say, in the Elks or a bowling league.

While some have claimed that being a member of an ascribed group can also serve to build up one's public skills,[312] which are essential for the civil society, this is often not the case. I fully agree with Linda McClain and James Fleming when they wonder about David Blankenhorn's claim that families are the primary place to prepare good *citizens*, for instance during dinner table talks.[313] Families, when they work well, lay the groundwork for good people, forming their character, not their political skills. Nor are families role models of democracy or a place to acquire the skills of participation in a voluntary association.

All this is not to deny that these ascribed or semi-voluntary groups are incompatible with the civil society; far from it. Indeed, they often serve as a very effective bulwark against the state. But they are not as attractive to civil society theory and practice as full-fledged voluntary associations.

The opposite is true for the good society. Families and communities of all kinds are mainstays of the moral infrastructure and informal social controls. The strong affective bonding these social units entail ensures their effectiveness as socialization units and mechanisms of social enforcement. They have a relatively strong hold on their members. In contrast, voluntary associations' hold on their members, on average, is much lighter and often has limited or no moral content. Bowling leagues or informal groups may foster some mores of their own (concerning fair play, punctuality, and such), but as a rule have very little impact as far as the main moral foundations of society are concerned. The same holds for chess clubs and, albeit somewhat less so, for choirs. (These are, of course, the examples given by Putnam of the mainstays of democracy, and the civil society.)

The prescriptive state is wary of both voluntary associations and ascribed social units. It uses its powers to abolish or co-opt ascribed groups as well as voluntary associations. Thus, both the Nazis and the USSR tried to suppress the family or use it for their own purposes. The same can be true of ethnic and religious communities.

The relationship of these distinctions to the law are as follows: the civil society prefers contracts over familial and other ascribed obligations, because contracts are voluntary while ascribed obligations are given. (This point was made as early as 1861 by Sir Henry Sumner Maine.)[314] The good society combines respect for ascribed relations (especially those of the family and community one is born into as distinct from one joins by marriage or mobility). The prescriptive state seeks to reach directly to individuals and is hostile to both ascribed and achieved relationships that are not state driven, derived, or controlled. Both the Nazis and the Communists (especially in the earlier era of the USSR) were rather hostile to the family and demanded that members put loyalty to the state and its laws above those of the ascribed relationship. However, these states had no more respect for achieved relations, like joining a labor union.

RIGHTS AND RESPONSIBILITIES

There is a strong affinity between the civil society and the championing of individual rights. The main reason is that individual rights are first and foremost claims against the government, meant explicitly to hold it at bay and to secure the private realm. The fact that individual rights are considered universal and not particularistic, bound to one group or community, further enhances the compatibility. Last but not least, such rights entail no social definition of the good other than their own goodness. Hence, practically all the numerous laws nourished by the Bill of Rights are standard fare of the civil society.

The key concept of the good society is often said to be responsibility, the sense that one is morally committed to attend to certain tasks such as taking care of one's children, helping one's friends, and assisting members of one's community. Whether these responsibilities are also ensconced in the law is of secondary importance because the good society is failing when it has to rely on the law as the first line of defense to shore up these responsibilities. To reiterate, responsibilities are first and foremost *moral* commitments.

Some communitarian writing has been interpreted, perhaps not without reason, as implying that communities are essentially social units that foster responsibilities but are hostile to rights. However, as I have argued extensively elsewhere,[315] and as a guiding theme of much this book, a good society can combine respect for individual rights while nourishing social responsibilities. Thus, there is no inherent contradiction between, say, the right to free speech, assembly, protection from unreasonable search and seizure, etc., and living up to one's responsibilities to one's children, friends and so on. And in those situations in which tension does arise between rights and responsibilities, the good society need not assume *a priori* that responsibilities have the higher claim. In short, a high respect for rights and for responsibilities can be combined. The main difference between the civil and the good society is that the first is rights focused, while the second one is concerned with balancing rights and responsibilities.[316] (The same holds for liberty and social order, not discussed here.) The core concept of the prescriptive state is duty. Duty entails obligations imposed on the citizens by law, and largely enforced by the law.

COMBINATIONS

Now that the basic elements and features of the three ideal types have been explored, one can turn to the question of combinations, especially that of whether a society can be both civil and good? For starters one should note that no society is completely free of any of the three basic types; all have some measure of state coercion, some shared definition of the good, and as a rule some civility, although sometimes it is hard to find. The question therefore concerns only those combinations in which two of these elements play a central role in the societal makeup.

While space will not allow me to demonstrate this point here, it seems clear that there is a considerable amount of tension between the civil society's focus on liberty and the good society's focus on the definition of shared values, which of course means that certain ranges of behavior are considered immoral. (In American history this issue arises in terms of what is the American genius, a society based on individual rights, republican virtues, or some combination of the two.)[317] However, to the extent that the good society relies on education and persuasion rather than coercion, the two kinds of societies can be reconciled.[318]

Finally, one may argue, as *A Call to Civil Society* does among many others, that the civil society relies on a moral base provided by earlier generations (a base sometimes defined as religious and as based on one particular scope of religious tradition, such as Judeo-Christian, Christian, or Protestantism).[319] Moreover, that as this base is eroded, the civil society is endangered. As *A Call to Civil Society* states,

> Because our civic truths are largely constitutional and procedural, they do not tell us how to pursue happiness or how to live a good life. Instead, they establish principles of justice for a society in which pluralism is a fact and freedom is a birthright. In addition to civic truths, then, our democracy depends upon moral truths.[320]

A communitarian readily sees the merit of the "basis" thesis but might well argue that the shared values in question could be religious or more broadly spiritual, or based on secular ethics, for instance on what Sanford Levinson called the constitutional faith.[321]

In Conclusion

The preceding analysis illustrates the merit of drawing a distinction between the civil and the good society (and between it and the prescriptive state). These concepts draw on rather different social philosophies, rely on different kinds of laws, and treat the laws they do rely on differently.

Moreover, their social formations—from voluntary associations to families and communities—play rather distinct roles and are viewed differently in the laws of these various kinds of societies. There is no law against collapsing all these differences and folding these conceptions into one, that of the civil society. However, this essay claims that such over-packing of the term is hindering sound analysis.

Chapter 12

Is Transparency the Best Disinfectant?[322]

"Sunshine is said to be the best of disinfectants; electric
light the most efficient policeman."

— Louis D. Brandeis
*Other People's Money, and How
the Bankers Use It* (1914), p. 92

Transparency is a highly regarded value, a percept used for ideological purposes, and a subject of academic study. The following critical analysis attempts to show that transparency is over-valued. Moreover, its ideological usages cannot be justified, because a social science analysis shows that transparency *cannot* fulfill the functions its advocates assign to it, although it can play a limited role in their service. We shall see that in assessing transparency one must take into account a continuum composed of the order of disutility and the level of information costs. The higher the score on both variables, the less useful transparency is. Moreover, these scores need not be particularly high to limit the extent to which the public can draw on transparency for most purposes.

TRANSPARENCY, WEAK AND STRONG, AND OTHER GOODS

Transparency is generally defined as a means that enables the public to gain information about the operations and structures of a given entity.[323] Transparency is often considered synonymous with openness and disclosure, although one can find some subtle differences among these terms.[324]

In public discourse, transparency is widely considered a good on the face of it, similar to privacy and free speech. Transparency is considered a self-evident good in Western society to the point that "we might almost say that 'more-transparent-than-thou' has become the secular equivalent of 'holier than thou' in modern debates over matters of organization and governance."[325] Transparency International, an organization that promotes transparency in many nations, both developing and industrialized, was founded in 1993 and has won much acclaim. Several progressive groups in many democratic

149

countries have been promoting the introduction of "sunshine" into legislation.[326] Reports indicate that transparency has been gaining ground "not only in state decision-making bodies but also in states' central banks, the international regimes to which they belong, and even in private companies within their borders."[327] Oxford Professor of Government Christopher Hood further documented this trend, within a 2006 book entitled *Transparency: The Key to Better Governance?*[328] Transparency has gained additional popularity in recent years as the lack of transparency in financial instruments has been deemed one of the major factors causing the 2008-2009 near-global economic crisis. Also, President Obama made increasing transparency one of the major themes of his 2008 election campaign.

In addition, transparency has an ideological application. This application differs from normative usages that merely hold that transparency is one feature of good government. The ideological usage of transparency holds that it can obviate the need for most if not all government controls. That is, transparency becomes a tool to fight off another position, that of regulation. Transparency plays such a role in arguments advanced by strong libertarians and laissez-faire conservatives.

In response to the near-global economic crisis of 2008-2009, which followed decades of de-regulation, many governments moved toward re-regulation. Various business groups opposed these re-regulation moves[329] and politicians from conservative parties argued against such changes.[330]

The editorial page of the *Wall Street Journal*, which is openly ideological, runs articles such as "Transparency is More Powerful than Regulation,"[331] and with lines such as "transparency is better than draconian regulation."[332] The argument is advanced that "better transparency is the surest way to make markets more efficient and less volatile. Market wisdom results when more people access better information."[333] The following analysis deals with this kind of transparency—its strong form—rather than with its weak, supplementary form. What is at issue is whether transparency can be the mainstay of delivering the promised goods, rather than whether it can make a contribution to their promotion.

To put it differently, *the critical question is whether transparency constitutes a reliable guidance mechanism that promotes good governance and sound markets under most circumstances— or whether it is a rather weak means that itself relies on other means of guidance and can supplement regulation but not serve as a main form of guidance.*[334]

I need to make two comments in order to properly focus the following discussion. The transparency I deal with here is public and not social. Communitarianism has long established that informal social controls can be very powerful. People have a profound need for approval from others, especially from people to whom they are related by bonds of affection—often members of their family, social group or community.[335] For such controls to work, these others must know how an ego is behaving. When people conceal their addictions or abuses from others, social control is often held in abeyance, while disclosure activates it.[336] However, the mechanisms at work in this situation are radically different from the kind of strong transparency studied in this paper; social controls are informal and voluntary. The focus here is on transparency mandated by the government, including annual audited statements by corporations and voluntary associations; campaign contribution disclosure; nutrition and ingredient labels for food; warning labels on hazardous materials; disclosure of terms of contracts and privacy policies; and numerous others. It is this kind of transparency that is held to provide substitution for government regulations, not for informal social controls.

Second, even advocates of strong transparency do not claim that it is an absolute value. Clearly there are significant situations in which transparency must be squared with other values, including security, private property (e.g., trade secrets and copyright protections), and privacy.[337] The best example of limits of transparency is the rationale for a secret ballot.

THE THEORY OF TRANSPARENCY

Both popular and academic texts lay out the ways transparency is expected to function. Although they are well known, I review these here to lay out the elements and mechanism on which transparency is believed to rely—which we shall see in effect are not available.

In the Economic Realm

According to the popular—and hence very well known—version of transparency, consumers control the direction of the economy by using their purchasing power to "vote" which business will succeed and which will fail.[338] For this consumer "sovereignty" to work, consumers must be able to know the attributes of the goods they are about to purchase. Hence, the introduction of labels that disclose the attributes of various food items, such as their caloric value, kinds and levels of vitamins, and so on. The transparency theory presumes that such disclosure will enable consumers to make informed choices and reward the businesses that provide the preferred products and discourage—at the margin, put out of business—those that disregard the consumers' preferences.[339]

Furthermore, transparency has a strong normative underpinning. "Respect for individual autonomy, responsibility, and decision-making is deeply entrenched in our culture and law. We believe that people can order their own economic affairs and, given sufficient information, can make their own personal assessments of the risks and benefits of transactions."[340] "Disclosure promotes fairness and empowers the investor with information to make smart investment choices,"[341] according to Chapman University law professor Susanna Kim Ripken.

In the Public Realm

The same basic argument is a very familiar part of the popular theory of democracy. "Greater openness and wider information sharing enable the public to make informed political decisions," writes World Bank economist Tara Vishwanath and the Brookings Institute's Daniel Kaufmann.[342] Transparency is said to be "the key for better government." Specifically, according to political philosopher Onora O'Neill, transparency "is supposed to discipline institutions and their office-holders by making information about their performance more public. Publicity is taken to deter corruption and poor performance, and to secure a basis for ensuring better and more trustworthy performance."[343] In short, "the more strictly we are watched, the better we behave," as English philosopher Jeremy Bentham put it.[344]

Campaign Finance Reform

In the 1970s, U.S. legislatures introduced new requirements that mandated the disclosure of campaign contributions. The Federal Election Commission (FEC) was founded in 1975. The FEC required that campaign contributions above $200 to those running for federal office be reported to it in a timely manner. The McCain-Feingold

Act of 2002 requires public disclosure of large donations to political campaigns, and this aspect of the law was upheld by the Supreme Court in 2003 on the grounds that disclosure of funding is vital for the American citizen to effectively assert his or her right to choose representatives.345

In Health Care

Transparency of medical organizations is critical for improving health care, according to Sen. Ron Wyden (D-OR).346 In 1975, *U.S. World and News Report* began issuing rankings on mortality in various hospitals to allow consumers to select those that perform better and deny patients to poor performers, assuming that such disclosure would either force them to improve their service or close down.347 The same argument was made in reference to disclosing data about the relative performance of various public schools.348

In Academic Treatments

There are a fair number of academic treatments of transparency that parallel and hence at least indirectly support the popular theory of transparency. These works are, as a rule, much more qualified and nuanced than the ideological texts, although some works, such as those by Milton Friedman, have a considerable ideological content. For instance, academic works by economists provide a major modification to the theory of transparency with the introduction of transaction costs—including the cost of collecting and processing information. It allows one to recognize that consumers and voters may not find it efficient to absorb and process all the disclosed information. That is, that sub-optimal processing of revealed information may actually serve to make optimal choices. (This is the case when the costs of additional collecting and processing of information, of additional "search," exceed the expected gains.)

Another major addition to the popular theory of transparency is the thesis that the public can utilize intermediaries, experts, technologies, heuristics. and choice architectures to help the processing of the information.349 As Jason Zweig points out, a 47-page mortgage can lull people into a false sense of security, as they mistakenly believe that more details means more honesty. However, as he sees it, with an intermediary defining a standard mortgage that is easy to understand, consumers may get less direct information but will gain information they can digest and use.350

EMPIRICAL STUDIES OF TRANSPARENCY

Given the high value put on transparency, its ideological currency, and scholarly interest, it is surprising to find that there are few empirical studies of the effects of transparency, especially of the strong kind under discussion here. Moreover, there seem to be no comparative studies of the use of transparency versus other means of regulation, to determine which is more effective. I am hardly the first or only one who notes this fact. There continues to be a dearth of studies empirically testing the theoretical claims of transparency advocates, even as legislation and institutional support for their case accumulates exponentially.[351]

Some of the few findings that are available deal with communitarian and not public transparency, namely of the kind used by communities for their members that is voluntary in nature rather than imposed by the government. One case in point is the study of "open-book" management. It refers to the sharing of financial information with everyone in a company. Moreover, the management also lays out the meaning of the financial information and points to ways the employees can contribute to the company's success. A 2005 survey found that 40 percent of the firms of "the five hundred fastest-growing private companies employed the practice in some fashion—far more than in the business community as a whole."[352] However, this study deals with the internal process of a company, not with the public at large.

The following are typical findings of the few studies that deal with public transparency. A study of nutrition labels[353] examined changes in nutrition labeling in grocery stores in New England from 1986 to 1989. It found that such labels affected consumer purchases—though the effect was small. For instance, the share of healthy milk bought rose .0012 in the first year. However, this type of effect was found only "in those food categories where differences in other quality characteristics (e.g. taste) are relatively small between more and less 'healthy' products."[354]

Other studies find that the introduction of warning labels enhances awareness of risk. In the first year after the introduction of alcohol warning labels in 1989, there was a slight increase in the public's perception of the risk associated with consuming alcoholic beverages. About 54 percent of the sample described alcoholic beverages as "very harmful" in 1990, compared to 50 percent of the sample a year earlier. The increase was somewhat larger among "heavy" drinkers.[355] Note that this study deals with awareness but not with changes in choices.

A study of disclosure statements in television ads in 2002 found that such disclaimers are providing little clarification for consumers. The study of 258 undergraduate students over a six-week period tested disclaimers in multiple ways. At times the students were explicitly told to pay attention to the disclosure statements and these statements were shown multiple times, yet the failure rate for recall remained high.[356] Another scholar concluded with regards to political financial disclosures, "There is no empirical evidence that this has resulted in a more aware electorate."[357]

A study of HMOs focused on 75 percent of these institutions that collected data on quality of care and voluntarily disclosed it. The quality of 382 commercial HMOs was observed between 1997 and 2000. The study found that the quality significantly improved among those HMOs that publicly disclosed quality information, "suggesting that public release of quality information can serve as a mechanism to improve quality in healthcare."[358] However, there are very few such studies and there is no evidence that these improvements do not wash out over time.

In short, there are relatively few studies of transparency, and several of those that are available deal with communitarian rather than government imposed transparency or with situations in which the information is easy to collect and process and the change in behavior required to benefit from it is not taxing.

Most important, none of these studies indicates that the effects of transparency are high enough to obviate the need for regulation, especially in those cases in which the harm done by a given activity or product is considerable (relatively high disutility) and the information is relatively complex (that is, the costs of processing the disclosed information are high for the user)

Given the paucity of empirical studies, I turn next to suggest that strong transparency *cannot* work.

A Critical Examination of Transparency

Strong Transparency Is But a Form of Regulation

The transparency often discussed as an alternative to regulation is in effect a form of regulation because it is required by the government. For instance, corporations are required by law to issue annual statements about their financial activities to the U.S. Securities and Exchange Commission. Most food manufacturers are effectively required by the Federal Food, Drug, and Cosmetic Act to place nutrition labels on their products,[359] and so on. Politicians who are running for federal offices are required by law to post campaign contributions with the FEC. That is, transparency is coercive, a label sometimes often affixed by opponents to regulations but which also applies to transparency.[360]

Additional regulation is required if the information released in order to meet the transparency requirements is to be *understandable* by consumers and voters. Unless the government requires disclosure in forms that the public finds digestible, the information is often released in ways that provide little de facto transparency.[361] This was once an issue with the small, legalistic, and opaque text on the back of airline tickets. It is a long-standing issue when people take out mortgages, credit cards, and car loans in the United States.[362]

Still more regulation is required to ensure the *veracity* of the released information. Thus, the Securities and Exchange Commission requires public companies to disclose their financial and operating information as defined by federal statutes, including net sales or operating revenues, income or losses from continuing operations, total assets, long-term obligations and redeemable preferred stock, every six months in the form of a portfolio snapshot at a particular point in time. This snapshot "can easily be manipulated by readjusting the composition just before and after the snapshot is taken—a well-documented practice known as *window dressing*."[363]

Another example of the manipulative disclosure concerns the hospital mortality rates: "The reduction in standardized mortality ratio...observed [after the implementation of disclosure of mortality rates] most likely reflects the changes in palliative care: fewer patients were admitted to die in hospital and more patients were discharged to die elsewhere."[364]

Political Action Committees (PACs), composed by special interest groups, regularly adopt names that very effectively conceal whom they are pushing for. For instance, try to guess with which political party the following PACs are linked: "All America," "America's Foundation," "American Dream," "America Works," and "American Leadership Council." (Answers: D, R, R, D, R.) The same holds for lobbies that represent various special interests.

Finally, like other regulations, the requirements to be transparent must be *enforced* by government. Thus, one reason transparency regarding campaign contributions does not disclose much is that when disclosure laws are violated, the matter goes before the deadlocked, minimally staffed, under-funded Federal Election Commission. If the commission does manage to find a grossly misleading disclosure, it is often months too late, well after the election is over.

In short, to a significant extent transparency is merely a form of regulation by other means. These observations are not taken into account by those who oppose regulation and who argue that transparency could obviate the need for regulation. A less dichotomous proposition is more defensible. Regulations come in different shades and forms; for instance, some regulations are more coercive than others (e.g., compare those that impose minor fines to those that require jailing offenders).[365] Also, some regulations outright ban certain products or activities while others merely require that safety measures be added to dangerous products (e.g., seat belts, motorcycle helmets, and, in some jurisdictions, child locks on guns) but do not ban those products. In this context, transparency stands out as a relatively light form of regulation, in the sense that meeting its requirements is much less restrictive of choice by producers and consumers than other forms of regulations.

The Limits of Knowing

Transparency, unlike other forms of regulation, has a major disadvantage because it assumes that those who receive the information released by producers or public officials can properly process the information and that their conclusions will lead them to reasonable action.[366] However, the well known and often cited findings of behavioral economics demonstrate that very often the public is unable to properly process even some rather simple information because of "wired in" congenital, systematic cognitive biases.[367]

Counterarguments do not seem to hold. The argument that these findings apply only to experimental conditions does not take into account that the same limitations have also been demonstrated in field studies.[368] The suggestion that it is rational for people to stop processing information when the cost of additional processing exceeds the benefit assumes that people can correctly assess the costs of information they have not yet collected, but there is next to no evidence that this is the case.[369]

None of this is to suggest that providing transparency where it is lacking has none of the desired effects, but only that often it cannot *by itself* suffice to serve the goals set for it, especially when consumers and voters must deal with even modestly complex information.

In today's "disclosure regime," "disclosure documents...are written by corporate lawyers in formalized language to protect the corporation from liability rather than to provide the investor with meaningful information,"[370] notes Susanna Kim Ripken. "The complexity and detail in disclosure documents can make them almost incomprehensible at times.... Disclosure cannot fulfill its communicative purpose if investors find it impenetrable and therefore ignore it."[371] Aware that "transparency mandates *disclosure* or *dissemination*, but does not require effective communication with any audience,"[372] these advocates state, "To be effective, information should be fair, reliable, timely, complete, consistent, and presented in clear and simple terms."[373] However, such information would be rather complex, containing assumptions, probabilities, and multiple correlations. Hence it is not surprising that it is far from demonstrated that information can be reasonable, complete, and comprehensible for most people, even those trained in statistics.[374] And behavioral economics and other studies, as noted above, consistently show that often people cannot process even relatively simple information.

In response to those who claim not all investors are "smart," the Efficient Capital Market Hypothesis defends transparency on the grounds that "the biases, errors in judgments, and decision-making shortcomings of uninformed investors are random and will cancel each other out in the market. Even if people are subject to errors and inconsistencies in decision-making, these fallibilities will be exploited and weeded out of the market by the more sophisticated, rational agents."[375] However, this theoretical hypothesis is not supported by evidence. Consumers were not protected by "more sophisticated agents" when they were sold sub-prime mortgages they could not possible pay for, and millions lost their homes; people who rely on brokers or financial advisers for investment advice are doing more poorly than those who invest in passive investment instruments such as index funds; consumers are not protected by private intermediaries from those who market foods that contain E. coli, melamine, or salmonella.

Nor, the record of the last two years reminds us, is the whole economic system protected from major crises by such agents. True, other factors are involved, such as irresponsible acts by consumers who were seeking speculative gains in real estates, individuals who consumed more than they earned by using credit cards, and so on, tendencies in turn fanned by changes in the culture and by marketing. However, people were not educated about, encouraged to deal with, or protected from these failings by "sophisticated agents."

In short, studies of processing information strongly favor adding stronger forms of regulation than those that merely require transparency, even if requirements to communicate are added.

INTERMEDIARIES: EVALUATION AND TRUST

Advocates of transparency respond to the findings of behavioral economics by suggesting that people need not process the information because they can rely on experts or leaders—above and beyond "smart" members of the masses.[376] For instance, people do not need to test appliances; they can rely on reports such as those issued by the Consumers Union or on a Good Housekeeping Seal of Approval. They do not have to read long legalistic language about the privacy policy of a corporation posted on its website; they can rely on the green TrustE icon which guarantees that a site is secure for private information,[377] and so on. That is, issues we face in dealing with the digestibility and veracity of what might be called first order information—we also face when dealing with intermediaries, that is with second order (rather than direct access), processed information.

This use of intermediary raises two related but not identical questions. One concerns information processing to the second degree, so to speak. The public does not have the cognitive capacities to determine which of these intermediaries provides information that is better processed than some other. Reference here is not to deliberate manipulation but to differences in the quality of the information processing due to differences in access to primacy information, resources available to the analysts, their skills and training, and the assumptions they make. A case in point is the ranking of colleges provided by various publications such as *U.S. News and World Report*, *USA TODAY*, and the *Princeton Review*, whose lists differ from one another and whose rankings have been a subject of considerable controversy.[378] There is no evidence that consumers can evaluate the relative reliability of these rankings any better than they can process the raw information on which these ratings draw.

Difficulties in digesting information that is released are common. A study of more than 47,000 elderly visitors to emergency rooms shows that people who use canes are seven times less likely to hurt themselves than those who use walkers.[379] But one cannot tell from this information whether or not those who use walkers should use canes, because differences in diminished capacity between those who use one means of support as compared to another have not been taken into account.

Hospital rankings have been issued by *U.S. News and World Report* and *Healthinsight.org*, among others, based on the data compiled by the Centers for Medicare and Medicaid available online for hospital comparisons. Users may well wish to avoid hospitals that have high morality rates; however, these are likely the best hospitals because they attract patients with severe illnesses. Rankings of high schools are issued by *U.S. News and World Report* drawing in part on the number of AP classes taken, which in turn is correlated with admission to "elite" colleges. However, these data do not inform the users of such rankings whether the schools' success is due to selection of students (e.g., "successful" schools draw a large number of their students from affluent neighborhoods) or due to the quality of education provided in the school. If one adds these and other such variables to the analysis of the information, the data become rather complex. The users of intermediaries (and the information processed by them) face many of the same problems individuals encounter when they deal directly with raw information.

Second, the old question of who will guard the guardians applies to intermediaries. As long as they are not regulated, the intermediaries can, and on some occasions do, manipulate their rankings. The TrustE label—assuring of privacy online—is granted to practically all who pay for it.[380] And far from indicating that a corporation that has such an icon provides strong privacy protection, which the icon means to many, it merely indicates that the corporation at issue is living up to whatever policy it announced, even when the small print states that it will sell to third parties whatever information the clients provide to it in the course of doing business with it.[381]

One may say that rankings and labels provided by the federal government can be trusted and save the consumer from having to find out on her own what the score is. However, a report on the "USDA Organic" label finds that it often applies to products that do not meet consumer expectations of organic—"foods without pesticides and other chemicals, produced in a way that is gentle to the environment." Instead, many products include ingredients that are not natural or environmentally friendly.[382]

In short, consumers and voters cannot evaluate or rely on intermediaries any more than they can rely on the original sources of information—especially if neither is closely regulated.

Information versus Choice

Transparency advocates tend to assume that if given information, individuals will use it to make improved decisions, from the viewpoint of these individuals. Actually, more than a generation ago we learned that "a curious feature of the growing demand for more information is the paucity of concrete evidence that past disclosures have made significant differences in consumer or market *behavior*."[383]

Data from psychological studies show that people "do not make rational choices when it comes to saving and investing activities... [and] information is beneficial only to the extent that it can be understood and utilized by the individual to whom it is directed.... Evidence suggests that when people are given too much information in a limited time, the information overload can result in confusion, cognitive strain, and poorer decision-making," concludes Susanna Kim Ripken.[384]

A survey found that only 11 percent of Medicare beneficiaries have sufficient knowledge to make an informed choice between newer Medicare+Choice options and the traditional fee-for-service program.[385]

Most important, in numerous situations even a well-informed person may find choice restricted, and must rely on other sources of control to be protected. Small investors with pension funds provided by their employers cannot affect the composition of theses funds or the selection of funds among which they may choose (if any is provided). In the case of health plans, the selection is likely to be even more limited and changes in the plans even less subject to individual preferences. Theoretically, a person could choose to seek another job with the preferred kind of pension or health plan, but the costs of such a shift are often very high. Hence, a case can be made that beyond being transparent, pension and health plans should be mandated to meet at least minimal standards. Even if one differs on this point, there is no denying that transparency has limited consequences when the choice is nil.

THE GUIDANCE CONTINUUM

To reiterate, the question is not, as the *Wall Street Journal* put it, whether "transparency is better than regulation" (which should be "better than other forms of regulation") but how much of the regulatory mission transparency can carry out. The preceding analysis suggests that it is fairly limited. The main factors that determine the extent to which one can rely on transparency without combining it with stronger regulatory means (sometimes referred to as substantive regulation)[386] are the degree of disutility (if the information is not heeded); the education level (whether people are likely to understand the information released); the culture of compliance (whether people trust and heed the information released)— and one's values. Clearly if the harm one seeks to prevent is great when the education level is low and when there is a strong tendency to ignore or not trust information released by the government or by corporations, transparency can be relied on even less than if all these readings are reversed.

Moreover, the preceding data suggest that the cut off point on the continuum which these variables form (I call it the *guidance continuum*)—the point at which transparency cannot be relied upon—is fairly close to the low end of the continuum. That is, even if the disutility and distrust are not high, compliance reasonable, and the level of education is considerable, transparency will often be insufficient for achieving a reasonable level of public protection.

162

Ultimately, though, it is a normative issue. If one values autonomy very highly and considers it morally acceptable if people suffer various ill effects as long as they were informed about the risks involved (or opportunities they miss), then one would lean toward relying more on transparency than if one holds that protecting people who cannot protect themselves from serious disutilities is morally justified.

Also, one should note that regulations have an "expressive" function—they express the community's shared values and they help to set norms. Relying on transparency indicates that the community considers the matter less consequential than if the activities or products at issue are banned or their provision is required.[387]

IN CONCLUSION

Transparency is a very popular concept. It reflects the conception that people are autonomous rational choosers who can govern themselves. Theoretically, transparency could be limited to voluntary disclosures. Thus, it could be promoted by consumers refusing to purchase items from sources that do not disclose their content, and investors refraining from investing in corporations that do not provide financial details. Indeed, some measure of such voluntary, communitarian disclosure is taking place because it generates good will and is considered "good business." However, to ensure the veracity of the information that is released, to promote releases that are comprehensible to the public and comparable to information released by other sources, and to secure that information will be regularly made available, often government regulation is required.

There are few empirical studies of the effects of transparency, and there seem to be none that compare its effects to other methods of regulation under the same conditions. However, other data— especially that evidence assembled by behavioral economists— strongly indicate that people are neither as able to process information nor to act on it as the transparency theory presumes. Hence, in situations in which adverse outcomes have a relatively high disutility (e.g., there is a high probability that they will cause death, serious bodily damage, or a loss of one's home or life's savings) or the information is complex (e.g., medical information), drawing on other sources of regulations in addition to transparency seems called for.

One should note that from a normative viewpoint the difference between transparency (which is relatively welcome by laissez-faire conservatives and libertarians and by academics whose assumptions parallel these ways of thinking) and government regulations (which the same sources consider an anathema) is smaller than it at first seems. Under numerous conditions, transparency has to be mandated or it is not provided, the forms of information disclosed must be prescribed—or even the more prepared users will be unable to divine the meaning of the released information—and its veracity must be assured. At the same time, other regulations are not necessarily highly coercive. Some merely provide incentives to those who follow public signals; others impose a minor fine and thus leave it to the regulated agent whether or not to comply (the fine on text messaging while driving in Virginia in 2009 was $20, and drivers had a very low probability of being caught in the act). Even for those regulations that ban an activity enforcement varies a great deal.

When all is said and done, there is room for increased, validated, and comprehensive transparency (and vetted intermediaries). However, it will not serve when the disutility and the information costs are high, and often even when they are not particularly high.

Chapter 13

Back to the Pillory?

Young drug dealers, caught for the first time peddling, should be sent home with their heads shaved and without their pants instead of being jailed: that was a suggestion I cautiously floated. My liberal friends rolled their eyes and stared at me with open dismay. When I tried to explain that if the same youngsters are jailed they are likely to graduate more hardened criminals than when they entered the stockades, that rehabilitation in prisons is practically unknown, and young people are often abused in jails, one of my friends stated that next thing I would mark people with scarlet letters. The others changed the subject.

A tragedy brought the merit of shaming back into public and scholarly discussion. We were discussing on NPR the raping and killing of a seven-year-old girl by a man in a lady's room in a Las Vegas casino. The media attention this time was not focused on the father, who left his child roaming the casino at 3:30 a.m., or on the rapist-assassin Jeremy Strohmeyer, but on the friend of the assassin, one David Cash. He accompanied Mr. Strohmeyer to the lady's room but did nothing to try to stop the savaging of Sherrice Iverson or to inform the police after the act.

In reaction, outraged Congressmember Nicholas Lampson drafted a Good Samaritan act that imposes severe punishments on those who do not stop a sexual crime against a child when they could do so at little risk to themselves, or who do not report such offenses to public authorities. UCLA law professor Peter Aranella, who joined the NPR conversation, argued that the punishment was too severe and suggested instead that a shorter jail sentence should suffice.[388] Elizabeth Semil from the National Association of Criminal Defense Lawyers, also on the panel, was even more critical of the Good Samaritan draft act. She pointed out: "Punitive legislation, criminal legislation, isn't the proper response." She also wondered out loud "whether making it criminal to fail to act is good public policy. In other words, is it going to assist in solving the problem? And my response to that is: absolutely not."[389] A typical letter to the editor of the *Sacramento Bee* opined, "I realize this is a popular issue, but the consequences of a law of this nature are terrifying.... Americans would be required to function as part of the government apparatus.... Maybe you know someone who takes cash in their business, but doesn't necessarily tell the IRS. You may go to jail for not turning that person in."[390] A commentator in Bergen, New Jersey's *Record* held forth, "As much as I'd like to encourage compassion and community, I think it's too late to legislate such morality."[391]

I, too, wondered if Americans should and could be turned into a nation of police informers, a role often despised not merely by their fellow citizens but even by the police themselves. And yet there is a strong sense that Mr. Cash behaved poorly (or worse) and others must do better. One looks for ways Good Samaritans may be fostered but in some less punitive way, best one that entails no jail terms.

I suggested shaming. Instead of jailing future Cashes, the law should require that the names of bad Samaritans be posted on a web site and in advertisements (paid for by the offenders) in key newspapers. Such posting would remove any remaining ambiguities concerning what society expects from people who can help others when there is no serious risk to their well-being. And those with a weak conscience or civic sense will be nudged to do that which is right by fearing that their names will be added to the list of bad Samaritans, their friends and families will chide them, and their neighbors will snicker.[392]

While there are no statistics on the matter, judges seem recently to try shaming more often than a decade or two ago, as a middle course between jailing offenders and allowing them to walk off scot free. Those convicted of driving under the influence of alcohol in Fort Bend County, Texas, must place "DUI" bumper stickers on their cars.[393] A child molester in Port St. Lucie, Florida was ordered by a judge to mark his property with a sign warning away children. The same judge ordered a woman convicted of purchasing drugs in front of her children to place a notice in the local newspaper detailing her offense.[394] Stephen J. Germershausen was ordered to place a four-by-six inch ad in his local Rhode Island newspaper, accompanied by his photo, reading, "I am Stephen Germershausen, I am 29 years old.... I was convicted of child molestation.... If you are a child molester, get professional help immediately, or you may find your picture and name in the paper..."[395] A Tennessee judge sentenced a convicted defendant to confess before a church congregation his crime of aiding in the sale of a stolen vehicle..[396] Syracuse puts embarrassing signs in front of buildings owned by slum lords, and Des Moines publishes their names in newspapers.[397]

Far from being widely hailed as a more humane and just way of punishing offenders and deterring others, judicial shaming has raised waves of criticism that put to shame my friends' reaction to my proposals. Nadine Strossen, president of the American Civil Liberties Union (ACLU), was rather gentle: "I'm very skeptical when criminologists and sociologists say that the best way to rehabilitate someone is to isolate him and put some sort of scarlet letter on him. We need to integrate criminals back into our community."[398] The ACLU's Mark Kappelhoff stated, "Gratuitous humiliation of the individual serves no societal purpose at all...and there's been no research to suggest it's been effective in reducing crime."[399] Judge Politan, U.S. District Court (N.J.), wrote similarly:

> [S]ocieties have often used branding or close equivalents thereto as means of making certain persons or groups of persons easily identifiable and thus, easily ostracized or set apart.... A clear example of such branding, justified by a social purpose wrongfully deemed acceptable by the populace, was the requirement in Nazi Germany that Jews wear the Star of David on their sleeve so that they might easily be identified.... This Court must determine whether Megan's Law and its attendant notification provisions amount to a branding of registrants with a "Mark of Cain" or a "Scarlet Letter," thus rendering them subject to perpetual public animus.[400]

Law professor (now dean) Erwin Chemerinsky is also concerned about shaming, claiming that "[t]he real measure of how civilized we are is the way we choose to punish people. It's not civilized to tell somebody 'you're going to sit in the stocks and we're going to throw stones at you.'"[401] Carl F. Horowitz, Washington correspondent for *Investor's Business Daily*, attacks shaming, which he writes includes public hanging, beheading of drug dealers, blacklisting, and boycotts.[402]

When I faced similar challenges from a class I teach at George Washington University, I suggested an examination of shaming suffers if one labels all punitive measures one disapproves of, and seeks to shun, as shaming. True or pure shaming entails only symbolic acts that communicate censure, ranging from relatively gentle acts such as according a student a C+ or sending a disruptive kid to stand in the classroom's corner, to such severe measures as marking the cars of convicted repeat drunk-drivers with glow-in-the-dark "DUI" bumper stickers. Shaming differs sharply from many other modes of punishment—public flogging, Singapore style, for instance—in that the latter inflict bodily harm, rather than being limited to psychic discomfort. While shaming has some untoward consequences of its own, it is relatively light punishment, especially if one takes into account that most other penalties shame in addition to inflicting their designated hurt.

I also stressed that shaming is morally appropriate or justified only when those being shamed are acting out of free will. To the extent that people act in ways that the law or prevailing mores consider inappropriate, but cannot help themselves from doing so (such as when those with a mental illnesses defecate in the streets or scream their head off at three a.m.), chiding them is highly inappropriate. They are to be helped, removed if need be, but hardly shamed.

When I tried to advance similar arguments on NPR, Elizabeth Semil would not have any of it; she instead would rely on education, celebrating those who conduct themselves as Good Samaritans rather than punishing those who do not.

> Instead of thinking about ways in which we can shame people, let's think about ways in which we can honor or hold up examples of the many heroes that we read about every week who risk their lives to save others; in other words, teaching by positive example children and adults that, indeed, this kind of behavior is rewarded and respected and admired.[403]

Such suggestions show that one's assessment of shaming is highly colored by one's assumption of human nature. Ms. Semil belongs to the sanguine camp that believes that people can be convinced to conduct themselves in a virtuous manner solely by means of praise, approbations, and words of encouragement, or by drawing on nonjudgmental responses, allowing the goodness of people to unfold. For those who share this view, shaming is not merely cruel but also unnecessary punishment; indeed, punishment in general is antisocial. Many of those who hold this view of human nature tend also to believe that people are good by nature; if they misbehave, either the demands imposed on them are unjust or their behavior reflects distorting forces which they neither caused nor are able to control (for instance, that they were abused by their own parents).

I file with those who hold that a world of only positive reinforcements, while in theory very commendable, is not within human reach, and that hence a society must—however reluctantly—also employ some forms of punishment. Granted, we should first determine whether the social demands are fair and reasonable, and to what extent we can rely upon positive inducements in given situations. But, at the end of the day, some form of disincentive—hopefully sparing and mostly of the gentle kind—cannot be avoided. Or, as Judge Ted Poe, a strong proponent of shaming penalties, put it, "...a little shame goes a long way. Some folks say everyone should have high self-esteem, but that's not the real world. Sometimes people should feel bad."[404]

An often overlooked feature of shaming, I should add, is that it is deeply democratic. Shaming reflects the community's values, and hence cannot be imposed by the authorities per se against a people. Thus, if being sent to the principal's office is a badge of honor in a person's peer culture, no shaming will occur in that situation. A yellow star, imposed to mark and shame Jews in Nazi Germany, is worn as a matter of pride in Israel. Thus, people are better protected from shaming that reflects values that are not shared by the community than from other forms of punishment, punishment that can be imposed by authorities without the specific consent of those who are governed.

Critics are quick to turn the communitarian tables on those who seek to use community to shame offenders by pointing out that communitarians have shown that communities are waning. Legal scholar Toni Massaro argues in the *Michigan Law Review* that shaming will be cogent and productive only if five conditions coexist.

> First, the potential offenders must be members of an identifiable group, such as a close-knit religious or ethnic community. Second, the legal sanctions must actually compromise potential offenders' group social standing. That is, the affected group must concur with the legal decisionmaker's estimation of what is, or should be, humiliating to group members. Third, the shaming must be communicated to the group and the group must withdraw from the offender—shun her— physically, emotionally, financially, or otherwise.

Fourth, the shamed person must fear withdrawal by the group. Finally, the shamed person must be afforded some means of regaining community esteem, unless the misdeed is so grave that the offender must be permanently exiled or demoted.[405]

But, Massaro adds, the "cultural conditions of effective shaming seem weakly present, at best, in many contemporary American cities."[406]

While granting that it is unfair to say that "Americans have no commonly shared instincts about crime or about shame," Massaro believes that "American subculturism, or cultural pluralism, is pronounced enough to make broad conclusions about our moral coherence suspect, and thus to undermine the likely effectiveness of widespread government attempts to shame offenders, absent significant decentralization of criminal law authority and the delivery of formal norm enforcement power to the local subcultures."[407]

Massaro and others who draw on communitarians' arguments do not take into account that while communities clearly are much weaker now than they were in, for instance, colonial days, they are not powerless, especially in smaller towns and in what have been called urban villages, numerous ethnic concentrations in big cities that form rather strong communities—Chinatown in New York City, for instance. Otherwise shaming would be no punishment at all. People are, however, very reluctant—ashamed—to drive around with a DUI marker on their car or to take ads in their town newspaper that contain their picture, apologizing for their offenses. Indeed, an accountant, who was sentenced to stand in his neighborhood with a sign "I embezzled funds" seemed deeply distraught when interviewed, and mused that he might have been better off if he had instead accepted a jail sentence. Hardly indifference. A woman convicted of welfare fraud in Eau Claire, Wisconsin preferred to be jailed than wear a sign admitting, "I stole food from poor people."

In arguing about these matters with liberal criminologists, I picked up a useful distinction between two kinds of shaming, one that isolates and is to be avoided, and one that reintegrates offenders into communities and is to be preferred. Liberal criminologists worry that once a person is shamed, he will be cut off from his community and withdraw into himself or worse, into a criminal subculture, and hence will be unlikely to be rehabilitated. Instead, criminologists suggest dealing with crimes in a way that restores people to good standing in their communities. The measures they favor include face-to-face meetings of the offenders and the victims, "facilitated" by community members; the offenders making amends (for instance, rebuilding a fence their car demolished); and closure, a ritual of reconciliation and forgiveness, all of which restore the offender to full membership in the community. David Karp, a criminologist, adds, "These efforts may be through social services or local economic efforts to change the social conditions of the offender's neighborhood."[408]

Reintegrative shaming may well be the best shaming there is, although the jury is out on whether it can be made to work, especially for offenders who are members of different communities than their victims, such as gang members. In effect, any kind of shaming will work only if it is couched in the reference terms of the community of the offenders—or if these terms can be changed as shaming occurs.

Our history offers some lessons on the working of shaming, mainly what happens to a good thing when it is driven too far, much too far. Most importantly, history teaches us the significance of the particular context. In colonial America shaming was very common, not merely one tool of punishment among others but a major one. Indeed, historians report it often worked so well, no prisons were deemed necessary in some colonies, for instance, in South Carolina. (Reference is only to white folks; slaves were savagely treated.)

One reason shaming was so powerful is that it took place in communities that were much smaller, tightly knit, and moralistic than any known to us today, on these shores. Stanford historian Lawrence Friedman describes them as "little worlds on their own, cut off from each other" and "small-town life [was] at its most communal—inbred and extremely gossipy." [409] Another historian, Roger Thompson, writes about Massachusetts that its communities were "well stocked with moral monitors who did not miss much in the goldfish-bowl existence of daily life." [410] Single people, who moved into colonies, were required to board with someone, so that the community could better keep an eye on them.

In contrast, today many Americans are members of two or more communities (for instance, at work and where they reside) and psychologically can shift much of their ego involvement from a community that unduly chastens them to another. While it was not practical for most individuals to escape from one community to another during colonial times, today the average American moves about once every five years, and in the process chooses to which community they are willing to subject themselves. Moreover, privacy at home is much greater, and the moral agenda of most communities is almost incomparably shorter.

In short, the colonial era shows us how little we now seek to shame about and how limited our ability to shame actually is. (Amy Gutmann, a liberal philosopher at Princeton University, once quipped that "communitarians seek Salem without witches," which the communitarians took as a scorching criticism. As I see it, we communitarians should, shamelessly, plead guilty as charged. We do favor communities in which moral mores are upheld without witch hunts, and maintain that in our kind of society this is possible.)

The purest form of shaming was "admonition." Law professor Adam Hirsch described it as follows:

> Faced with a community member who had committed a serious offense, the magistrates or clergymen would lecture him privately to elicit his repentance and a resolution to reform. The offender would then be brought into open court for formal admonition by the magistrate, a public confession of wrongdoing, and a pronouncement of sentence, wholly or partially suspended to symbolize the community's forgiveness.[411]

"The aim was not just to punish, but to teach a lesson, so that the sinful sheep would want to be back to the flock," writes Friedman.[412]

The emphasis on reintegrative justice should appeal to the progressive criminologists who seek to restore it, although for others it may evoke the image of a Soviet or Chinese trial. Having witnessed one of these, what offended me most was not the shaming per se but the kind of matters people were shamed for, having conceived a second child and listened to the BBC.

While pure (merely symbolic) shaming was employed in the colonial era and long thereafter, often it was mixed with other forms of punishment such as fines, whipping, and worse. Stocks and pillories combined holding people up for public ridicule, with confining their movements, exposing them to the elements, and at least a measure of physical discomfort.

Friedman describes another common shaming measure, which was to make the culprit—here, a thief—wear for six months

> a "Roman T, not less than four inches long and one inch wide, of a scarlet colour, on the outside of the outermost garment, upon the back, between the shoulders, so that all times to be fully exposed to view, for a badge of his or her crime." A robber had to wear a scarlet R; and a forger, a scarlet F, "at least six inches long and two inches wide."[413]

But, unlike the DUI signs today, wearing of these insignia was proceeded by a public whipping in a considerable number of cases.

All said and done it is easy to see why shaming as practiced in earlier periods, or in other kinds of societies, has left it in ill-repute. We best think about shaming in terms of how different our much more liberal and tolerant society may adapt it to our needs rather than be swayed by an anachronistic image.

Most important, one must not evaluate any social policy in itself but must compare it to others. The existing criminal justice system jails millions of people, about half of them for non-violent crimes mainly dealing in controlled substances. Offenders are incarcerated for ever long periods, in harsher conditions, with fewer opportunities for parole. Still, the system rehabilitates very few, and the recidivism rate is very high. And the system imposes high charges on the taxpayers. A year in jail costs the public about the same as a year at one of our nation's most costly colleges.[414] Ergo, society is keen to find some new, more effective, and more humane and less costly than other modes of deterrence. Whether it works, and for which kinds of offenders, we are about to find out, that is, if our well-meaning progressive friends will allow us to proceed.

Chapter 14

The U.S. Sentencing Commission on Corporate Crime: A Critique

In this essay, I argue that when commissions do not include in their analyses major social and political forces that will affect the implementation of their recommendations, their work is incomplete. The United States Sentencing Commission first disregarded these forces and as a result had to redraft its recommendations drastically. After several twists and turns, it ended up with some creative responses to pressures by the business community. The commission tried to follow suggestions made on the basis of neoclassical economists; however, these proved to be impossible to implement and in conflict with basic values.

During the Carter Administration's first year, the President convened a task force on energy. Disdaining Washington politics, Carter instructed the task force to formulate the best energy policy possible, without regard to questions of political support. The panel came up with a package of measures—strongly leaning toward conservation rather than production enhancement—that was sure to raise the powerful opposition of oil, gas, and drilling corporations, as well as other business groups and conservatives, all of whom were leaning toward enhanced production as the answer to energy shortages.

The panel also included in its package a recommendation to expand the nation's reliance on nuclear energy. This was sure to antagonize environmentalists, outrage consumer groups—at least as championed by Ralph Nader—and aggravate most liberals, who tend to be antinuclear. As a result, when the package was sent to Congress, it had next to no political support, having alienated both conservatives and liberals as well as the main political players on both sides. Congress basically ignored these policy proposals.

Moreover, the apolitical nature of the package and its failure in Congress weakened the ability and credibility of the President. In a sense, it might be said that by sending Congress an unsupported policy proposal, Carter lost twice.

The question that the United States Sentencing Commission in its work on corporate crime and other task forces and commissions face is whether they should do their jobs without regard to political considerations. The answer to the question, in my opinion, should vary according to what one means by "political." Surely such policy-advancing groups cannot and should not take into account the thousands of special-interest groups that roam Washington, tailoring a policy to please all, or even most, of them. Such a policy would end up as perverted as our current tax code with hundreds of special clauses favoring numerous small groups, rather than being in line with the public interest.

On the other hand, major constituencies must be taken into account. Implementation problems cannot be ignored in policy analysis; otherwise, policy analysis becomes a form of utopian writing. In effect, as I have argued elsewhere, full policy analysis contains constituency analysis.[415] This does not mean that all constituent positions must be accepted on their face. Creative policy analysts design options that allow policymakers to move one or more constituencies from opposition to support, forming new combinations of groups that will lead to winning coalitions.

The U.S. Sentencing Commission initially acted as if this political problem did not exist. Possibly because its first report, on individual sentencing, moved from its submission to law without a hitch—largely because it was tough on street crime and hence had built-in support—the commissioners may have assumed that the same would happen with their treatment of corporate crime. Perhaps the commissioners failed to anticipate problems because they were caught up in other battles, especially with neoclassical economists and between the more and less conservative members of the commission. The apolitical nature of the work was further exacerbated by the fact that neither the press nor various interest groups paid much attention to what the commission was doing in its rather closeted deliberations. Indeed, when I had lunch with the chairman of the commission, Judge William Wilkins, Jr., on February 14, 1990, the day of the first hearing, he stated unequivocally that he believed that the commission's recommendations would become law within a few months.

The results of the commission's work on corporate sentences were the first-draft guidelines, published in November 1989 and subject to public hearing on February 14, 1990. While the commission asked for comments, it offered only two options, and the difference between them was minimal. One option provided for fines ranging from two to three times the amount of damage caused, or illicit gains obtained, by a corporation. The second established a 32-level sliding scale of fines that was dependent on the severity of the offense. It was like asking a person who had been dealing drugs all his life and was suddenly caught whether he would prefer to be hanged or shot.

The guidelines required the introduction of huge fines, up to one-third of $1 billion, for crimes that had previously resulted in fines of tens of thousands of dollars. The maximum fine provided for in the guidelines was $364 million. In contrast, four-fifths of all corporate convictions between 1975 and 1976 resulted in fines of $5000 or less. Between 1984 and 1987, the average corporate fine was $48,000, and 67 percent of the fines were $10,000 or less. Consider some specific cases: Eli Lilly & Company, the pharmaceutical manufacturer, was fined $25,000 for a guilty plea to a misdemeanor charge for failing to inform the government of four deaths and six illnesses related to its arthritis drug Oraflex.[416] Though the company was charged with only a misdemeanor, the drug was linked to at least 26 deaths in the United States and even more from its sale overseas.[417] In another example, of the 60 banks convicted of money laundering between 1982 and 1990, 25 received fines of $10,000 or less.

The predictable result was a firestorm of opposition. Major corporations (and the lawyers who worked for them) and trade associations (and the columnists close to them) severely criticized the commission's recommendations. At the hearing on February 14, the National Association of Manufacturers' representative testified, "The proposed guidelines...are extremely harsh, punitive, unwarranted, and will place many businesses on the threshold of insolvency." The American Corporate Counsel Association added that the draft was "critically flawed." In the press, warnings were issued that if the draft guidelines "become law this year, the judge might wind up managing a major corporation"[418] or that "a single misadventure by an unauthorized low-level employee in a remote plant could have threatened a corporation with a multimillion-dollar fine."[419]

Liberal groups that might have approved of the commission's recommendations were barely aware of the hearings and initially played a rather minor role in the process. Late testimony was submitted by the Natural Resources Defense Council and a small group of environmental lobbies, but other public-interest and consumer-advocacy groups did not mobilize their constituencies.

The result was to be expected: the commission withdrew its recommendations and promised to reconsider them. Then, forewarned but either disinclined or unable to marshal constituency support, it swung full force in the opposite direction. Its new set of recommendations, released on March 6, 1990, drastically scaled back most of the penalties, in some cases as much as 97 percent! For example, under the commission's original guidelines, a level-10 offense carried a penalty of up to $64,000; the new option reduced its ceiling to $17,500. Level-25 dropped from a hefty $136 million to $580,000. The maximum proposed penalty dropped from $364 million to about 3 percent of that, or $12.6 million. It should be noted that because they started from such a high base, these new fines were still higher than those typically imposed on corporations, which tend to be—with the exception of fines for environmental crimes—trivial.

These much diluted and weakened guidelines were still not acceptable to the basic political lineup. Liberal groups, alerted by me, now entered the arena, though rather weakly. Consumer groups were still not interested, and environmentalists focused largely on their cut. Overall, liberal groups had little influence in Washington at this point, with the first Bush Administration at the height of its power.

Business groups, high on their recent victory over the commission's draft, went in for the kill. They wanted the commission either to withdraw its conclusions completely and go back to study the matter or to adopt only *recommended* penalties. The National Association of Manufacturers and others demanded "adoption of voluntary policy statements rather than mandatory guidelines," despite the fact that mere recommendations would leave local judges— elected and far from immune from local politics and other influences—to pass sentences as they saw fit. The White House was successfully drafted to help the business community restrain the commission. Then-Deputy Attorney General Donald Ayer had issued a strong letter of support to the commission in February; the letter was withdrawn, however, shortly after a meeting between members of the Business Roundtable and White House Counsel C. Boyden Gray resulted in an "inquiry" from the White House to the Justice Department.[420] The press was also brought into the act on both sides, including a full-page article of mine in the *Washington Post*[421] and analyses in the *New York Law Journal*[422] and the *Wall Street Journal*.[423]

Given the new political constellation, the commission, buffeted and bobbed by forces it neither understood nor controlled, issued its final report on May 1, 1991 on all but environmental crimes. It had finally been pushed into an acceptable formula. In the report, the commission enhanced somewhat the reduced penalties—a sop to the critical press and the liberals—but provided a list of extenuating circumstances that allowed offending corporations to reduce easily the remaining penalties to small amounts, if not to zero. The mitigating factors included:

- occurrence of the offense despite the existence of an effective compliance program designed to prevent and detect violations;
- lack of knowledge of the offense on the part of high-level management;
- prompt reporting of the offense to governmental authorities;
- full cooperation in any investigation; and
- clearly demonstrated recognition and acceptance of responsibility for criminal conduct.

When the fine is first set, the defendant is given a culpability score of 5, indicating no increase or reduction in the penalty. Corporations can then subtract various points for meeting the mitigating factors. For example, the existence of an effective compliance program subtracts three points and reduces the fine to 40 percent of the original amount. If the corporation meets all of the last three criteria, it can subtract five points and reduce the penalty to only five percent of the original fine.

In the process, though, the commission stumbled onto a rather important concept. Given the present political reality, it is difficult to go after major corporations and penalize them on a level that would deter future crimes.[424] Therefore, it makes sense to close the barn door before the horse bolts; that is, prevention has much to recommend itself over relying exclusively on after-the-fact, acute treatment.

The commission made the existence of internal plans that operate to inhibit criminal conduct, and serious efforts to make them stick, a major way to mitigate penalties if a corporation were caught committing a crime. The guidelines defined in detail an effective compliance program, including designation of a specific high-level person to be responsible for the program, written policies and reporting procedures, and mandatory participation in training programs by employees. To the extent that corporations would respond by introducing more of these compliance programs, the more corporate crime will be curbed, at least when it is not orchestrated from the highest level.

In sum, to those who believe that commissions should do what is right, disregarding all other considerations, the U.S. Sentencing Commission failed. Its mountain of deliberations and studies produced a molehill of enforcement. To those who believe that commissions should take implementation problems into account in their policy analyses, the commission zigzagged itself into a position that has some merit. It could have done much better, however, but probably only in a less pro-business environment and only if liberal groups had mobilized more effectively to support its work.

NEOCLASSICAL FANTASIES

The commission's deliberations and product provide details for an important study of the consequences of applying neoclassical economics to public affairs. The theory turned out to be even less applicable than when it is applied to intramarket choices. Moreover, the moral issues involved stood out clearly.

At issue are twin questions: on what basis should the size of the punishment for a crime be determined, and what role should the moral values of a community play in such a determination? Neoclassical economists argue that the basis should be considerations of costs and benefits: the costs of a crime should exceed the loot or benefits. Thus, if a corporation made a profit of $6 million from selling an unsafe product and the fine were, say, $7 million, it would refrain from committing this crime. Second, neoclassical economists imply—and occasionally explicitly state—that the question of moral values need not enter the picture at all. Thus the fact that the community finds some crimes more abhorrent than others or wishes to use the penalties to send a message about the importance of some values—say, not betraying your country by selling certain high-tech items to the enemy—should not be a factor. An economist who testified before Congress about what he considered to be the commission's wrongheaded concern with just punishment stated,

"'Justice' and its cognate forms are high-sounding words, but they cannot be permitted to operate as trump cards in sentencing policy.... [J]ustice was served by basing organizational sentences on the level of harms caused or threatened by offenses."[425] People are assumed to be moved by self-interest and not values. The law, neoclassicists argue, should work on corporations' calculations of profit and loss rather than try to affect their preferences by affecting their values.[426]

The commission found this approach impossible to follow, and it dropped its staff economists and consultants. In a much-publicized resignation, Commissioner Michael K. Block, a University of Arizona economics professor, essentially resigned over the commission's refusal to use calculations of social harm as derived from past fine levels as the sole basis for determining fine levels.[427]

What went wrong? First of all, the economists' approach turned out to be unempirical. To pursue their recommendations, the commission needed to take detection ratios into account. These come into the picture because courts must assume that not all crimes are detected and punished. Therefore, the penalties must be higher as detection ratios decrease; otherwise, a corporation might rationally calculate that since it has only, say, a 1 in 10 chance of being caught, even if the fine is somewhat larger than the gains of violating the law, it is still more profitable to proceed and disregard the law. To stay with this example, if the benefit of a violation is $6 million, the fine would have to be not $7 million but at least $60 million to be an effective deterrent.

It is hardly surprising that the commission found, however, that the detection ratios for most crimes are very difficult to establish. After all, to do so requires knowing the number of crimes that have been committed but remain uncovered. Moreover, even if in some areas the size of the ratio can be estimated roughly, it would be nearly impossible to litigate on such estimates. For example, the prosecution might claim that the detection ratio is five (1 of 5 is caught) for consumer fraud, while the defense might argue that the ratio is three. How could such a dispute be settled?

Another problem for the commission was the generally pro-business bent of neoclassical economists and their consequent assumption that detection ratios are very high and because of this the fines should be set rather low. Gary Becker, for instance, assumes a 50 percent detection rate: "[If the illegal] act does $1 million worth of harm with a 50% chance of going unpunished, then the fine would be $2 million. Fines of this size would force companies to think longer and harder before committing white-collar crime."[428] Jeffrey Parker, a former commission staff member, suggested that the actual detection ratio was 1 in 10 to 1 in 20.[429] From what little we know about the subject, however, we can glean that the ratios are much lower; 1 out of 50 may be closer to the mark.

We gain this estimate when we see that in some areas very few corporations are convicted—crime is actually very common. Consider the fact that the Resolution Trust Corporation, established to manage the savings and loan bailout, reports that criminal fraud was discovered in 60 percent of the savings institutions seized by the government in 1989.[430] Another example is reported by a study by the U.S. Department of Justice. The study looked at almost 600 of the largest U.S. publicly owned manufacturing, wholesale, retail, and service corporations with annual sales of $300 million or more. It showed that during 1975 and 1976 "over 60 percent had at least one enforcement action initiated against them [actions were all federal—administrative, civil, and criminal].... [M]ore than 40 percent of the manufacturing corporations engaged in repeated violations."[431] In contrast, there are very few convictions in these areas, well below one percent.

As a result, fines would have to be set at astronomical figures to satisfy the neoclassical economists' criteria, and such fines would often put convicted corporations out of business. While this might well deter others, it is politically unrealistic, and probably not in the public interest, to put a major corporation out of business and throw thousands out of work because it happens to be the one corporation that was caught.

The commission also felt strongly that certain crimes need to be severely punished, even if one cannot calculate the costs. Thus it granted various conditions for departures above the maximum fine levels, including criminal acts that threaten national security, that target vulnerable victims—such as the elderly or disabled—or that involve a foreseeable risk of death or serious injury.[432]

All this remains of interest with respect not merely to the commission's report but to all those who try to apply neoclassical economics to the study of crime, and more generally to public choice and other matters of public policy.

CORPORATE REHABILITATION AND COMMUNITY SERVICE

The least attention was paid in hearings and in the press to two interesting ideas that the commission explored. The first is corporate rehabilitation. The way the commission worded the idea, it sounded more like a partially suspended sentence: in the case of corporations that could not pay their full fines—and thus presumably were insufficiently deterred from repeating their crime—the court could oversee certain activities for a period of up to five years. For example, the court could require the defendant to provide regular financial reports, to notify the court of adverse changes in the company's business or financial position, to publicize its offense,[433] and to submit to unannounced audits of its books or interrogation of knowledgeable individuals. Such corporations, in effect, would need a judge's approval to pay dividends, obtain new financing, or enter into a merger with another corporation.

This led to an outcry that the commission would create a situation "tantamount to having the courts running a commercial enterprise" and that "such restrictions will lead to loss of jobs and the eventual demise of any business faced with probation."[434] Such complaints disregarded the fact that the commission's recommendation dealt only with convicted criminals.

As I see it, the commission's idea deserves further consideration. Close supervision of a corporation—especially if it is convicted of a pattern of wrongdoing carried out over a period of years—seems appropriate until it is established that the corporation has been rehabilitated. My own version of the same basic idea is for corporations to be sentenced to rehabilitation even when no other penalty is exacted or even if they are able to pay their fine in full. Imagine, for instance, a corporation that is found to have systematically neglected the safety of its consumers. It seems socially productive to put it on a five-year diet of closer inspections. If it is found to have truly mended its ways, the inspectors should report that the firm has been rehabilitated and fully restore it to membership among decent and law-abiding corporations. One can further imagine that if the transition were not complete, the court could extend the period of rehabilitation, and thus send a signal to consumers to be particularly wary; or the court might lift the standing ahead of schedule if a corporation were making particularly strong corrections in its practices in favor of consumer protection.

Even more interesting is the idea of community service. The commission suggested that a corporation could be required to perform community service that is directly related to its crime when the defendant "possess[es] knowledge, facilities, or skills that uniquely qualify it to repair damage caused by the offense or to take preventive action."[435] This applies to the related question of who the criminal is. Corporate representatives argue that corporations "are extraordinarily law-abiding" and that most "are composed of morally and ethically honorable people who genuinely try to comply with the law."[436] They claim that when the law is violated, it is "frequently because of the unauthorized act of an employee."[437]

The fact is, though, that violations of the law are orchestrated all too often by management and that the profits often flow not to an employee but into corporate coffers. Take, for example, the case of Beech-Nut, which systematically adulterated the contents of its infant apple juice, a product that generations of mothers had trusted. Top managers clearly helped to orchestrate the adulteration. When they were caught red-handed, far from desisting, they shifted to mixed juices, in which the adulteration was more difficult to detect. Later, facing an imminent federal indictment, they attempted to sell these products in Third World countries.[438]

Many other cases have a similar structure, from the homicide conviction of three Film Recovery Systems executives in Illinois for the death of an employee caused by inhaling cyanide fumes on the job;[439] to a 15-year conspiracy by the VSI Corporation, the nation's largest aircraft fastener manufacturer and a subsidiary of Fairchild Industries, to falsify test reports on parts;[440] to purchases of top-secret Pentagon documents giving arms manufacturers illegal competitive advantages. The commission collected data showing that in large, publicly held firms, 25 percent of the time a top executive knew of the criminal activity, and in 33 percent of the cases, a manager knew.[441] Under those conditions, it seems quite proper to penalize management and the corporation.

One way to proceed is to demand that the corporation perform community service as part of its punishment—or as the only punishment when the violation is not particularly troubling. This could be achieved by the corporation's using its facilities and resources to arrange for, say, soup kitchens for the homeless if it previously sold adulterated food; sending its executives to do volunteer work in emergency rooms if they deliberately built cars that became fire bombs when hit from the rear; or requiring its board to work in Veterans Administration hospitals if the corporation profited from systematically falsifying test records on drugs, declaring them safe when they were not.

Here it may be said that a politically confused and buffeted commission saw through the neoclassical economists' mumbo jumbo and opened the gate to some imaginative sentencing.

Chapter 15

Minorities and the National Ethos

The relationship between minorities (whether native or immigrant) and the national community raises numerous issues that have been often explored, with various positions carefully spelled out. This essay focuses on one key question: how can the inevitable tension between the rights of members of minorities and the national particularistic values (or national ethos) be curbed?

ON THE CONTEXT OF THESE DELIBERATIONS

It cannot be stressed enough that at issue here is not whether the rights of the members of these minorities should be fully respected, or whether they should benefit from some kind of government-led affirmative action programs or be compensated for past injustices, or even whether minorities as groups ought to command some additional rights.[442] One can readily favor the minorities in all these regards and still not necessarily hold that the national community should significantly attenuate, let alone give up, its national ethos.

The term national ethos refers to the particularistic values, traditions, identity and vision of the future (or "destiny") of the given nation. The term "nation" implies a community invested in a state. Communities are social collectivities whose members are tied to one another by bonds of affection and at least a core of shared values.[443] The term is best contrasted with the notion of national character, which tends to imply that all the members of a given nation have the same basic psychological profile and the same behavioral traits. In contrast, national ethos merely suggests that the relevant collectivity has the said attributes, but many members may not internalize them nor view them in a positive light. Hence, the fact that in a given nation there are some groups—say, Native Americans in the United States or Kurds in Turkey—who do not see themselves as part of the national community, or who may seek to form a nation of their own, does not belie the fact that most citizens' first loyalty in political matters is devoted to "the" nation. However, if there is no sizeable majority that is committed to the nation, if for instance most citizens of Belgium see themselves first as Walloons or Flemings, it follows that Belgium is not much of a nation. The same is true for the Kurds, Shia, and Sunnis in Iraq and for the various groups that make up Afghanistan. (The phrase "not that much of a nation" may seem too colloquial, but it serves to capture a thesis that being a nation is variable and not a dichotomy. The extent to which a state has the features of a community, and hence is a nation, varies from one state to another and over time. Thus the U.S. became much more of a nation after the American Civil War and the post-war reconstruction period than it was before.)

The context of these deliberations is *nations*, because despite strong arguments and major efforts to form more encompassing communities, especially in Europe, the nation continues to be the community that often commands the loyalty of the overwhelming majority of the citizens in cases of conflict between the nation and these more extensive communities. As Anthony Smith of the London School of Economics put it, "who will feel European in the depths of their being, and who will willingly sacrifice themselves for so abstract an ideal? In short, who will die for Europe?"[444] In contrast, Alasdair MacIntyre's statement that to ask people to die for their country is like asking them to die for the telephone company[445] seems sociologically particularly uninformed.

True, less encompassing communities, especially ethnic groups, such as the Basques, Scots, and Walloons, often command even stronger loyalties than the nation. However, given that the matters at issue are sorted out largely in national courts and legislatures and more generally in national politics, the nation is for many countries the arena in which the issues at hand are worked out.

Practically all the examples and evidence cited below are from nations considered constitutional democracies because only in such nations—ones that respect rights (by definition)—can one explore the relationship between rights and the national ethos. However, this normative analysis applies equally to other nations, although of course they must first develop their commitments to rights before they face the tensions such commitments pose for the relationship between rights and the national ethos.

ABOLISH THE ETHOS?

The Thesis

Radical multiculturalists advocate for resolving this tension by abolishing the particularistic values of nations, that is, those values which differentiate the one national community from another. This entails "neutralizing" their distinct sense of history, identity, and future—in short, their national ethos. They argue that the state should strive for normative neutrality centered around the protection of rights that all share, and should not foster a distinct conception of the common good and the particularistic commitments it entails. Or, that the values to be promoted should be those that ease the said conflict, such as tolerance, diversity, rights, and due process.

To illustrate: in 1999, the prominent British historian Linda Colley delivered a lecture entitled "Britishness in the 21st Century" as part of then Prime Minister Tony Blair's series of "Millennium Lectures." She argued that given an increasingly diverse population, and the bitterness and alienation caused by the "ancestral and visceral" idea of British identity, this identity should be discarded and replaced by a renovated "political and functional" idea of British citizenship.[446] A similar vision was promoted in 2002, when the political theorist Lord Bhikhu Parekh chaired the Commission on the Future of Multi-Ethnic Britain, whose widely-discussed report concluded that because the United Kingdom had become a territory which English, Scottish, Welsh, West Indian, Pakistani and other such groups inhabit like tribes resting next to each other with little in common, and following different sets of values,[447] in order to avoid offending or injuring any of these groups, the government should avoid promoting any "fixed conception of national identity and culture."[448]

Political theorists like Etienne Tassin, in an effort to reconcile social inclusion and political legitimacy, have promoted a type of "constitutional patriotism" which "refuses any convergence between culture and politics."[449] According to these theorists, allegiance to institutions and respect for justice and rights should be valued over a sense of shared associations, language, and culture.

Jamie Mayerfeld of the University of Washington goes further than even many radical multiculturalists, stating that almost all forms of group identity are undesirable, national identity being by far the worst. He suggests that people should be motivated by a type of "civic consciousness" in which citizens would "be united by a commitment to a constitutional order that protects individual rights, authorizes a fair scheme of social cooperation, and establishes procedures for democratic decision-making."[450] According to Mayerfeld, "principle, not identity, should be the glue that binds the polity."[451] (Along similar lines, several liberals argue that the state of Israel must give up its Jewishness because otherwise the Israeli Palestinian minority will not feel fully at home, and they will continue to see themselves as second-class citizens.[452] One such argument can be found in Bernard Avishai's *The Hebrew Republic*.[453])

Empirical Concerns

An empirical study of this matter, I suggest, would show that although a national ethos can be edited or recast (in effect, it continually is), it cannot be abolished outright. A state cannot avoid institutionalizing one set of particularistic values or another.

The issue at hand can be readily illustrated by exploring national policies regarding the weekly day of rest. If a nation rules that all businesses must be closed on Sunday—this offends the sensibilities of those Jews for whom Saturday is the day of rest, and Muslims, for whom it is Friday. At first it may seem that the state could become neutral on this matter by allowing those who prefer to open their businesses on Sunday as long as they close it on some other day of the week. However, given that public institutions such as the government offices, courts, mail delivery, etc. will be closed on Sunday, along with the majority of the businesses if we are dealing with a nation in which there is a Christian majority, minorities would still feel out of place.[454] They are like those pupils in a public school in countries in which prayers are conducted who are not required to participate—which was the practice in the United States until quite recently. These pupils feel awkward and are often subject to social discrimination by their peers.

Only if all shops, especially all public offices, were closed on all three days would the state attain the kind of neutrality sought by radical multiculturalists—at least with regard to rest days. (That this, unless these advocates would also fight for those minorities who are atheist and would feel offended by such stately treatment of religions.)

Even more difficult is to imagine how one would treat all holidays that have a particularistic meaning, such as Christmas, Easter, Independence Day (which in the case of Israel, Israeli-Palestinians know as Catastrophe Day),[455] and Columbus Day (which troubles some Native Americans).[456] Reference is not merely to actions of the state, but to common norms. For instance, on Atonement Day—the holiest of holidays for Jews—driving is not banned by Israeli law; nevertheless, the entire Jewish population refrains from driving, including the adamant secularists. Israeli-Palestinians can drive their cars any place they want on that day, but there is no way to make them feel that this Jewish holiday is not a special national day and that they are not outsiders in some way.

Whether a state bans or permits gay marriages, it is far from neutral on the institution. In the first case, it extends the institutionalizing of individual rights, ignoring the values and sentiments of sizeable religious minorities and its own historical traditions; in the second case, it refuses to extend the institutionalization of individual rights, sticks to its historical traditions, and refuses to heed a growing segment of its progressive citizens.

Nor can one neutralize the particularistic effects of the "mother" tongue (or tongues). Multiculturalists correctly point out that the primary language of a given nation contains a particularistic bias. If the tongue is English, people will be more inclined to read books and magazines, follow news, and even identify with nations whose primary language is English. In contrast, if it is French, Russian, Chinese, or some other, their biases would run in a different direction. Hence, conflicts over which language should be the dominant one tend to be highly emotional and on occasion violent.[457] Attempts to neutralize the issue by making two or more languages co-equal (e.g., in Canada and in Switzerland) still leave a particularistic bias (due to those languages not chosen) and tend to fail, as one language remains the dominant one (e.g., English in Canada, and German in Switzerland).

In short, the rights of the members of minorities can be fully respected, but, from an empirical perspective, the particularistic conceptions of the common good, invested in the national community, the national ethos, cannot be abolished. It can only be modified and attenuated. And if one approximates such neutrality, it often means that there is only a very weak national ethos, which in turn leads to civil strife, as the ethos is a major source of sociological cohesion that keeps nations stable and one.

Prudential Concerns

In addition to the empirical facts that lead one to doubt the attainability of the kind of society that the radical multiculturalists advocate, there are prudential reasons not to seek to erase the national ethos despite its particularistic normative content. Public policies that seek to abolish the national ethos are perceived as a major attack on identity and psychological well-being by the majority of the citizens.[458]

Radical multicultural drives seem to be one major reason a growing number of members of the majority in many countries in Europe are supporting conservative, or right wing, or even nationalistic political parties and movements that promise to restore the traditional values and that have strong anti-minority (and/or anti-immigrant) positions. Thus, parties and policies that are perceived as attacking national identity—and more generally, the national ethos—add to other forces that are fanning xenophobia and nativism.[459]

Given the very wide opposition to erasing the national ethos, even if such public policies were somehow introduced, they would be unlikely to be sustained. Indeed, Tony Blair, a master politician, flirted with Linda Colley's ideas on vacating Britishness for only a very short period,[460] and no other public leader of any import has picked them up in the UK in the following years. Lord Parekh's report was roundly criticized and its multicultural recommendations were not adopted or even seriously considered. On the contrary, citizenship tests that assess the extent to which new immigrants at least show familiarity with the particularistic culture have been introduced in Britain, Holland, and Germany, among other nations.

Normative Objections

Although a national ethos can be attenuated to some extent and often to good effect (e.g., when nationalism is reduced)—and it can be recast over time, by taking into account the values and preferences of minorities—if significantly eroded, the nation, as a community invested in a state, will lose its capacity to provide human nurturing and to contribute to human flourishing.

Mountains of data, recently reviewed and augmented by Robert Putnam and Francis Fukuyama, and long before them by Robert Bellah and his associates[461] and scores of other sociologists,[462] show that when communities are thin or absent, people suffer physically (e.g., are more prone to have a great variety of major illnesses as well as to recover from illness more slowly)[463] and psychologically (e.g., are more prone to be depressed, have low self-esteem, or be disoriented).[464] The absence of communal bonds causes people to feel detached, alienated, and powerless. Such a community deficit leads some to withdraw from society, or act out in antisocial ways.

For hundred of millions of people, nations are a major source of such communal affiliation, even if they are merely imagined communities. Communitarians have long shown that individual identity —a core element of the liberal image of the person—is insufficiently explained by liberal philosophy and is profoundly linked to community. Michael Sandel notes that we cannot understand ourselves but "as the particular persons we are—as members of this family or community or nation or people, as bearers of this history, as sons and daughters of that revolution, as citizens of this republic."[465]

Our capacity to act as reasoned people relies greatly on our being anchored in relatively thick communities. Moreover, community-wide conceptions of the good provide criteria used in finding which shared decision-making and which public policies are legitimate. They thus help curb strife and gridlock.

Communities, importantly, also provide informal social controls that reinforce the moral commitments of their members and which in turn help make for a largely voluntary social order. The most effective way to reinforce norms of behavior is to build on the fact that people have a strong need for continuous approval from others, especially from those with whom they have affective bonds of attachment.[466] Communities, thus, can strengthen adherence to social norms. Neo-communitarians see this persuasive power as a key function of communities, in part because it allows the role of the state and its coercive means to be greatly curtailed, as it is replaced by drawing on informal social controls built into communities, to promote the common good. Given that the national ethos helps to maintain the national community, it helps to maintain this source of human flourishing.

Theoretically, a loss of national ethos can be compensated for by providing a new community that is more encompassing, say a regional one like the EU. But, so far, all such community-building endeavors have failed to provide a new community thick enough to provide the kind of flourishing that national communities provide.

Furthermore, as the EU's difficulties in making Turkey a member and in absorbing nations such as Romania and Bulgaria make clear, regional communities have a particularistic ethos of their own.

To the extent that attempts are made to replace the national ethos with those of smaller communities within one and the same state, one finds that such developments lead to difficulties in forming state-wide policies, which require shared core values and a commitment to the common good to justify inevitable sacrifices. At worst, such developments invite secession and civil war. The first situation is illustrated by Belgium. The second by the breakup of Czechoslovakia and Yugoslavia, as well as the civil wars that rage among ethnic, confessional, and other tribal-like communities in countries like Iraq and Afghanistan, in parts of Pakistan, and in other states in which the national community is weak.

Finally, it is hard to see principled reasons that the sensibilities of the majority should be disregarded as the way to address those of the minorities. This is especially true, as we shall see shortly, because there are other ways to proceed. To reiterate one more time, reference here is not to rights. The rights of all members of minority groups are to be fully respected, whether or not such observation discomforts the majority. They should not be denied the right to vote, assemble, worship, speak, and so on, even if, for example, the majority fears that a given minority will use these rights to promote terrorism.[467] (Note, reference is to speaking, not acting. Minorities have no right to act violently.)

Given, as we have seen, that the flourishing of all people entails nurturing communities, *societal designs that combine the nurturing communities of both minorities and of the majority are more conducive to flourishing than those that require abolishing the national ethos and which offend the sensibilities of the majority.*

DIVERSITY WITHIN UNITY

Diversity Within Unity (DWU) is a societal design that meets the requirement just laid out.[468] Essentially, it assumes that all citizens will embrace a core of values (the unity element) while being not just allowed, but welcomed, to follow their own subcultures on other matters (the diversity elements). The DWU thus differs from both radical multiculturalism, which maximizes diversity, and full blown assimilation, which maximizes unity. (Diversity Within Unity is not to be confused with "unity in diversity," which is one of those oxymorons only a politician could love. It implies that increased diversity by itself will lead to greater unity, which is at least a very different idea from the one here advanced.)

I already outlined in some detail the reasons radical multiculturalism should be rejected. The same holds for full blown assimilation, which demands that immigrants and other minority members assimilate to the point that they become indistinct from native citizens (a common expectation in France, for instance). Such a degree of assimilation is often difficult to achieve and unnecessary for social peace and community building, and it entails sacrificing the culturally enriching effects of diversity.

The images used for depicting these positions are telling. The melting pot is used to depict a society in which all differences are melted down. A salad bowl is used to depict a society in which various groups are tossed together but each maintains its original color and flavor. Diversity Within Unity is akin to a mosaic which is richer for the difference in size and color of its pieces but which also has a shared frame and glue—which can be recast but not abandoned. (In the United States, in numerous ethnic events, both the American flag and that of the country of origin are displayed, and the national anthem of both countries is sung. If one overlooks either element, one tends to arouse considerable consternation as either not being a "good American"—or as not loyal to one's sub group. The very widespread use of a hyphen, to indicate both one's origin and one's Americanism is another expression of the DWU design.)

Next, a list is provided as to which elements belong in the unity side and which in the diversity side. However, it is important to keep in mind that (a) even if one divides this list in a different manner, the approach itself may be still of merit. (b) The elements that are considered essential for the unity part itself can be recast over time. (c) Finally, one should acknowledge that although I suggest that DWU is a preferable societal design compared to the others already cited, it is likely not to fully satisfy either the minorities or the majority, as it seeks adaptations from both sides.

The next step is to sort out which elements are part of the framework, and which can be particularized or remain particularistic. On the unity side: Minorities must accept the core values of the society (including the respect for individual rights, mutual tolerance and civility, and respect for the environment); obey the laws (until they are changed, if a given minority considers them a violation of their values); learn the nation's language(s); and share not only in the assets history has bequeathed to the nation, but also in its burdens. For example, as an immigrant to America I cannot claim that I had nothing to do with slavery and hence have no need to concern myself with making up for past injustices, and yet also claim that I am entitled to the rights that the Founding Fathers institutionalized. Similarly, a new German cannot pride himself on the achievements of Kant, Goethe, and Bach without also sharing responsibility for the Holocaust. In short, minorities cannot reject the national ethos, although they can seek to modify it, and often succeed. (The ways this can be achieved—as well as the difficulties involved—can be studied when various national states undertake to re-write the text books used in schools, which include parts that offend various minorities, and when debates take place as to which works colleges should include in their "core" curriculum.[469])

On the diversity side: There is no sociological reason to prevent people from practicing their own religion or study a second language that appeals to them either as the language of the country of origin (in the case of immigrants) or to which they have historical attachments (e.g., native minorities such as the Catalans). Similarly, differences in cuisine, dance, arts, and music enrich the national community rather than undermine it. Personal legal matters and personal disputes can be settled by various ethnic/religious/tribal authorities, including marriage, divorce, burial, and mediation, as long as (a) all parties involved truly consent to submit to these authorities, and (b) no individual rights are violated. (This is a common practice regarding Jewish minorities in Europe, and it is being extended to Muslim ones.)

DWU favors allowing minorities institutionalized opportunities to promote changes in all these elements through actions from seeking to change the laws to reconstructing and revising the national history (for instance, by changing the text books used to teach it); from adjusting their new nation's relationship with other nations of particular interest to fighting for social justice. However, as long as such changes have not been adopted, the relevant laws and public policies must be heeded.[470]

At the same time, every group in society is free to maintain its distinct subculture—those policies, habits, and institutions that do not conflict with the shared core—as well as a strong measure of loyalty to its country of origin, as long as this does not trump loyalty to the society in which it lives if these loyalties come into conflict. Cuisine, by itself of limited import, serves as an effective symbol for my point. A generation ago, there was a national cuisine in many nations, such as the United States and the United Kingdom, although there were always local variations and changes over time. One still can identify the national cuisines today, but in most cities a large variety of other cuisines are prepared and consumed both privately and in public places such as restaurants, conferences, and banquets. There is no reason to suggest that anything was lost in the process, or that all citizens should be expected, say in Britain, to enjoy warm beer and eat shepherd's pie. In short, the diversity of cuisine enriches a society rather than threatening its unity. The same holds for many other diversity elements already listed.

The *addition* of ethnic holidays to the national, "unity" holidays enriches; for instance, the celebration of St. Patrick's Day and Cinco de Mayo.[471] Ethnic minorities can also "sit out" national holidays, as Israeli-Palestinians do, and a fair number of African Americans did in the days they celebrated Kwanza and not Christmas. (Kwanza used to be much more of a withdrawal and protest holiday than it has become in recent years.[472])

It is true that if the DWU design is applied, the members of many minorities will tend to exhibit some sense of deprivation, based in whole or in part on societal realities. These realities can be addressed, for instance by certain kinds of affirmative action, as well as various rituals and even reparations (ranging from apologies for slavery or for the injustice done to Japanese Americans to including Imams in opening prayers of public events). However, one should recognize that although these societal realities—and sentiments they generate—can be treated, they may persist to some extent for considerable periods of time. Similarly, there are likely to be differences at the margins about exactly where the line lies between the diversity and the unity elements, for instance regarding animal rights. (For example, ritual slaughter as practiced by various religious groups is considered a violation of animal rights by some cities but not by others. In the United States, the line was partially drawn after a minority religious group brought a successful case to the Supreme Court.[473])

Applying the DWU design to schools raises many complex questions concerning the balance between required and elective courses, parallel school systems (for instance Jewish and so-called Koran schools as well as bilingual education), public financing of private schools, and many other issues, which we have explored elsewhere and which cannot be treated within the limits of this chapter.[474]

The DWU design often benefits when considerable local autonomy is granted to those minorities that are concentrated in given areas. Examples include British devolution to the Scots and Welsh, Canadian devolution to the Québécois, and Spanish devolution to the Basques and Catalans. However, this assumes that these minorities will refrain from violence, not secede (as the Slovaks did in Czechoslovakia), and will embrace the unity elements. Attempts to form separate sovereign territories for minority groups within the nation state in which they constitute a minority — for instance, as Henry Milton did with his call for the Republic of New Africa[475] — violate the basic DWU design.

The DWU design is familiar to Americans to the point that it may be considered a natural part of social reality, although the design has been criticized from both multicultural and right wing perspectives.[476]

Moreover, a fair number of limited attempts have been made in the United States to break away from this design and to move toward other ones. Other nations, including most European ones and Japan, find the DWU design much more alien, one that may suit "immigration societies" like the United States, but not their nations. They tend to favor strong assimilationist designs, especially in France, where even collection of information along racial lines is illegal and minorities are given little autonomy. However, growing immigration and increased minority membership is forcing these nations to consider changes in their societal designs and move toward the DWU one, whether or not they welcome these changes. At the same time, attempts to treat the problem at hand by trying to abolish the national ethos have practically died out, a loss—for reasons laid out in the first part of this essay—that should not be mourned.

PERMISSIONS AND CREDITS

The chapters in this anthology are adapted and updated from the author's contributions to academic journals and other sources listed below; the author appreciates their original editorial assistance and, where applicable, permission to republish a version of the work.

Terrorists: Neither Soldiers nor Criminals
From *Military Review* (July-August 2009), pp. 108-118. This article is reprinted with the permission of *Military Review*, the Professional Journal of the US Army, Combined Arms Center, Fort Leavenworth, Kansas. It was originally published in the July-Aug. 2009 issue.

How Liberty is Lost
From *Society*, Vol. 40, No. 5 (July/August 2003), pp. 44-51. Reprinted with kind permission from Springer Science+Business Media.

Privacy and Security in the Digital Age
From the *Harvard Journal of Law & Technology*, Vol. 15, No. 2 (Spring 2002), pp. 258-290.

UAS: The Moral and Legal Case
From *Joint Force Quarterly*, Issue 57, No. 2 (April 2010), pp. 66-71. This chapter first appeared in *Joint Force Quarterly*, Issue 57, Second Quarter, 2010.

Scanners: A Threat to Privacy?
Published online October 9, 2010, by *The New Republic*, at http:// www.tnr.com/article/politics/78250/private-security-virtual-strip-search.

A Right Above All Others
Azure, Fall, 2008, no. 33, pp. 25-28. Published with permission of *Azure*.

The Normativity of Human Rights is Self-Evident
From *Human Rights Quarterly*, Vol. 32, No. 1 (February 2010), pp. 187-197.

DNA Tests: Protect Rights and the Common Good
From *DNA and the Criminal Justice System: The Technology of Justice*, David Lazer, editor, (MIT Press, 2004), pp. 197-223.

Second Chances and Social Forgiveness in the Digital Age
From *The American Scholar*, Vol. 78, No. 2 (Spring 2009), pp. 35-41.
Copyright © by Amitai Etzioni.

Social Norms: The Ways They Are Formed, Transformed, and Affect the Social Order
From *Law & Society Review*, Vol. 34, No. 1 (2000), pp. 157-178, in Symposium on Norms, Law, and Order in the City. Copyright © 2000 by Law and Society Association.

Law in Civil Society, Good Society, and the Prescriptive State
From *Chicago-Kent Law Review*, Vol. 75, No. 2 (2000), pp. 355-377.

Is Transparency the Best Disinfectant?
From *The Journal of Political Philosophy*, Vol. 18, No. 4 (December 2010), pp. 389-404.

Back to the Pillory
From *The American Scholar*, Vol. 68, No. 3 (Summer 1999), pp. 43-50. Copyright © by Amitai Etzioni.

The U.S. Sentencing Commission on Corporate Crime: A Critique
From *Annals of American Academy of Political and Social Science*, Vol. 525 (January 1993), pp. 147-156, and first published by SAGE.

Minorities and the National Ethos
From *Politics*, Vol. 29, No. 2 (June 2009), pp. 100-110.

NOTES

Chapter 1

1 *Griswold v. Connecticut*, 381 U.S. 479 (1965).

2 *Whitney v. California*, 274 U.S. 357 (1927) (Brandeis, J., joined by Holmes, J., concurring).

3 Michael B. Mukasey, "Remarks Prepared for Delivery by Attorney General Michael B. Mukasey at the American Enterprise Institute for Public Policy Research," (lecture, American Enterprise Institute, Washington, D.C., July 21, 2008).

4 Samantha Power, "Our War on Terror," *New York Times*, July 29, 2007, at http://www.nytimes.com/2007/07/29/books/review/Power-t.html?_r=1 (accessed April 23, 2010).

5 Wesley K. Clark and Kal Raustiala, "Why Terrorists Aren't Soldiers," *New York Times*, August 8, 2007, at http://www.nytimes.com/2007/08/08/opinion/08clark.html (accessed April 23, 2010).

6 David Rieff, "Policing Terrorism," *New York Times*, July 22, 2007, late edition, sec. 6.

7 Benjamin Wittes and Zaahira Wyne, "The Current Detainee Population of Guantánamo: An Empirical Study" Brookings Institution, Oct. 21, 2009, 1, http://www.brookings.edu/reports/2008/~/media/Files/rc/reports/2008/1216 _detainees_wittes/1216_detainees_wittes_supplement.pdf (accessed November 14, 2010).

8 Senate Committee on the Judiciary, *Improving Detainee Policy: Handling Terrorism Detainees within the American Justice System*, 110th Cong., 2nd sess. (2008), testimony of Wittes.

9 This basic definition is derived from that which is common to most definitions, as there is no accepted single definition of terrorism or terrorists. Bruce Hoffman defines terrorism briefly as "the deliberate creation and exploitation of fear through violence or threat of violence in the pursuit of political change" [Bruce Hoffman, *Inside Terrorism* (New York: Columbia University Press, 1998), 43.]. Tamar Meisels defines it as "the intentional random murder of defenseless non-combatants, with the intent of instilling fear of mortal danger amidst a civilian population as a strategy designed to advance political ends" [Tamar Meisels, "The Trouble with Terror: The Apologetics of Terrorism—a Refutation," *Terrorism and Political Violence*, 18 (2006): 480]. Boaz Ganor defines it more simply as "the deliberate use of violence aimed against civilians in order to achieve political ends" [Boaz Ganor, "The Relationship Between International and Localized Terrorism," Jerusalem Center for Public Affairs Jerusalem Issue Brief, 4:6 (2005), http://www.jcpa.org/brief/brief004-26.htm]. Title 18, Section 2331 of the U.S. Code defines international terrorism as activities that "involve violent acts or acts dangerous to human life that are a violation of criminal laws... appear to be intended— (i) to intimidate or coerce a civilian

population; (ii) to influence the policy of a government by intimidation or coercion; or (iii) to affect the conduct of a government by mass destruction, assassination, or kidnapping; and ... occur primarily outside the territorial jurisdiction of the United States...."

10 Caleb Carr, *The Lessons of Terror: A History of Warfare Against Civilians*, Revised edition (New York: Random House, 2003), 6; Boaz Ganor, "Defining Terrorism: Is One Man's Terrorist Another Man's Freedom Fighter?" International Policy Institute for Counter-Terrorism, Herzlia, Israel. September 24, 1998, http://www.ict.org.il/ResearchPublications/tabid/64/Articlsid/432/currentpage/1/Default.aspx; Albert J. Bergesen and Omar Lizardo, "International Terrorism and the World-System," *Sociological Theory* no. 22 (2004): 50.

11 Department of Defense, *Nuclear Posture Review Report* (April 2010), 10, http://www.defense.gov/npr/docs/2010%20Nuclear%20Posture%20Review%20Report.pdf.

12 Sharon Begley, "Deterring a 'Dirty Bomb,'" *Newsweek*, April 26, 2010; Joint Working Group of the American Physical Society and the American Association for the Advancement of Science, *Nuclear Forensics Role, State of the Art, Program Needs*, (2008), 23, available at http://www.aps.org/policy/reports/upload/Nuclear-Forensics-Report-FINAL.pdf.

13 Amitai Etzioni, "Unmanned Aircraft Systems: The Moral and Legal Case," *Joint Force Quarterly* 57, no. 2 (2010): 66-71. This reality is discussed in detail in Chapter 4.

14 Amitai Etzioni, *Security First* (New Haven, Conn.: Yale, 2007); Etzioni, *The Moral Dimension: Toward a New Economics* (New York: Free Press, 1988).

15 David Chandler, *International Statebuilding: The Rise of Post-Liberal Governance* (New York: Routledge Press, 2010), 101-21.

16 Matthew Waxman, "Administrative Detention of Terrorists: *Why* Detain, and Detain *Whom*?" *Journal of National Security Law and Policy*, no. 3 (2009): 12-13.

17 Ruth Wedgwood and Kenneth Roth, "Combatants or Criminals? How Washington Should Handle Terrorists," *Foreign Affairs*, May/June 2004, at http://www.foreignaffairs.com/articles/59902/ruth-wedgwood-kenneth-roth/combatants-or-criminals-how-washington-should-handle-terrorists.

18 Tung Yin, "Ending the War on Terrorism One Terrorist at a Time: A Noncriminal Detention Model for Holding and Releasing Guantanamo Bay Detainees," *Harvard Journal of Law and Public Policy*, 29 (2005): 155.

19 John Ashcroft, "Success and Strategies in the Effort to Liberate Iraq," April 17, 2003, http://www.usdoj.gov/archive/ag/speeches/2003/041703effortsliberateIraq.htm (accessed April 23, 2010).

20 Waxman, "Administrative Detention of Terrorists," 11.

21 John Schwartz, "Path to Justice, but Bumpy, for Terrorists," *The New York Times*, May 1, 2009.

22 Robert Chesney and Jack Goldsmith, "Terrorism and the Convergence of Criminal and Military Detention Models," *Stanford Law Review,* no. 60 (2008): 1081.

23 Waxman, "Administrative Detention of Terrorists," 12-13.

24 Yin, "Ending the War on Terrorism One Terrorist at a Time," 155.

25 Goldsmith, "Terrorism and the Convergence of Criminal and Military Detention Models," 1081.

26 Chesney, ibid.

27 Amos N. Guiora, "Quirin to Hamdan: Creating a Hybrid Paradigm for the Detention of Terrorists," *Florida Journal of International Law,* 19 (2007): 529.

28 One may ask why I hold that this third approach is very unpopular despite the fact that both books received rave reviews, as did my much more limited attempt to deal with this issue in *The Financial Times* on August 22, 2007. I reached this conclusion by noting that despite the warm welcome to these texts, so far they have been almost completely ignored by policy makers, most legal scholars, and most assuredly by advocates of human and individual rights.

29 It remains to be worked out what should be considered torture. It can be defined so broadly that it would block most interrogation techniques—for instance, if it encompasses a ban on humiliating the detainees and it leaves up to them to define what is humiliating—or so narrowly that waterboarding and many other cruel measures would be allowed as long as they do not lead to organ failure. It goes without saying that the suggested guidelines' use would be much hampered unless the definition is worked out, presumably somewhere in between these two extremes.

30 Guiora, "Quirin to Hamdan," 529.

31 Rajiv Chandrasekaran, "From Captive To Suicide Bomber," *Washington Post,* February 28, 2009.

32 Terrorism Act 2006, 2006, c. 11, §25 (U.K.).

33 Waxman, "Administrative Detention of Terrorists: *Why* Detain, and Detain *Whom?*"

34 Jack Goldsmith and Neal Katyal, "The Terrorists' Court," *New York Times,* July 11, 2007.

35 Ibid.

36 Ibid.

37 Benjamin Wittes, *Law and the Long War* (New York: Penguin Press, 2008), 11-16.

38 Ibid., 164-178.

39 Ibid., 165.

40 Phil Hirschkorn, "Civil rights attorney convicted in terror trial," CNN.com, Feb. 14, 2005, http://www.cnn.com/2005/LAW/02/10/terror.trial.lawyer/ (accessed December 24, 2010).

41 Nor can they be tried as soldiers, as much of the evidence is not admissible in military commissions either. On May 15, 2009, President Obama announced his intentions to continue to use military commissions to try suspected terrorists, among other venues. According to his announcement, these commissions will be different from the Bush Administration Commissions. The outline of changes he provided, however, was vague:

> First, statements that have been obtained from detainees using cruel, inhuman and degrading interrogation methods will no longer be admitted as evidence at trial. Second, the use of hearsay will be limited, so that the burden will no longer be on the party who objects to hearsay to disprove its reliability. Third, the accused will have greater latitude in selecting their counsel. Fourth, basic protections will be provided for those who refuse to testify. And fifth, military commission judges may establish the jurisdiction of their own courts.

Office of the Press Secretary, The White House, *Statement of President Barack Obama on Military Commissions*, May 15, 2009, http://www.whitehouse.gov /the_press_office/Statement-of-President-Barack-Obama-on-Military-Commissions/ (accessed November 14, 2010).

42 For more discussion, see Amitai Etzioni, *How Patriotic is the Patriot Act?* (New York: Routledge, 2004). The larger problem of preserving security without sacrificing liberty or democracy is explored here in Chapter 2, and the specific dilemma of digital is examined in Chapter 3.

43 Etzioni, "Unmanned Aircraft Systems: The Moral and Legal Case." See also Chapter 4 on UAS.

Chapter 2

44 American Civil Liberties Union, "Insatiable Appetite," October 15, 2002, available at http://www.aclu.org/national-security/insatiable-appetite-govern ments-demand-new-and-unnecessary-powers-after-september-/ (accessed November 14, 2010).

45 Wendy Kaminer, "Ashcroft's Lies," *The American Prospect*, July 15, 2002, at 9.

46 Peter Fritzsche, *Germans Into Nazis* (Cambridge: Harvard University Press, 1998), 7, 8 (historians tend to "understand Nazism as the outcome of extra-ordinary hardship more than of popular mobilization," while author further argues that Nazism specifically [not just the fall of Weimar] was no accident and not just a response to internal disaster, but recognizing "traumas and scarcities" explanation of many historians).

47 Theodore Abel, *The Nazi Movement: Why Hitler Came to Power* (New York: Atherton, 1966, rpt'd from a 1938 Prentice-Hall ed.), 39, 121, 127, 166. The book is readily available in a more modern edition, entitled simply *Why Hitler Came Into Power* (Cambridge: Harvard University Press, 1986), with similar pagination.

[48] Kurt Sontheimer, "Anti-Democratic Thought in the Weimar Republic," as translated by John Conway, ed., *The Path to Dictatorship, 1918-1933: Ten Essays* (New York: Praeger, 1967), 44.

[49] Sheri Berman, "Civil Society and the Collapse of the Weimar Republic," *World Politics* 49, no. 3 (1997): 424.

[50] Arthur Schram and Arthur van Riel, "Weimar Economic Decline, Nazi Economic Recovery, and the Stabilization of Political Dictatorship," *Journal of Economic History*, no. 53 (1993): 75.

[51] Fritz Stern, "Introduction," in John Conway, ed., *The Path to Dictatorship, 1918-1933: Ten Essays* (New York: Praeger, 1967), xx.

[52] E. J. Feuchtwanger, *From Weimar to Hitler: Germany 1918-33* (New York: St. Martin's Press, 1993), 316 (calling that reality the "most pervasive cause of Weimar's failure").

[53] E.g., Stuart A. Scheingold, *The Politics of Law and Order: Street Crime and Public Policy* (1984; reprint, New Orleans: Quid Pro Books, 2010).

[54] The flight traffic rates noted, and those to follow, are adapted from the Bureau of Transportation Statistics, *e.g.*, "Sum: Number of Passengers by Month for 2001."

[55] *Los Angeles Times* Poll, September 13-14, 2002.

[56] National Public Radio/Kaiser/Kennedy School Poll on Civil Liberties, Oct. 31-Nov. 12, 2001.

[57] Ibid.

[58] These various poll results were summarized in two *New York Times* stories by Richard L. Berke, from January 23, 1994 (at A1) and June 5, 1996 (A1).

[59] *USA Today*/CNN/Gallup Poll, October 13-18, 1993.

[60] On the political and deterrent effects of shaming punishments, and the Fay example, see generally Amitai Etzioni, *The Monochrome Society* (Princeton, N.J.: Princeton University Press, 2001). Shaming and alternate punishments in the present book are explored in Chapter 13.

[61] *Newsweek* Poll, April 7-8, 1994.

[62] Rich Connell & Richard Serrano, "L.A. Is Warned of New Unrest," *Los Angeles Times*, October 22, 1992, A1.

[63] Lucy Soto, "Delegation Makes Its Presence Known," *Atlanta Journal & Constitution*, March 2, 1995, A3.

[64] ABCNews.com Poll, May 31-June 4, 2000.

[65] *USA Today*/CNN/Gallup Poll, October 23-25, 1998.

[66] The paragraph's reported crime rates are drawn from the FBI's *Crime in the United States: Uniform Crime Reports*, for the years 1996 (p. 10), 1999 (p. 10), and 2001 (p. 11).

Chapter 3

[67] See Amitai Etzioni, *The Limits of Privacy* (1999) (analyzing boundaries and contours of privacy right from a communitarian perspective).

[68] As reported for 2009 by ITU at http://www.itu.int/ITU-D/ict/. ITU is the United Nations agency for communications technologies. Similar figures have been reported over the years at www.ctiawireless.com.

[69] See http://www.itu.int/ITU-D/ict/ (using Statistics field). The figure is also reported from ITU sources at http://www.internetworldstats.com/am/us.htm. Earlier reports from Nielson-Netratings.com are similar, e.g., 228 million users in the U.S. in 2009, or 74.1%.

[70] 18 U.S.C. §§ 3122-3123 (2000). See generally *United States v. Giordano*, 416 U.S. 505, 549 n.1 (1974); *Smith v. Maryland*, 442 U.S. 735 (1979); 18 U.S.C. § 2518 (2000).

[71] Christian Schultz, "Unrestricted Federal Agent: 'Carnivore' and the Need to Revise the Pen Register Statute," *Notre Dame L. Rev.* 76: 1215, 1221-23 (2001); Terrence Berg, "www.wildwest.gov: The Impact of the Internet on State Power to Enforce the Law," *BYU L. Rev.* 2000: 1305 (2000); Joginder S. Dhillon & Robert I. Smith, "Defensive Information Operations and Domestic Law: Limitations on Government Investigative Techniques," *Air Force L. Rev.* 50: 135 (2001); Paul Taylor, "Issues Raised by the Application of the Pen Register Statutes to Authorize Government Collection of Information on Packet-Switched Networks," *Virginia J.L. & Tech.* 6: 4 (2001). See also U.S. Department of Justice, *Field Guide on the New Authorities (Redacted) Enacted in the 2001 Anti-Terrorism Legislation* § 216A, available stored at http://epic.org/privacy /terrorism/DOJ_guidance.pdf (accessed November 14, 2010).

[72] Steven Levy, *Crypto: How the Code Rebels Beat the Government* (New York: Viking, 2001), 310-11.

[73] Deborah Russell & G.T. Gangemi, Sr., "Encryption," in Lance Hoffman, ed., *Building Big Brother* (New York: Springer-Verlag, 1995), 10-11; Dorothy E. Denning and William E. Baugh, Jr., "Encryption and Evolving Technologies as Tools of Organized Crime and Terrorism," *Trends in Organized Crime* 3, no. 1 (1997): 1-64.

[74] See ECPA, 18 U.S.C. § 2518(11) (2000).

[75] 18 U.S.C. § 2518(11)(b) (2000).

[76] Intelligence Authorization Act for Fiscal Year 1999, Pub. L. No. 105-272, § 604, 112 Stat. 2396, 2413 (1998) (codified as amended at 18 U.S.C. § 2518(11)(b) (2000)).

[77] As collected and analyzed in Bryan R. Faller, "The 1998 Amendment to the Roving Wiretap Statute: Congress 'Could Have' Done Better," *Ohio St. L.J.* 60: 2093 (1999). See, e.g., *United States v. Petti*, 973 F.2d 1441, 1444-45 (9th Cir. 1992).

[78] Tom Ricks, "A Secret U.S. Court Where One Side Always Seems to Win," *Christian Science Monitor* , May 21, 1982, at 1.

[79] *Olmstead v. United States*, 277 U.S. 438, 466 (1927).

[80] 389 U.S. 347, 351 (1967).

[81] *Katz*, 389 U.S. at 361 (Harlan, J., concurring).

[82] E.g., Jonathan Laba, "If You Can't Stand the Heat, Get Out of the Drug Business: Thermal Imagers, Emerging Technologies, and the Fourth Amendment," *Calif. L. Rev.* 84: 1347, 1470-75 (1996); Anthony Amsterdam, "Perspectives on the Fourth Amendment," *Minn. L. Rev.* 58: 349, 384-85 (1974). See also Richard Julie, Note, "High Tech Surveillance Tools and the Fourth Amendment: Reasonable Expectations of Privacy in the Technological Age," *Am. Crim. L. Rev.* 37: 127, 131-32 (2000); *State of Louisiana v. Reeves*, 427 So. 2d 403, 425 (La. 1982) (Dennis, J., dissenting).

[83] 45 M.J. 406, 417 (C.A.A.F. 1996).

[84] 979 F. Supp. 1177, 1185 (S.D. Ohio 1997).

[85] 973 F.2d 1441, 1444 (9th Cir. 1992) (quoting a 1987 Supreme Court case).

[86] *Petti*, 973 F.2d at 1444.

[87] See 18 U.S.C. § 2518(11)(b)(iv) (2000); 18 U.S.C. § 2518(12) (2000).

[88] See generally *The "Carnivore" Controversy: Electronic Surveillance and Privacy in the Digital Age: Hearing Before the Senate Comm. on the Judiciary*, 106th Cong., statement of Donald M. Kerr, Assistant Director, Laboratory Division, FBI.

[89] As explained by the detailed Affidavit of Randall S. Murch, at 3-4, available at http://epic.org/crypto/scarfo/murch_aff.pdf (October 4, 2001) (accessed November 14, 2010).

[90] See *United States v. Scarfo*, 180 F. Supp. 2d 572 (D.N.J. 2001). See generally "Judge Orders Government to Explain How 'Key Logger System' Works," *Andrews Computer & Online Indus. Litig. Rep.*, Aug. 14, 2001, at 3.

[91] See Affidavit of R.S. Murch, at 6-7 (October 4, 2001).

[92] See Lou Dolinar, "Upping the Pressure; With New Tools and Laws, Authorities Can Target Suspects' Computers with Accuracy," *Newsday*, December 12, 2001, at C8.

[93] Ted Bridis, "Congressional Panel Debates Carnivore as FBI Moves to Mollify Privacy Worries," *Wall Street Journal*, July 25, 2000, A24.

[94] ACLU, "Urge Congress to Stop the FBI's Use of Privacy-Invading Software," http://www.aclu.org/action/carnivore107.html (as of August 9, 2001), quoted in Shel Holtz, *Public Relations on the Net: Winning Strategies* (New York: Amacom Books, 2002), 73.

[95] ACLU, http://www.aclu.org/action/carnivore107.html (as of February 5, 2002).

[96] See, e.g., *The "Carnivore" Controversy: Electronic Surveillance and Privacy in the Digital Age: Hearing Before the Senate Comm. on the Judiciary*, 106th Cong., statement of Donald M. Kerr, Asst. Dir., FBI, as well as his earlier testimony of July 2000 before the 105th Congress. See generally Ted Bridis,

"Congressional Panel Debates Carnivore," *Wall Street Journal*, July 25, 2000, A24.

97 I.I.T. Research Institute, *Independent Technical Review of the Carnivore System: Final Report* (December 8, 2000), available at http://epic.org /privacy/carnivore/carniv_final.pdf (accessed November 14, 2010).

98 Ibid.

99 John Schwartz, "Wiretapping System Works on Internet, Review Finds," *New York Times*, November 22, 2000, A19 (quoting Henry Perritt Jr.).

100 Bruce Schneier, "Uncle Sam is Listening," *Salon*, December 20, 2005, available at http://www.salon.com/news/opinion/feature/2005/12/20/surveillance (accessed November 14, 2010).

101 Barton Gellman, "The FBI's Secret Scrutiny," *Washington Post*, November 6, 2005.

102 E.g., Declan McCullagh and Anne Broache, "NSA Cooperation: OK for E-mail, IM Companies?," *Cnet News*, October 27, 2007, at http://news.cnet.com/NSA-cooperation-OK-for-e-mail,-IM-companies/2100-7348_3-6214609.html (accessed November 14, 2010).

103 Ron Wyden, "Rights that Travel," *Washington Post*, December 10, 2007, A19.

104 Russ Feingold, Oct. 25, 2001, Floor statement.

105 "The Enemy Within: Liberty and Security," *Economist* 373, no. 8396, October 9, 2004, 1.

106 See, e.g., U.S. Department of Justice, *Field Guide on the New Authorities (Redacted) Enacted in the 2001 Antiterrorism Legislation*, § 216, available at http://epic.org/privacy/terrorism/DOJ_guidance.pdf (accessed November 14, 2010), and discussion in this chapter above.

107 These accountability mechanisms are discussed further in Amitai Etzioni, "Implications of Select New Technologies for Individual Rights and Public Safety," *Harv. J. L. & Tech.* 15: 257, 282-90 (2002). The "second balance" analysis is applied particularly as to DNA sampling and testing, below, in Chapter 8.

Chapter 4

108 Jane Mayer, "Predator War," *The New Yorker* (October 26, 2009), available at http://www.newyorker.com/reporting/2009/10/26/091026fa_fact_mayer/ (accessed November 14, 2010).

109 Jane Mayer, *The Dark Side: The Inside Story of How The War on Terror Turned into a War on American Ideals* (New York: Doubleday, 2008).

110 Jane Mayer, "Predator War," *The New Yorker* (October 26, 2009) (quoting former CIA officer).

111 Ann Scott Tyson, "Less Peril for Civilians, But More for Troops," *Washington Post*, September 23, 2009, A1.

112 Jane Mayer, "Predator War," *The New Yorker* (October 26, 2009) (discussing international law). Mayer adds, "Many lawyers who have looked at America's drone program in Pakistan believe that it meets these basic legal tests."

113 E.g., Peter M. Cullen, "The Role of Targeted Killing in the Campaign against Terror," *Joint Forces Quarterly* 48, no. 1 (2008); David Kretzmer, "Targeted Killing of Suspected Terrorists: Extra-Judicial Executions or Legitimate Means of Defence?," *European J. Int'l L.* 16, no. 2 (2005), 171; Steven R. Ratner, "Predator and Prey: Seizing and Killing Suspected Terrorists Abroad," *Journal of Political Philosophy* 15, no. 3 (2007).

114 As discussed in Chapter 1.

115 Jane Mayer, "Predator War," *The New Yorker* (October 26, 2009) (quoting Singer, author of *Wired for War* (New York: Penguin, 2009)).

116 Ibid. (ellipses in original). Dudziak is a professor of law at the University of Southern California.

Chapter 5

117 An earlier version of this chapter recently appeared in online form in *The New Republic*, as "Private Security: In Defense of the 'Virtual Strip-Search'" (October 9, 2010), available at http://www.tnr.com/article/politics/78250/private-security-virtual-strip-search/. The author is indebted to Radhika Bhat for research assistance. It is included in this book by permission of *The New Republic*.

118 As is discussed in the Preface and detailed in, *inter alia*, Amitai Etzioni, *The Limits of Privacy* (New York: Basic Books, 1999).

119 The useful SARS example, and the larger concept of crediting both individual rights and community needs, are discussed in Etzioni, *The New Golden Rule* (New York: Basic Books, 1996).

120 For example, the German site bild.com: http://www.bild.de/BILD/news /bild-english/world-news/2009/12/31/pregnancy-body-piercings-genitals/ what-can-naked-scanners-really-see.html/ (December 31, 2009) (accessed November 18, 2010).

121 See, for instance, http://en.wikipedia.org/wiki/File:Backscatter_x-ray_image _woman .jpg / (accessed November 18, 2010).

122 See John Hughes, "Airport 'Naked Image' Scanners May Get Privacy Upgrades," *Bloomberg News*, September 7, 2010, available at http://www .bloomberg.com/news/2010-09-08/airport-naked-image-scanners-in-u-s-may- get-avatars-to-increase-privacy.html/ (accessed November 18, 2010).

123 American Civil Liberties Union, *ACLU Backgrounder on Body Scanners and "Virtual Strip Searches"* (January 8, 2010), available at http://www .aclu.org/technology-and-liberty/aclu-backgrounder-body-scanners-and-%E2% 80%9Cvirtual-strip-searches%E2%80%9D/ (accessed November 18, 2010).

124 CBSNews.com, "Poll: 3 in 4 Support Airport Body Scans" (January 11, 2010), available at http://www.cbsnews.com/stories/2010/01/11/earlyshow/main608 0816.shtml/ (accessed November 18, 2010).

125Electronic Privacy Information Center, "Whole Body Imaging Technology and Body Scanners" (2010), available at http://epic.org/privacy/airtravel/back scatter/ accessed November 18, 2010). EPIC's position on the use of ISP intercepts is discussed in Chapter 3.

126 Jeffrey Rosen, "Nude Awakening: The Dangerous Naked Machines," *The New Republic*, January 29, 2010 (emphasis added), available at http://www .tnr.com/article/politics/nude-awakening/ (accessed November 18, 2010).

127 American Civil Liberties Union, *ACLU Backgrounder on Body Scanners and "Virtual Strip Searches"* (January 8, 2010).

128 This concept of the Fourth Amendment as a decidedly communitarian regime is further explored in Chapter 8, and there applied to the particular problem of DNA testing. It is also a part of the analysis explored in Chapter 3 on digital intercepts.

Chapter 6

129 On security versus individual rights from a communitarian perspective, see Chapter 3 on technological issues of privacy in the digital age and, in Chapter 5, the specific balancing context of TSA scanners. Both concerns are valid and worthy of protection.

130 Chapter 7 explores the core concept of the primacy of life in the normative debate over international "human rights."

131 As detailed above in Chapter 2.

132 See the discussion of Gates and the "shoot first" response, in Chapter 2 and the sources detailed there.

133 See generally Alexander Lukin, "Russia's New Authoritarianism and the Post-Soviet Political Ideal," *Post-Soviet Affairs* 25, no. 1 (2009): 66 (exploring several fundamental reasons for the increasing popularity of Putin's authoritarian approach, beyond usual explanation of captive media). For comparison to the social and economic necessities that in part brought the Weimar Republic down, see Chapter 2.

Chapter 7

134 The author is indebted to Alex Platt for several rounds of comments on previous drafts of an article, which appeared earlier this year in *Human Rights Quarterly* [vol. 32, no. 1, February 2010, at 187-197], from which this chapter is drawn (and adapted by permission of The Johns Hopkins University Press).

135 I am not the first to describe human rights as a "self-evident" moral claim. See, e.g., Louis Henkin, *The Age of Rights* (New York: Columbia University Press, 1990), 2.

136 Michael Ignatieff, "The Attack on Human Rights," *Foreign Affairs* 80, no. 6 (2001), 102-116.

137 John Locke, *Second Treatise on Government*, Ch. 2, § 6, C.B. Macphearson, trans. (Indianapolis: Hackett Publishing Co., 1980).

138 *Southern Pacific Company v. Jensen*, 244 U.S. 205, 222 (1917) (Holmes, J., dissenting) (rejecting majority's reliance on a particular economic theory of capitalism and property ownership as built into the common law and Constitution, and thus as immutable despite majoritarian will and the progression of philosophical and economic theory over the years).

139 Michael S. Moore, *Law as a Functional Kind*, in Robert George, ed., *Natural Law Theory: Contemporary Essays* (Oxford: Clarendon Press, 1992), 188-242, at 188.

140 Joel Feinberg, "The Nature and Value of Rights," in Patrick Hayden, ed., *The Philosophy of Human Rights* (St. Paul, Minn.: Paragon House, 2001).

141 United Nations Office of the High Commissioner on Human Rights, "International Covenant on Civil and Political Rights," and "International Covenant on Economic, Social and Cultural Rights" (1966) (the latter known as "ICESCR," and available at http://www2.ohchr.org/english/law/cescr.htm/ (accessed November 18, 2010)). The Covenants share Article 1, which states: "All peoples have the right of self-determination. By virtue of that right they freely determine their political status and freely pursue their economic, social, and cultural development."

142 See, e.g., Alasdair MacIntyre, *After Virtue* (South Bend, Ind.: University of Notre Dame Press, 1984).

143 Rhoda Howard, *Human Rights and the Search for Community* (Boulder, Co.: Westview Press, 1995).

144 It might be said that I argue that human rights need no case to be made for them, but I am making one: against those who seek to support human rights by basing them on other concepts.

145 Ethicist Peter Singer, also discussed in Chapter 4, may be the only one who contests this point. He writes famously: "If I am walking past a shallow pond and see a child drowning in it, I ought to wade in and pull the child out.... It makes no moral difference whether the person I can help is a neighbor's child ten yards from me or a Bengali whose name I shall never know ten thousand miles away." Peter Singer, "Famine, Affluence, and Morality," *Philosophy and Public Affairs* 1, no. 1 (1972), 229, 231-232. For a more detailed refutation of Singer on this point, see Amitai Etzioni, "Are Particularistic Obligations Justified?," *The Review of Politics* (Autumn 2002), 573-598.

146 Some added arguments as an afterthought, to examine and account for a moral sense which they already recognized. In other words, this is where ethics and moral philosophy comes in.

147 See Louis Henkin, *The Age of Rights* (New York: Columbia University Press, 1990).

148 As epistemologist Robert Audi writes, "Since premises are not needed as a ground for justified belief of a self-evident proposition, there is also no basis for demanding an independent argument in every case where there is an appeal to

the self-evident."Audi, "Self-Evidence," *Philosophical Perspectives* 13 (1999), 233.

149 Charles Taylor, *Sources of the Self: The Making of the Modern Identity* (Cambridge, Mass.: Harvard University Press, 1989), 5.

150 Ibid., 5-8.

151 Ibid., 7.

152 Michael P. Zuckert argues that Jefferson, following John Locke and others, took self-evident truths to "serve as the most fundamental sort of premise, what in mathematics are called axioms." Zuckert, "Self Evident Truth and the Declaration of Independence," *Review of Politics* (Summer 1987), 322.

153 Alvin Plantinga, "Is Belief in God Rational?," in C. F. Delaney, ed., *Rationality and Religious Belief* (South Bend, Ind.: University of Notre Dame Press, 1979).

154 See Bernard Williams, *Truth and Truthfulness* (Princeton, N.J.: Princeton University Press, 2002). Williams argues that accuracy and sincerity are "virtues of truth."

155 Martin Buber, *I and Thou* (New York: Scribners, 1970).

156 Private communication with the author, Berlin, June 1, 2003.

157 Amartya Sen, "Human Rights and Asian Values," *The New Republic*, July 14-21, 1997.

158 Abdullah Ahmed An-Na'im, ed., *Human Rights in Cross-Cultural Perspectives: Quest for Consensus* (Philadelphia: University of Pennsylvania Press, 1992).

159 Richard Rorty, "Human Rights, Rationality, and Sentimentality," in Patrick Hayden, ed., *The Philosophy of Human Rights* (St. Paul, Minn.: Paragon House, 2001), 246.

160 See, e.g., Rorty, "Human Rights, Rationality and Sentimentality," ibid.; Stanley Fish, "Don't Blame Relativism," *The Responsive Community*, 12 (2002), 27-31.

161 Rorty, "Human Rights, Rationality, and Sentimentality," ibid., 254.

162 See, e.g., Dale Jamieson, "When Utilitarians Should be Virtue Theorists," *Utilitas* 19, no. 2 (2007), 160-183.

Chapter 8

163 See generally Amitai Etzioni, *The Moral Dimension: Toward a New Economics* (New York: Free Press, 1988); Amitai Etzioni, *How Patriotic is the Patriot Act?: Freedom versus Security in the Age of Terrorism* (New York: Routledge, 2004).

As to applying communitarian analysis to particular thorny dilemmas of "other rights," as this Section involves, see, e.g., Etzioni, *The Common Good*, ch.

3 (Cambridge, Mass.: Polity Press, 2004) (First Amendment rights of children and the problem of access to speech and the Internet in such forums as libraries), as well as my 2001 essay for the *Chronicle of Higher Education*, "Are Liberal Scholars Acting Irresponsibly on Gun Control?," (April 6, 2001), exploring the Second Amendment issue of gun control (before the *Heller* decision at the Supreme Court). The latter remains available at http://aladinrc.wrlc.org/bitstream/1961/1045/1/B350.pdf / (accessed November 18, 2010).

In this Section, specific application will be given toward such other interests as the privacy right involved with DNA technologies (in this chapter; and related to the balancing of privacy interests introduced in Chapter 3 regarding ISP and cellphone tracking, and Chapter 5 regarding TSA scanners). Chapter 9 explores the social and privacy considerations that the long tail of the Internet imposes on those with a past they would rather [others] forget. The issues of digital tracking and DNA technologies were introduced as well in *The Common Good*, ch. 4-5 (2004).

[164] For a fuller description of this kind of communitarianism, see Amitai Etzioni, *The New Golden Rule* (New York: Basic Books, 1996).

[165] As introduced in the Preface.

[166] Alan Ehrenhalt, *The Lost City: The Forgotten Virtues of Community in America* (New York: Basic Books, 1996 [pbk. revised ed. of 1995 book studying Chicago values in the 1950s]).

[167] E.g., Michael Walzer, *Interpretation and Social Criticism* (Cambridge, Mass.: Harvard University Press, 1987); Robert Bellah, et al., *Habits of the Heart* (Berkeley: University of California Press, 1985); Michael Sandel, *Liberalism and the Limits of Justice* (Cambridge: Cambridge University Press, 1981 [and his 2nd ed. in 1998]). See also Charles Taylor, *The Ethics of Authenticity* (Cambridge, Mass.: Harvard University Press, 1992); Michael Sandel, ed., *Liberalism and Its Critics* (New York: New York University Press, 1984).

[168] Etzioni, *The New Golden Rule* (New York: Basic Books, 1996).

[169] For more on this point, see Chapters 1 and 2, and Etzioni, *How Patriotic is the Patriot Act?* (2004).

[170] For further examples of such warrantless, suspicionless searches that have been ruled permissible under the Fourth Amendment, see Michael Froomkin, "The Metaphor is the Key: Cryptography, the Clipper Chip, and the Constitution," *U. Penn. L. Rev.* 143 (1995), 709, 824-825.

[171] As discussed in detail in Etzioni, *How Patriotic is the Patriot Act?* (2004), and introduced here in Chapter 1.

[172] See also Sally Howell and Andrew Shryock, "Cracking Down on Diaspora: Arab Detroit and America's 'War on Terror'" (March 14, 2003) (discussing pre-invasion sentiments and actions), available at http://www.umich.edu/~biid/cvs/Cracking%20Down.pdf/ (accessed October 14, 2010).

[173] See Amitai Etzioni, *The Moral Dimension: Toward a New Economics* (1988).

174 See, e.g., Jeffrey Rosen, "A Watchful State," *New York Times Magazine,* October 7, 2001, 38; Jeffrey Rosen, *The Naked Crowd: Reclaiming Security and Freedom in an Anxious Age* (New York: Random House, 2004).

175 Quoted in Kenneth Jost, "DNA Databases: Does Expanding. Them Threaten Civil Liberties?," *CQ Researcher* 9, no. 20 (May 28, 1999), 451, 451, available at http://www.denverda.org/DNA_Documents/CQ%20DNA%20Database%20Art icle.pdf/ (accessed November 18, 2010). Jost also quotes a federal prosecutor as saying, "It's one of the most accurate technologies we have." Ibid.

176 Césare Beccaria, *On Crimes and Punishments* (1764), Aaron Thomas and Jeremy Parzen, trans. (Toronto: University of Toronto Press, 2008).

177 Lois Romano, "When DNA Meets Death Row, It's the System That's Tested," *Washington Post,* December 12, 2003, A1.

178 Kevin Flynn, "Fighting Crime with Ingenuity, 007 Style: Gee-Whiz Police Gadgets Get a Trial Run," *New York Times,* March 7, 2000, B1.

179 Radio Interview with Dr. Paul Ferrara, Director of Virginia Division of Forensic Science, "Discusses Gathering of DNA Evidence," *All Things Considered,* National Public Radio, July 27, 2000.

180 It has been widely documented that eyewitness accounts are unreliable. As Justice William Brennan wrote in his opinion in *United States v. Wade,* "The vagaries of eyewitness identification are well known; the annals of criminal law are rife with instances of mistaken identification." 388 U.S. 218, 228 (1967).

Gary L. Wells and Eric P. Seelau summarize findings regarding eyewitness identification: "Although there is no way to estimate the frequency of mistaken identification in actual cases, numerous analyses over several decades have consistently shown that mistaken eyewitness identification is the single largest source of wrongful convictions." Wells and Seelau, "Eyewitness identification: Psychological Research and Legal Policy on Lineups," *Psychology, Public Policy & Law* 1, no. 4 (1995), 765, 765, available at http://blog.lib.umn.edu/jbs/soc3101/EyewitnessIdentificationWellsSeelou.pdf/ (accessed October 4, 2010). The error rate is so high, and not perceived properly by juries, that an issue has arisen in evidence law as to whether expert witnesses on the unreliability of such evidence should be admissible.

181 Even this cannot be assumed with full confidence given that in a few instances rapists have intentionally left other people's semen behind.

182 National Public Radio, "Crime Labs under Scrutiny around the U.S. for Producing Evidence that Wrongly Convicts People for Felonies," *Weekend Edition,* May 12, 2001; John F. Kelly and Phillip K. Wearne, *Tainting Evidence: Inside the Scandals at the FBI Crime Lab* (New York: The Free Press 1998).

183 Kelly and Wearne, *Tainting Evidence,* ibid. Further, the Office of the Inspector General reported that FBI employee Jacqueline Blake falsified lab documents. The report also lists and explains several vulnerabilities in the FBI lab's protocol and practice. Office of the Inspector General, The FBI DNA Laboratory, *A Review of Protocol and Practice Vulnerabilities* (May 2004), available at http://www.usdoj.gov/oig/special/0405/index.htm/ (accessed November 14, 2010).

184 Rosie Cowan and David Hencke, "Row Over 'Blank' CCTV Tapes at Station," *The Guardian,* August 23, 2005, 8.

185 As detailed in Chapter 3, "The Second Balance."

Chapter 9

186 An earlier version of this chapter appeared as an article in *The American Scholar* [vol. 78, no. 2 (Spring 2009)], which was co-written by Radhika Bhat. It is reproduced here with the kind permission of Ms. Bhat, whom the author thanks for her contribution, and of *The American Scholar.*

187 Samuel D. Warren & Louis D. Brandeis, "The Right to Privacy," *Harv. L. Rev.* 4, no. 5 (December 15, 1890), 193. This influential study is reprinted in *The Right to Privacy* (New Orleans: Quid Pro Books, 2010), in a monograph which contains some of the offending news clippings and recounts in its Foreword the *paparazzi* and newspaper incidents which fomented the article.

188 See generally Amy Gajda, "What If Samuel D. Warren Hadn't Married a Senator's Daughter?: Uncovering the Press Coverage that Led to 'The Right to Privacy,'" *Mich. St. L. Rev.* 2008: 35 (2008); William L. Prosser, "Privacy," *Calif. L. Rev.* 48: 383 (1960); Amitai Etzioni, *The Limits of Privacy* (New York: Basic Books, 1999).

189 Beth Givens, "Public Records on the Internet: The Privacy Dilemma" (April 19, 2002; revised March 2006), available at http://www.privacyrights.org /ar/onlinepubrecs.htm (accessed November 14, 2010).

190 Ann Zimmerman and Kortney Stringer, "As Background Checks Proliferate, Ex-Cons Face a Lock on Jobs," *Wall Street Journal,* August 26, 2004.

191 Brad Stone, "If You Run a Red Light, Will Everyone Know?," *New York Times,* August 3, 2008 (discussing CriminalSearches.com and interviewing its founder).

192 Patrick A. Langan and David J. Levin, *Bureau of Justice Statistics Special Report: Recidivism of Prisoners Released in 1994* (June 2002), available at http://bjs.ojp.usdoj.gov/content/pub/pdf/rpr94.pdf/ (accessed November 14, 2010).

193 See, e.g., David Lisak and Paul Miller, "Repeat Rape and Multiple Offending Among Undetected Rapists," *Violence and Victims,* 17: 73 (2002), available at http://www.innovations.harvard.edu/cache/documents/1348/134851.pdf (accessed November 14, 2010).

194 Cheryl W. Thompson, "Poor Performance Records Are Easily Outdistanced ," *Washington Post,* April 12, 2005, A1.

195 Ibid.

196 Pope Brock, *Charlatan: America's Most Dangerous Huckster, the Man Who Pursued Him, and the Age of Flimflam* (New York: Crown, 2008).

197 Robert Barnoski, *Sex Offender Sentencing in Washington State: Has Community Notification Reduced Recidivism?* (Olympia, Wash.: Washington

State Inst. for Pub. Pol'y, 2005), available at http://www.wsipp.wa.gov/rptfiles/ 05-12-1202.pdf/ (accessed November 14, 2010).

[198] Donna Schram and Cheryl Milloy, *Community Notification: A Study of Offender Characteristics and Recidivism* (Olympia, Wash.: Washington State Inst. for Pub. Pol'y, 1995), available at http://www.wsipp.wa.gov/rptfiles /chrrec.pdf/ (accessed November 14, 2010). See also Peter Finn, *Sex Offender Community Notification* (Washington, D.C.: National Institute of Justice [Dept. of Justice], 2007), available at http://www.ncjrs.gov/txtfiles/162364.txt (accessed November 14, 2010).

[199] WKYC.com News, "Should Mayor's Criminal Past Keep Him from Serving?" (May 12, 2008), available at http://www.wkyc.com/news/regional/akron_ article.aspx?storyid=89350/ (accessed November 20, 2010).

[200] See, e.g., Akron.com, "Lakemore Officials Respond to Fiscal Emergency Status" (August 16, 2010), available at http://www.akron.com/akron-ohio-community-news.asp?aID=10068/ (accessed November 20, 2010).

[201] Themes of shaming, community approval, and prevention of criminal behavior through such social processes are discussed in Chapter 13 and explored more deeply throughout Amitai Etzioni, *The Monochrome Society* (Princeton, N.J.: Princeton University Press, 2001).

Chapter 10

[202] For examples of early law and society works, see Donald Black, *The Behavior of Law* (New York: Academic Press, 1976); Lawrence M. Friedman, *The Legal System: A Social Science Perspective* (New York: Russell Sage Foundation, 1975); Robert L. Kidder, *Connecting Law and Society: An Introduction to Research Theory* (Upper Saddle River, N.J.: Prentice Hall, 1983); Richard Lempert and Joseph Sanders, *An Invitation to Law and Social Science: Desert, Disputes, and Distribution* (Philadelphia: University of Pennsylvania Press, 1986); and Jerome H. Skolnick, *Justice Without Trial: Law Enforcement in Democratic Society* (New York: Macmillan, 3d ed. 1994). A modern summary of the movement and its perspectives is found in Kitty Calavita, *Invitation to Law and Society* (Chicago: University of Chicago Press, 2010).

[203] See Cass Sunstein, "Social Norms and Social Roles," *Colum. L. Rev.* 96 (1996), 903; Sunstein, "Preferences and Politics," *Philosophy and Public Affairs* 20, no. 3 (1991); Robert C. Ellickson, "Law and Economics Discovers Social Norms," *J. Legal Stud.* 27 (1998), 537; Lawrence Lessig, "The Regulation of Social Meaning," *U. Chi. L. Rev.* 62 (1995), 943; Lessig, "The New Chicago School," *J. Legal Stud.* 27 (1998), 661; Dan Kahan, "Social Influence, Social Meaning, and Deterrence," *Va. L. Rev.* 83 (1997), 349; Kahan, "What Do Alternative Sanctions Mean?," *U. Chi. L. Rev.* 63 (1996), 591; Eric Posner, "Law, Economics, and Inefficient Norms," *U. Penn. L. Rev.* 144 (1996), 1697; Richard Epstein, "Enforcing Norms: When the Law Gets in the Way," *The Responsive Community* 7 (Fall 1997), 4; Dennis Chong, "Values Versus Interests in the Explanation of Social Conflict," *U. Penn. L. Rev.* 144 (1996), 2079. For an informal discussion, see Jeffrey Rosen, "The Social Police," *The New Yorker*, October 20 & 27, 1997, 170.

[204] E.g., Epstein, "Enforcing Norms," *The Responsive Community* 7 (Fall 1997), 4.

[205] A reviewer pointed out that there is "no single law and economics." It is of course true that there are significant differences within any school, but what makes them into a paradigm, is that these divergent views share certain core assumptions, concepts and perspectives. When I refer to law and economics, law and society, and law and socio-economics, I mean their shared paradigm.

[206] Socio-economics was founded as a discipline in 1989. The International Association of Socio-economics soon featured all the attributes of a scholarly association, including an elected group of officers, a journal, and a series of books.

[207] Robert C. Ellickson, *Order Without Law: How Neighbors Settle Disputes* (Cambridge, Mass.: Harvard University Press, 1991), 138.

[208] Epstein, "Enforcing Norms," *The Responsive Community* 7 (Fall 1997), 7.

[209] Tracey Meares, "Drugs: It's a Question of Connections," *Val. U. L. Rev.* 31 (1997), 579, 594.

[210] Robert D. Cooter, "Law and Unified Social Theory," *Journal of Law and Society* 22 (1995), 50.

[211] Amartya Sen, "Rational Fools," *Philosophy and Public Affairs* 6 (1977), 317; Lester Thurow, *The Zero-Sum Society* (New York: Basic Books, 1980).

[212] Lawrence Lessig, for example, argues that the neoclassical paradigm assumes stable preferences:

> [This assumption is made] [n]ot because economists are so silly as to actually believe they are fixed, but because most of the techniques of economics, like any system of knowledge, function only when certain structures are taken for granted. Usually this discussion is in the context of the evolution of custom, but a custom is no less valuable for our purposes than a direct discussion of social meaning: Custom is just a particular form of social meaning, less symbolic in general, but generated and transformed by the same mechanisms that affect social meaning. Economists aim to understand both custom's origin and its persistence, and it is in tracking this understanding of a custom's persistence that the most useful parallels to the regulation of social meaning can be drawn.
>
> There is nothing about positing a change in preferences, however, that is inconsistent with even Gary Becker's conceptions of the stability of preferences. As he has explained, what his account presumes is the stability of "meta-preferences," not particular preferences.

Lessig, "The Regulation of Social Meaning," *U. Chi. L. Rev.* 62 (1995), 943, 1005 n.207. See also Milton Friedman, "The Methodology of Positive Economics," in *Essays in Positive Economics* (Chicago: University of Chicago Press, 1953).

[213] I refer to the neoclassical paradigm rather than economics because the former is now widely applied in social sciences that do not deal with economic behavior.

See generally Amitai Etzioni, *The Moral Dimension: Toward a New Economics* (New York: Free Press, 1988).

214 See Gary S. Becker and Kevin M. Murphy, "A Theory of Rational Addiction," in Gary S. Becker, ed., *Accounting for Tastes* (Cambridge, Mass.: Harvard University Press, 1996), 50.

215 See Mark Blaug, "The Empirical Status of Human Capital Theory: A Slightly Jaundiced Survey," *Journal of Economic Literature* 14, no. 3 (1976), 827, 837. See also Amitai Etzioni, *The Moral Dimension: Toward a New Economics* (1988).

216 Wassily Leontief, "Interview: Why Economics Needs Input-Output Analysis," *Challenge* (March/April 1985), 27.

217 See Etzioni, *The Moral Dimension: Toward a New Economics*, 141-142.

218 Eric A. Posner, "Law, Economics, and Inefficient Norms," *U. Penn. L. Rev.* 144 (1996), 1697, 1699.

219 Lessig, "The Regulation of Social Meaning," *U. Chi. L. Rev.* 62 (1995), 943, 1044.

220 Sunstein, "Social Norms and Social Roles," *Colum. L. Rev.* 96 (1996), 903, 939.

221 Ibid., 935.

222 See Kingsley Davis, *The Human Society* (New York: MacMillan, 1949).

223 On the difference between treating people as a product of their social status versus the creation of their project, see Arthur Schlesinger, Jr., *The Disuniting of America: Reflections on a Multicultural Society* (Knoxville, Tenn.: Whittle Books, 1991).

224 Intrinsic affirmation refers to the sense one has when one acts in a manner consistent with one's moral commitments. This sense is often treated, particularly by reductionists, as if it were just another source of satisfaction (i.e., pleasure). However, these acts often entail pain or deferred gratification, and the feelings they generate are far more complex than mere satisfaction. For additional discussion, see Amitai Etzioni, *The Moral Dimension: Toward a New Economics* (New York: Free Press, 1988).

225 See generally Richard McAdams, "The Origin, Development, and Regulation of Norms," *Mich. L. Rev.* 96 (1997), 338, 381. See also Robert D. Cooter, "Decentralized Law for a Complex Economy: The Structural Approach to Adjudicating the New Law Merchant," *U. Penn. L. Rev.* 144 (1996), 1643, 1662. Shame can be turned into guilt, a point not discussed here.

226 See Dan M. Kahan, "What Do Alternative Sanctions Mean?," *U. Chi. L. Rev.* 63 (1996), 591. In Chapter 13, the notion of social norm enforcement of law through shame, and Professor Kahan's thesis, are further explored.

227 Alan Lewis, *The Psychology of Taxation* (New York: Palgrave MacMillan, 1982).

228 This statement raises an important question: when should social norms be challenged on normative grounds? Dealing with this issue would take the

discussion too far off track. See Etzioni, *The Moral Dimension*, 217-257 (for discussion of the selection and critical assessment of core societal values).

229 George J. Stigler and Gary S. Becker claim that preferences are fixed. "[O]ne does not argue over tastes," they reason, "for the same reason that one does not argue over the Rocky Mountains—both are there, will be there next year, too, and are the same to all men." Stigler and Becker, "De Gustibus Non Est Disputandum," *American Economic Review* 67 (1977), 76. Later, Becker retreated somewhat from this position. It is still very widely held by neoclassical economists.

230 Robert C. Ellickson, *Order Without Law: How Neighbors Settle Disputes* (Cambridge, Mass.: Harvard University Press, 1991), 156.

231 Robert D. Cooter, "Law and Unified Social Theory," *Journal of Law and Society* 22 (1995), 50.

232 See Charles Lindbloom, *The Intelligence of Democracy: Decision Making through Mutual Adjustment* (New York: Free Press, 1965). See also Herbert A. Simon, *Administrative Behavior: A Study of Decision Making Processes in Administrative Organizations*, 4th ed. (New York: Free Press, 1997); Amartya Sen, "Rational Fools," *Philosophy and Public Affairs* 6 (1977).

233 See, for a list of seminal socio-economic writings, The Communitarian Network, *Communitarian Bibliography*, available at http://www.icps.gwu.edu/communitarian-bibliography/ (accessed December 24, 2010).

234 Lawrence Kohlberg, "Moral Development," in David Sills, ed., *International Encyclopedia of the Social Sciences* (New York: MacMillan, 1968), 483.

235 Martin L. Hoffman, *Childrearing Antecedents of Moral Internalization* (unpublished manuscript, on file with the author). See also Hoffman, "Moral Internationalization, Parental Power, and the Nature of Parent-Child Interaction," *Developmental Psychology* 11 (1975), 228-239; Hoffman, "Child-rearing Practices and Moral Development: Generalizations from Empirical Research," *Child Development* 34 (1963), 295-318.

236 Cooter, Book Review, "Against Legal Centrism," *Calif. L. Rev.* 81 (1993), 417, 426-427.

237 McAdams, "The Origin, Development, and Regulation of Norms," *Mich. L. Rev.* 96 (1997), 338, 376.

238 Ibid., 380-381.

239 Lessig, "The Regulation of Social Meaning," *U. Chi. L. Rev.* 62 (1995), 943, 957-962.

240 Cooter calls this process internalization as well. Yet the phenomenon he describes is not necessarily compatible with common usage of the term. See Cooter, "Decentralized Law for a Complex Economy," *U. Penn. L. Rev.* 144 (1996), 1643, 1643.

241 Ibid., 1662.

242 Ibid., 1662 (footnotes omitted).

243 Lawrence Kohlberg, "Moral Stages and Moralization," in Thomas Lickona, ed., *Moral Development and Behavior* (New York: Holt, Rinehart and Winston, 1976), 31, 32-35.

244 Though Kohlberg himself clearly does believe that "moral stage is a good predictor of action" (ibid., 32).

245 Ibid.

246 See Stigler and Becker, "De Gustibus Non Est Disputandum," *American Economic Review* 67 (1977), 76, discussed as noted above.

247 While it often flows from authority figures or elites to followers, this need not always be the case. Members of a community can work out a shared position in which peers persuade those who may initially have differed on normative issues, drawing on non-rational means. For additional discussion, see the examination of moral dialogues in Etzioni, *The Moral Dimension*, 85-118. Moral dialogues are also seen to be important to human rights, as explored above in Chapter 7.

248 Chapter 15 explores the dilemma of respecting sub-cultures and different religions while preserving a national ethos, and the idea of the "melting pot."

249 Stigler and Becker write: "A consumer may indirectly receive utility from a market good, yet the utility depends not only on the quantity of the good but also the consumer's knowledge of its true or alleged properties." Stigler and Becker, "De Gustibus Non Est Disputandum," 84.

250 Ibid., 83-84.

251 Becker acknowledges the significant effect of habits acquired during childhood, and concedes that these may make little sense as the individual grows up. Yet far from conceding the possibility of non-rational behavior, Becker argues that this is the case because "it may not pay to try to greatly change habits as the environment changes." Becker, "Habits, Addictions, and Traditions," in *Accounting for Tastes*, 118, 127.

Again, not a bit of evidence is provided concerning the costs of changing habits as compared to losses incurred by not changing them. See also Lessig, "The Regulation of Social Meaning," *U. Chi. L. Rev.* 62 (1995), 943 (on habits).

252 McAdams, "The Origin, Development, and Regulation of Norms," *Mich. L. Rev.* 96 (1997), 338, 358.

253 Ellickson, *Order Without Law: How Neighbors Settle Disputes*, 167 (emphasis in original). Note that "cooperative" is synonymous with "rational" in the language of the Prisoner's Dilemma.

254 Robert Axelrod, *The Evolution of Cooperation* (New York: Basic Books, 1984).

255 Robert Cooter, "Normative Failure Theory of Law," *Cornell L. Rev.* 82 (1997), 947, 950-951.

256 See Robert Shiler, "Stock Prices and Social Dynamics," *Brookings Papers on Economic Activity* 2 (1984), 457-498. See also Gary S. Becker, "Norms and the Formation of Preferences," in *Accounting for Tastes*, 226.

257 See Douglas C. North, *Structure and Change in Economic History* (New York: Norton, 1981).

258 Aaron Wildavksy, "Choosing Preferences by Constructing Institutions: A Cultural Theory of Preference Formation," *American Political Science Review* 81, no. 3 (1987).

259 Cooter uses this example to illustrate rational reasoning. Actually it is a prime example of persuasion by appeal to values the actor already holds, rather than appeal to facts and logic. See Cooter, "Decentralized Law for a Complex Economy," *U. Penn. L. Rev.* 144 (1996), 1643, 1661.

260 Talcott Parsons, *The Structure of Social Action* (New York: McGraw Hill, 1937).

261 This can be empirically demonstrated. In situations where respect for tradition prevails, changing instrumental factors will not modify behavior, or at least, only if this is carried to great extremes. Most people will not eat human flesh, however hungry they are, if they are not members of a culture whose social norms legitimates cannibalism. There are, of course, limited exceptions to this rule under extreme conditions. See Piers Paul Read, *Alive: The Story of the Andes Survivors* (Philadelphia, Penn.: J.B. Lippincott Co., 1974) (for reports of cannibalism among survivors of a plane crash in the remote Andes mountains); A. W. Brian Simpson, *Cannibalism and the Common Law* (Chicago: University of Chicago Press, 1984) (history behind yachting disaster and the later famous trial of the men who ate crewman Richard Parker, *Regina v. Dudley and Stephens*, 14 Q.B.D. 273 (1884)).

262 Chong, "Values Versus Interests in the Explanation of Social Conflict," *U. Penn. L. Rev.* 144 (1996), 2079, 2101.

263 Ibid., 2094-2095.

264 Ibid., 2132.

265 Lessig, "The Regulation of Social Meaning," *U. Chi. L. Rev.* 62 (1995), 943, 1006 (citation omitted).

266 See Gordon Tullock, *Private Wants, Public Means: An Economic Analysis of the Desirable Scope of Government* (New York: Basic Books, 1970).

Chapter 11

267 National Commission on Civic Renewal, *A Nation of Spectators: How Civic Disengagement Weakens America and What We Can Do About It*, Final Report of The National Commission on Civic Renewal (Washington, D.C.: Island Press, 1999); Council on Civil Society, Institute for American Values, *A Call to Civil Society: Why Democracy Needs Moral Truths* (New York: Institute for American Values, 1998).

268 See Amitai Etzioni, *The Spirit of Community: Rights, Responsibilities, and the Communitarian Agenda* (New York: Touchstone, 1994).

269 Etzioni, *The Spirit of Community: Rights, Responsibilities, and the Communitarian Agenda* (1994); Etzioni, *The New Golden Rule: Community and Morality in A Democratic Society* (New York: Basic Books, 1997).

270 Bernard Susser, *Political Ideology in the Modern World* (Upper Saddle River, N.J.: Allyn and Bacon, 1995), 277.

271 John A. Hall, "In Search of Civil Society," in John A. Hall, ed., *Civil Society: Theory, History, Comparison* (Cambridge, Mass.: Polity Press, 1995), 25.

272 Victor Perez-Diaz, "The Possibility of Civil Society," in John A. Hall, ed., *Civil Society: Theory, History, Comparison* (Cambridge, Mass.: Polity Press, 1995), 80, 81.

273 Neera Chandhoke, *State and Civil Society: Explorations in Political Theory* (Thousand Oaks, Cal.: Sage, 1995), 9.

274 For older derivations of the phrase, see Dennis H. Wrong, *The Problem of Order* (New York: Free Press, 1994), 87-88; Dominique Colas, *Civil Society and Fanaticism: Conjoined Histories*, trans. Amy Jacob (Stanford: Stanford University Press, 1997), xv, 9, 24-25, 33.

275 Susan H. Williams, "A Feminist Reassessment of Civil Society," *Indiana L.J.* 72 (1997), 425; Linda C. McClain and James E. Fleming, "Some Questions for Civil Society-Revivalists," in Symposium on Legal and Constitutional Implications of the Calls to Revive Civil Society, *Chi.-Kent L. Rev.* 75 (2000), 301.

276 Robert N. Bellah, *The Good Society* (New York: Vintage Books, 1992).

277 Jean Bethke Elshtain, *Democracy on Trial* (New York: Basic Books, 1995), 16.

278 Peter L. Berger and Richard John Neuhaus, "Response," in Michael Novak, ed., *To Empower People: From State to Civil Society* (Washington, D.C.: American Enterprise Institute, 1996), 148-149.

279 Robert Fine and Shirin Rai, eds., *Civil Society: Democratic Perspectives* (Portland, Ore.: Frank Cass, 1997); Benjamin R. Barber, *A Place for Us: How to Make Society Civil and Democracy Strong* (New York: Hill and Wang, 1998); E.J. Dionne, Jr., ed., "Why civil society? Why now?," *Brookings Review* 15, no. 4 (Fall 1997), 4-8; Robert D. Putnam, *Making Democracy Work: Civic Traditions in Modern Italy* (Princeton, N.J.: Princeton University Press, 1993).

280 Robert D. Putnam, "Bowling Alone, Revisited," *The Responsive Community* 5, no. 2 (Spring 1995), 18, 18.

281 Nancy L. Rosenblum, *Membership and Morals: The Personal Uses of Pluralism in America* (Princeton, N.J.: Princeton University Press, 1998).

282 Amitai Etzioni and Robert P. George, "Virtue and State: A Dialogue," *The Responsive Community* 9, no. 2 (Spring 1999), 54, 54-66.

283 For more discussion, see Charles K. Rowley, ed., *Classical Liberalism and Civil Society* (Northampton, Mass.: Edward Elgar, 1997).

284 John Rawls, *Political Liberalism* (New York: Columbia University Press, 1996), 382-383.

285 Michael Walzer, "The Concept of Civil Society," in Michael Walzer, ed., *Toward a Global Civil Society* (Providence, R.I.: Berghahn Books, 1995), 7, 16.

286 For discussion of these as compared to reasoned deliberations, see Amitai Etzioni, *The New Golden Rule*, 102-110. For their application to human rights, see Chapter 7 above.

287 For discussions of the moral voice, see Amitai Etzioni, *The New Golden Rule*, 119-159.

288 William Kymlicka, *Contemporary Political Philosophy: An Introduction* (New York: Oxford University Press, 1990), 219-220.

289 See William R. Lund, "Taking Autonomy Seriously," *The Responsive Community* 9, no.1 (Winter 1998/1999), 10, 20.

290 Elizabeth Frazer and Nicola Lacey, *The Politics of Community: A Feminist Critique of the Liberal-Communitarian Debate* (Toronto: University of Toronto Press, 1993); Susan Moller Okin, *Justice, Gender and the Family* (New York: Basic Books, 1989).

291 Amitai Etzioni, *The Limits of Privacy* (New York: Basic Books, 1999), 183-216.

292 Benjamin R. Barber, *A Place For Us: How to Make Society Civil and Democracy Strong* (New York: Hill and Wang, 1998).

293 Harry C. Boyte and Nancy N. Kari, *Building America: The Democratic Promise of Public Work* (Philadelphia: Temple University Press, 1996).

294 Etzioni, *The New Golden Rule*, 160-188.

295 Vincent N. Campbell and Richard A. Bond, "Evaluation of a Character Education Curriculum," in David C. McClelland, ed., *Education for Values* (New York: Irvington Publishers, 1982), 134.

296 Amy Gutmann, *Democratic Education* (Princeton, N.J.: Princeton University Press, 1987). Compare to William A. Galston, *Liberal Purposes: Goods, Virtues, and Diversity in the Liberal State* (New York: Cambridge University Press, 1991).

297 For additional discussion of this subject, see Eamonn Callan, *Creating Citizens: Political Education and Liberal Democracy* (Oxford: Clarendon Press, 1997), 44-47.

298 See Robert D. Putnam, *Making Democracy Work: Civic Traditions in Modern Italy* (Princeton, N.J.: Princeton University Press, 1993).

299 Ibid., 90.

300 The relevant differences are instrumental, rather than principled or normative (for example, the relative size, the level of public education, etc.).

301 See Suzanna Sherry, "Without Virtue There Can Be No Liberty," *Minn. L. Rev.* 78 (1993), 61. A somewhat similar point is made by the noted civil theorist Benjamin Barber. While Barber is a fan of voluntary associations generally, he warns against those that are so "privatistic, or parochial, or particularistic" that they undermine democracy. He writes: "Parochialism enhances the immediate

tie between neighbors by separating them from alien 'others,' but it subverts the wider ties required by democracy—ties that can be nurtured only by an expanding imagination bound to no particular sect or fraternity." See Benjamin R. Barber, *Strong Democracy: Participatory Politics for a New Age* (Berkeley: University of California Press, 1984), 234-235.

302 Peter L. Berger and Richard John Neuhaus, "Response," in Michael Novak, ed., *To Empower People: From State to Civil Society* (Washington, D.C.: American Enterprise Institute, 1996), 149-150.

303 Michael Walzer, "The Concept of Civil Society," in Michael Walzer, ed., *Toward a Global Civil Society* (Providence, R.I.: Berghahn Books, 1995), 25.

304 For further discussion and criticism of this conception of civil society, see Jean Cohen, "Interpreting the Notion of Civil Society," in Michael Walzer, ed., *Toward a Global Civil Society* (1995), 35.

305 See Amitai Etzioni, *The New Golden Rule*, 217-257.

306 Ibid., Ch. 8.

307 David Boaz, "Enemies of Civil Society," *Cato Policy Report* (July/August 1999), 2.

308 E.J. Dionne, Jr., ed., "Why civil society? Why now?," *Brookings Review* 15, no. 4 (Fall 1997), 5.

309 Robert D. Putnam, "Bowling Alone, Revisited," *The Responsive Community* 5, no. 2 (1995), 18-33.

310 Jean Bethke Elsthtain, *Democracy on Trial* (New York: Basic Books, 1995), 5.

311 See, for instance, *A Call to Civil Society*, 7.

312 See, e.g., David Blankenhorn, "Conclusion: The Possibility of Civil Society," in Mary Ann Glendon and David Blankenhorn, eds., *Seedbeds of Virtue: Sources of Competence, Character, and Citizenship in American Society* (New York: Institute for American Values, 1995), 271.

313 Linda C. McClain and James E. Fleming, "Some Questions for Civil Society-Revivalists," *Chi.-Kent L. Rev.* 75 (2000), 301, 331-336 (commenting on David Blankenhorn's chapter from the preceding footnote).

314 See "Henry Sumner Maine," in David L. Sills, ed., *International Encyclopedia of the Social Sciences* 9 (New York: Macmillan & Free Press, 1968), 530-532.

315 Amitai Etzioni, *The New Golden Rule*.

316 See, e.g., Section I above. Nor need a society abandon its national ethos in order to guarantee that a minority's *rights* are ensured, as is discussed below in Chapter 15.

317 For discussion see Louis Hartz, *The Liberal Tradition in America: An Interpretation of American Political Thought Since the Revolution* (New York: Harcourt, 1955). In response to Hartz, see Isaac Kramnick, *Republicanism and Bourgeois Radicalism: Political Ideology in Late Eighteenth-Century England and America* (Ithaca, N.Y.: Cornell University Press, 1990); J.G.A. Pocock, *The Machiavellian Moment: Florentine Political Thought and the Atlantic Repub-*

lican Tradition (Princeton, N.J.: Princeton University Press, 1975); Rogers M. Smith, "Beyond Tocqueville, Myrdal, and Hartz: The Multiple Traditions in America," *American Political Science Review* 87 (1993), 549, 553-554, 559.

[318] For much more discussion, see Etzioni, *The New Golden Rule*, 34-57.

[319] See Max Weber, *The Protestant Ethic and the Spirit of Capitalism*, Talcott Parsons trans. (New York: Routledge, 1992).

[320] Council on Civil Society, Institute for American Values, *A Call to Civil Society: Why Democracy Needs Moral Truths* (New York: Institute for American Values, 1998), 12.

[321] See Sanford Levinson, *Constitutional Faith* (Princeton, N.J.: Princeton University Press, 1988), 90-121; and Etzioni, *The New Golden Rule*, 217-258.

Chapter 12

[322] The author is indebted to S. Riane Harper for extensive research assistance on a previous version of this essay.

[323] David Heald, "Varieties of Transparency," in Christopher Hood and David Heald, eds., *Transparency: The Key to Better Governance?* (New York: Oxford University Press, 2006), 26; Bernard I. Finel and Kristin M. Lord, "The Surprising Logic of Transparency," *International Studies Quarterly* no. 43 (1999), 316.

[324] "Openness might therefore be thought of as a characteristic of the organization, where transparency also requires external receptors capable of processing information made available." Heald, "Varieties of Transparency," 26.

[325] Christopher Hood, "Transparency in Historical Perspective," in *Transparency: The Key to Better Governance?*, 9.

[326] Transparency International, the National Democratic Institute, and the site Openthegovernment.org are examples of organizations promoting more transparency in government.

[327] Finel and Lord, "The Surprising Logic of Transparency," 315.

[328] Hood, "Transparency in Historical Perspective," in *Transparency: The Key to Better Governance?*, 15.

[329] Steven Thomma and Kevin G. Hall, for McClatchy, "President Rolls Out Financial Regulation Proposal," *The Spokesman-Review*, June 18, 2009.

[330] Gene Healy, "Obama's Statist Ambitions," *DC Examiner*, June 30, 2009; Mark Calabria, "Cato Scholar Comments on the Obama Administration's Financial Regulation Reforms," June 17, 2009, available at http://www.cato.org /pressroom.php?display=ncomments&id=242 (accessed November 22, 2010).

[331] L. Gordon Crovitz, "Transparency is More Powerful than Regulation," *Wall Street Journal*, March 30, 2009, available at http://online.wsj.com/article/ SB123837223623167841.html (accessed November 22, 2010).

332 Richard H. Thaler and Cass R. Sunstein, "Disclosure is the Best Kind of Credit Regulation," *Wall Street Journal*, August 13, 2008.

333 Ibid.

334 I use the term guidance rather than control because it captures the observation that as a rule, regulations merely point to preferred choices and are rarely fully coercive in their adaptation. For more discussion, see Amitai Etzioni, *The Active Society* (New York: Free Press, 1968).

335 Dennis H. Wrong, *The Problem of Order: What Unites and Divides Society* (Cambridge, Mass.: Harvard University Press, 1995).

336 Ibid. For the comparison of social controls and disclosure in the context of criminal activity and shaming, see Chapter 13, and in the context of corporate crime and sentencing, see Chapter 14.

337 Patrick Birkinshaw, "Transparency as a Human Right," in David Heald and Christopher Hood, eds., *Transparency: The Key to Better Governance?* (New York: Oxford University Press, 2006), 50; Finel and Lord, "The Surprising Logic of Transparency," at 320; Mark Landler, "Experts Say Full Disclosure May Not Always Be Best Tactic in Diplomacy," *New York Times*, June 17, 2009; Kristin M. Lord, *The Perils and Promise of Global Transparency* (Albany: State University of New York Press, 2006), 3; Warren Bennis, "The New Transparency," in Warren Bennis, Daniel Goleman, et al., *Transparency: How Leaders Create a Culture of Candor* (San Francisco: Jossey-Bass, 2008), 11. For further discussion, see also Albert Breton, Gianluigi Galeotti, Pierre Salmon and Ronald Wintrobe, *The Economics of Transparency in Politics* (Burlington, Vt.: Ashgate, 2007).

338 M. Joseph Sirgy and Chenting Su, "The Ethics of Consumer Sovereignty in an Age of High Tech," *Journal of Business Ethics* 28 (November 2002), 2.

339 Ibid., 1.

340 Susanna Kim Ripken, "The Dangers and Drawbacks of the Disclosure Antidote: Toward a More Substantive Approach to Securities Regulation," *Baylor L. Rev.* 58 (2006), 195. See also Jerry Brito and Jerry Ellig, "An Accountability Agenda," *Regulation* 31, no. 4 (2008/9), 5.

341 Ripken, "The Dangers and Drawbacks of the Disclosure Antidote," 153-154.

342 Tara Vishwanath and Daniel Kaufmann, "Toward Transparency: New Approaches and their Application to Financial Markets," *World Bank Research Observer* 16, no. 1(2001), 41.

343 Onora O'Neill, "Transparency and the Ethics of Communication," in *Transparency: The Key to Better Governance?*, 13.

344 Jeremy Bentham, unpublished, from the manuscripts of Jeremy Bentham in the Library of University College London.

345 *McConnell v. Federal Election Commission* (02-1674), 540 U.S. 93 (2003).

346 Ron Wyden, "Transparency: A Prescription Against Malpractice," *Public Health Reports* 110, no. 4 (1995), 380; see also Clayton Christensen, "What

---

Obama's Health Care Team Can Learn from Massachusetts," *Harvard Business Review,* Jan. 22, 2009.

[347] See Michael B. Rothberg, Elizabeth Morsi, Evan M. Benjamin, Penelope S. Pekow and Peter K. Lindenauer, "Choosing The Best Hospital: The Limitations of Public Quality Reporting," *Health Affairs* 27, no. 6 (2008), 1680-1687.

[348] Jay Mathews, "FAQ: Best High Schools," *Newsweek,* May 17, 2008, available at http://www.newsweek.com/id/137415/ (accessed November 22, 2010); Andrew J. Rotherman, "In Politics of School Reform, Transparency Doesn't Equal Accountability," *U.S. News and World Report,* May 14, 2009, available at http://www.usnews.com/articles/opinion/2009/05/14/in-politics-of-school-reform-transparency-doesnt-equal-accountability.html (accessed November 22, 2010).

[349] Richard Thaler and Cass Sunstein, *Nudge: Improving Decisions about Health, Wealth and Happiness* (New Haven, Conn.: Yale University Press, 2008).

[350] Jason Zweig, "About Time: Regulation Based on Human Nature," *Wall Street Journal,* June 20-21, 2009.

[351] Martin N. Marshall, Paul G Shekelle, et al., "The Public Release of Performance Data," *JAMA* 283, no. 14 (April 12, 2000), 1866.

[352] Bennis, "The New Transparency," 108-109.

[353] For example: Scott B. Keller, Mike Landry, Jeanne Olson, Anne M. Velliquette, Scot Burton and J. Craig Andrews, "The Effects of Nutrition Package Claims, Nutrition Facts Panels, and Motivation to Process Nutrition Information on Consumer Product Evaluations," *Journal of Public Policy and Marketing* 16, no. 2 (1997), 256-269; Scot Burton, Abhijit Biswas and Richard Netemeyer, "Effects of Alternative Nutrition Label Formats and Nutrition Reference Information on Consumer Perceptions, Comprehension, and Product Evaluations," *Journal of Public Policy and Marketing* 13, no. 1 (1994), 36-47; John C. Kozup, Elizabeth H. Creyer and Scot Burton, "Making Healthful Food Choices: The Influence of Health Claims and Nutrition Information on Consumers' Evaluations of Packaged Food Products and Restaurant Menu Items," *Journal of Marketing* 67, no. 2 (2003), 19-34.

[354] Mario F. Teisl and Alan S. Levy, "Does Nutrition Labeling Lead to Healthier Eating?," *Journal of Food Distribution Research* 28, no. 3 (1997), 19-26.

[355] Michael B. Mazis, Louis A. Morris, et al., "Evaluation of the Alcohol Warning Label: Initial Survey Results," *Journal of Public Policy and Marketing* 10, no. 1 (1991), 229-241, at 239-240.

[356] Fred W. Morgan and Jeffery J. Stoltman, "Television Advertising Disclosures: An Empirical Assessment," *Journal of Business and Psychology* 16, no. 4 (2002), 515-535, at 535.

[357] Jeffrey Kraus, "Campaign Finance Reform Reconsidered: New York's Public Finance Program After Fifteen Years," *Forum* 3, no. 4 (2006), 20. See also Nathaniel Persily and Kelli Lammi, "Perceptions of Corruption and Campaign Finance: When Public Opinion Determines Constitutional Law," *U. Penn. L. Rev.* 153 (2004), 119-120.

358 Kyoungrae Jung, "The Impact of Information Disclosure on Quality of Care in HMO Markets," presented at iHEA 2007 6th World Congress: Explorations in Health Economics Paper (abstract and download available at SSNR: http://ssrn.com/abstract=992234).

359 21 U.S.C. § 301 et seq. (1938), as amended over the years. For example, the, Nutrition Labeling and Education Act of 1990 gives the FDA the authority to require nutrition labeling of most foods it regulates.

360 William Walker, "Some Reflections on Transparency in the Contemporary Security Environment," *Disarmament Forum* 2 (2003), 55, available at http://www.unidir.org/pdf/articles/pdf-art1912.pdf/ (accessed November 22, 2010).

361 "Card Statements Blind Consumers to Debt Traps," Communication Research Institute, Melbourne, Australia (June 2009), available at http://communication.org.au/news/news/Card-statements-blind-consumers-to-debt-trap/16,1.html/ (accessed November 22, 2010).

362 Sara Hansard, "Insurers, Banks Criticize Obama's Proposed Consumer Watchdog Agency," *Investment News*, June 24, 2009.

363 Prat, "The Wrong Kind of Transparency," 93. See also Heald, "Transparency As an Instrumental Value," in Christopher Hood and David Heald, eds., *Transparency: The Key to Better Governance?* (New York: Oxford University Press, 2006), 62; Lord, *The Perils and Promise of Global Transparency*, 5; Bennis, "The New Transparency," 112-113.

364 Kaveh G. Shojania and Alan J. Forster, "Hospital Mortality: When Failure is Not a Good Measure," *Canadian Medical Association Journal* 179, no. 2 (2008), 155.

365 In Chapter 14, various severities of fines and punishments and their economic effects are considered in the context of corporate crime.

366 Ann Florini, ed., *The Right to Know: Transparency for an Open World* (New York: Columbia University Press, 2007), 4.

367 Daniel Kahneman, Jack Knetsch and Richard Thaler, "Anomalies: The Endowment Effect, Loss Aversion, and Status Quo Bias," *Journal of Economic Perspectives* 55 (1991), 193-206; J. Edward Russo and Paul J. H. Shoemaker, *Decision Traps* (New York: Simon and Schuster, 1989); Arthur Lefford, "The Influence of Emotional Subject Matter on Logical Reasoning," *Journal of General Psychology* 34 (1946), 127-151; Amos Tversky and Daniel Kahneman, "Judgment under Uncertainty: Heuristics and Biases," *Science* 185 (1974), 1124-1131; Marco Cipriani and Antonio Guarino, "Herd Behavior and Contagion in Financial Markets," *B.E. Journal of Economics* 8, no. 1 (2008); Robert H. Frank, Thomas Gilovich and Dennis T. Regan, "Does Studying Economics Inhibit Cooperation?," *Journal of Economic Perspectives* 7, no. 3 (1993), 159-171.

368 Brigitte Madrian and Dennis Shea, "The Power of Suggestion: Inertia in 401(k) Participation and Savings Behavior," *Quarterly Journal of Economics* 116 (2002), 1149-1225; Kahneman, Knetsch and Thaler, "Anomalies"; Uri Gneezy and Aldo Rustichini, "Incentives, Punishment, and Behavior," in C. F. Camerer, G. Lowenstein and M. Rabin, eds., *Advances in Behavioral Economics* (Princeton, N.J.: Princeton University Press, 2004), 573-589.

369 Gordon Malkiel Burton, *A Random Walk Down Wall Street: Including a Life Cycle Guide to Personal Investing*, 7th ed. (New York: Norton, 1999).

370 Ripken, "The Dangers and Drawbacks of the Disclosure Antidote," 186.

371 Ibid., 185.

372 Onora O'Neill, "Transparency and the Ethics of Communication," 81 (emphasis added).

373 Vishwanath and Kaufmann, "Toward Transparency: New Approaches and their Application to Financial Markets," 43. See also Onora O'Neill, "Transparency and the Ethics of Communication," 88-89; Virginia A. Sharpe, "Science, Bioethics, and the Public Interest: On the Need for Transparency," *Hastings Center Report* 32 (2002), 24.

374 Ripken, "The Dangers and Drawbacks of the Disclosure Antidote," 163.

375 Ripken, "The Dangers and Drawbacks of the Disclosure Antidote," 178.

376 Helen Margetts, "Transparency and Digital Government," in *Transparency: The Key to Better Governance?*, 201; Richard H. Thaler, "Mortgages Made Simple," *New York Times*, July 5, 2009.

377 See http://www.truste.com/.

378 E.g., Elizabeth F. Farrell and Martin Van Der Werf, "Playing the Rankings Game," *Chronicle of Higher Education*, May 25, 2007; Glen Kersten, "Grading on the Curve: College Ratings and Rankings," *Points of Reference*, January 2000; Eric Hoover, "Liberal-Arts College Group Plans to Help Develop Alternative to Commercial Rankings," *Chronicle of Higher Education*, June 20, 2007.

379 Jean DerGurahian, "Canes, Walkers Tied to Many Injuries in Seniors: CDC," June 29, 2009, available at http://www.modernhealthcare.com/article/20090629/REG/306299953 (accessed November 22, 2010).

380 *Wired* Blogs, "Report: TrustE Sites Twice As Likely to Be Bad Actors," September 26, 2006, at http://www.wired.com/threatlevel/2006/09/report_truste_s/ (accessed November 22, 2010).

381 Ibid. See also Eric L. Lane, "Consumer Protection in the Eco-mark Era: A Preliminary Survey and Assessment of Anti-Greenwashing Activity and Eco-mark Enforcement," *John Marshall Rev. Intel. Prop. L.* 9, no. 3 (2010), 742 (examining Greenlist, Energy Star, and similar industry ratings of pro-environmentalism that are industry sponsored and use criteria that may not promote accurate consumer information while appearing ostensibly objective).

382 Kimberly Kindy and Lyndsey Layton, "Purity of Federal 'Organic' Label Is Questioned," *Washington Post*, July 3, 2009. See also Heald, "Transparency As an Instrumental Value," 70; Onora O'Neill, "Transparency and the Ethics of Communication," 75.

383 George S. Day, "Assessing the Effects of Information Disclosure Requirements," *Journal of Marketing* 40 (1976), 42.

384 Ripken, "The Dangers and Drawbacks of the Disclosure Antidote," 159-160 (footnotes omitted).

385 William M. Sage, "Regulating Through Information," *Colum. L. Rev.* 99 (1999), 1729.

386 See Ripken, "The Dangers and Drawbacks of the Disclosure Antidote."

387 Ibid., 149; Note, "Disclosure as a Legislative Device," *Harvard L. Rev.* 76 (1963), 1273-1293.

Chapter 13

388 See Panel (Ray Suarez, host), "Good Samaritan Laws," *Talk of the Nation*, October 1, 1998, Transcript #98100102-211.

389 Ibid.

390 Letter to the Editor, *Sacramento Bee*, September 20, 1998, F4.

391 Ann Sjoerdsma, "Is America Too Dangerous for a 'Good Samaritan Law'?," *The Record* (Bergen, N.J.), September 16, 1997.

392 Panel, "Good Samaritan Laws," *Talk of the Nation*, October 1, 1998, Transcript #98100102-211. The larger sociological issues of shaming and juvenile crime, and the need for alternative punishments and the use of *social* instead of legal controls, are explored throughout Amitai Etzioni, *The Monochrome Society* (Princeton: Princeton University Press, 2003). In the present book's Chapter 14, the author notes the related issue of potential alternative punishments, including publicizing the offense and rehabilitation, for *corporate* crime.

393 Dan M. Kahan, "What Do Alternative Sanctions Mean?," *U. Chi. L. Rev.* 63 (1996), 635, cited in "Sentencing Lawbreakers to a Dose of Shame," in "Civic Renewal," *CQ Researcher*, March 21, 1997, 252.

394 Jan Hoffman, "Crime and Punishment: Shame Gains Popularity," *New York Times*, January 16, 1997, A1, cited in "Sentencing Lawbreakers to a Dose of Shame," *CQ Researcher*, March 21, 1997, 252.

395 Toni M. Mossaro, "Shame, Culture, and American Criminal Law," *Michigan L. Rev.* 89 (1991), 1880, 1881 (discussing and citing 1989 article from *Arizona Republic*). See generally Anne-Marie McAlinden, *The Shaming of Sexual Offenders: Risk, Retribution and Reintegration* (Oxford: Hart Publishing, 2007), 42-46, 165-195.

396 Massaro, ibid., 1888 (citing 1984 article from *National Law Journal*).

397 Pam Belluck, "Forget Prisons: Americans Cry Out for the Pillory," *New York Times*, October 4, 1998, A4, A5.

398 Quoted in "Sentencing Lawbreakers to a Dose of Shame," *CQ Researcher*, March 21, 1997, 252.

399 Quoted in Tony Allen-Mills, "American Criminals Sentenced to Shame," *Sunday Times*, April 20, 1997.

400 Quoted in American Civil Liberties Union (ACLU Media), "ACLU Answers: Megan's Law," received by fax, December 3, 1996.

⁴⁰¹ Ibid. See also ACLU, "Megan's Law Prompts Fairness Question in Online Notification of Sex Offenders," January 19, 1999, available at http://www aclu .org/content/megans-law-prompts-fairness-question-online-notification-sex-offenders/ (accessed November 3, 2010) ("Notification laws will not prevent sex offenders from committing crimes, the ACLU said but rather will victimize rehabilitated ex-offenders and their families. Those in stable environments have the highest likelihood of staying out of trouble. Attacking the family unit by publicizing this information will only make ex-offenders more likely to reoffend."); McAlinden, *The Shaming of Sexual Offenders: Risk, Retribution and Reintegration* (2007), 42-46.

Note that the ACLU fax and its previous press releases on the subject ostensibly quoted from USC law professor Evan Cherminsky, but it is apparent they meant Erwin Chemerinsky, dean of UC-Irvine's new law school, who previously taught at USC.

⁴⁰² Carl F. Horowitz, "The Shaming Sham," *The American Prospect*, March-April 1997, 71.

⁴⁰³ Panel, "Good Samaritan Laws," *Talk of the Nation*, October 1, 1998.

⁴⁰⁴ Quoted in Michael Grunwald, "Shame Makes Comeback in Courtrooms," *Boston Globe*, December 28, 1997, A1.

⁴⁰⁵ Toni M. Mossaro, "Shame, Culture, and American Criminal Law," *Michigan L. Rev.* 89 (1991), 1880, 1883 (footnotes omitted).

⁴⁰⁶ Ibid., 1921.

⁴⁰⁷ Ibid., 1923. See also Dan Markel, "Wrong Turns on the Road to Alternative Sanctions: Reflections on the Future of Shaming Punishments and Restorative Justice," *Tex. L. Rev.* 85 (2007), 1385.

⁴⁰⁸ David R. Karp, "The Judicial and Judicious Use of Shame Penalties," *Crime and Delinquency* 44, no. 2 (April 1998), 292.

⁴⁰⁹ Lawrence M. Friedman, *Crime and Punishment in American History* (New York: Basic Books, 1994), 36-37.

⁴¹⁰ Quoted in ibid., 37.

⁴¹¹ Adam J. Hirsch, "From Pillory to Penitentiary: The Rise of Criminal Incarceration in Early Massachusetts," *Michigan L. Rev.* 80 (1982), 1179, 1224. Dr. Hirsch is a historian and currently a law professor at Florida State's law school.

⁴¹² Lawrence M. Friedman, *Crime and Punishment in American History*, 37.

⁴¹³ Ibid., 75 (citation omitted).

⁴¹⁴ See generally, e.g., John Schmitt, Kris Warner, and Sarika Gupta, "The High Budgetary Cost of Incarceration," Center for Economic and Policy Research, Washington, D.C. (June 2010), available at http://www.cepr.net/documents /publications/incarceration-2010-06.pdf/ (accessed November 22, 2010).

Chapter 14

[415] Amitai Etzioni, *The Responsive Society: Collected Essays on Guiding Deliberate Social Change* (San Francisco: Jossey-Bass, 1991), Ch. 5.

[416] This relatively small Oraflex fine has recently been contrasted with massive settlements, fines, and whistleblower lawsuits under the *qui tam* action and related statutes, all levied over the past few years, as discussed in David Evans, "Pfizer Broke the Law By Promoting Drugs for Unapproved Uses," *Bloomberg News*, November 9, 2009, available at http://www.bloomberg.com/apps/news?pid=newsarchive&sid=a4yV1nYxCG0A/ (accessed November 18, 2010).

[417] Philip Shenon, "Report Says Eli Lilly Failed to Tell of 28 Deaths," *New York Times*, August 27, 1985, A16.

[418] Victoria Toensing, "Corporations on Probation: Sentenced to Fail," *Legal Times*, February 12, 1990.

[419] Robert J. Giuffra, "Sentencing Corporations," *American Enterprise* (May-June 1990).

[420] Neil A. Lewis, "White House Aide Intervenes on Tough Fines for Businesses," *New York Times*, April 29, 1990.

[421] Amitai Etzioni, "Going Soft on Corporate Crime," *Washington Post*, April 1, 1990.

[422] Barbara Franklin, "Corporate Penalties: Model Sentencing Guide Rewards Good Behavior," *New York Law Journal*, March 29, 1990.

[423] Stephen Wermiel and Martha Brannigan, "Sentencing Panel Puts Off Debate on Guidelines for Corporate Fines," *Wall Street Journal*, April 11, 1990.

[424] The treatment of Exxon after the Valdez spill is the exception, not the rule; also, in general, environmental groups are more powerful than other groups that support penalties on corporations, such as consumer and other liberal groups.

[425] Testimony of Jeffrey Parker before U.S., Congress, House, Committee on the Judiciary, Subcommittee on Criminal Justice, 101st Cong., 2d sess., May 24, 1990, pp. 463-464.

[426] A fuller discussion of this issue can be found in papers from "A National Conference on Sentencing of the Corporation," George Mason University Law School, Fairfax, Va., October 25, 1990.

For a much more complete discussion of the issue or moral values versus cost/benefit analysis, see Amitai Etzioni, *The Moral Dimension: Toward a New Economics* (New York: Free Press, 1988). For a fuller discussion of corporate crime, deterrent fines, preventative education and methods, and the more recent imposition of penalties and reporting requirements under the Sarbanes-Oxley Act of 2002, see the author's chapter with Derek Mitchell, "Corporate Crime," in Henry N. Pontell and Gilbert L. Geis, eds., *International Handbook of White-Collar and Corporate Crime* (New York: Springer, 2006), Ch. 1.

[427] For further discussion of the commission, see the proceedings of the Cato Institute's (Center for Constitutional Studies') conference "Corporate Sentenc-

ing: The Guidelines Take Hold," Washington, D.C., October 31, 1991. Dr. Block remains Professor Emeritus at Arizona's Eller College of Management.

[428] Gary S. Becker, "The Economic Approach to Fighting Crime," *Business Week*, October 28, 1985, 20.

[429] Parker testimony before House Subcommittee on Criminal Justice, May 24, 1990.

[430] Thomas C. Hayes, "Sick Savings Units Riddled by Fraud, FBI Head Asserts," *New York Times*, April 12, 1990.

[431] Marshall B. Clinard, *Illegal Corporate Behavior* (Washington, D.C.: Department of Justice, 1979), 108. For recent recidivism studies and summaries of Clinard's and other such studies, see Xia Wang and Kristy Holtfreter, "Illegal Corporate Behavior: An Organizational Perspective," Presented at Annual Meeting of American Society of Criminology, May 24, 2009, indexed at http://www.allacademic.com/meta/p126843_index.html/ (accessed November 22, 2010).

[432] See U.S. Sentencing Commission, Draft Guidelines, November 5, 1990, § BC5.

[433] The sociology and preventative implications of similar shaming methods were explored, in the context of juvenile crime and other street crime, in Chapter 13.

[434] Testimony of James Carty of the National Association of Manufacturers before U.S. Congress, House, Committee on the Judiciary, Subcommittee on Criminal Justice, 101st Cong., 2d sess., May 24, 1990, 244.

[435] Federal Register, 55(214): 46612, November 5, 1990.

[436] Testimony of Joseph diGenova before U.S. Sentencing Commission, February 14, 1990.

[437] Testimony of John Borgwardt of Boise Cascade Corporation before U.S. Sentencing Commission, February 14, 1990.

[438] James Traub, "Into the Mouths of Babes," *New York Times Magazine*, July 24, 1988. See also Leonard Buder, "Beech-Nut Is Fined $2 Million for Sale of Fake Apple Juice," *New York Times*, November 14, 1987, A1.

[439] "3 Executives Get 25 Years in Worker's Death," *New York Times*, July 2, 1985. The conviction was later reversed on technical grounds.

[440] "Maker of Aircraft Fasteners Pleads Guilty to Conspiracy," *New York Times*, May 12, 1990.

[441] See Parker testimony before House Subcommittee on Criminal Justice, May 24, 1990, at 446.

Chapter 15

[442] See William Kymlicka, *Liberalism, Community and Culture* (New York: Oxford University Press, 1989).

443 Amitai Etzioni, *The New Golden Rule: Community and Morality in a Democratic Society* (New York: Basic Books, 1996), 127.

444 Anthony Smith, *Nations and Nationalism in the Global Era* (Cambridge, Mass.: Polity Press, 1995).

445 Quoted in John Horton and Susan Mendus, eds., *After MacIntyre: Critical Perspectives on the Work of Alasdair MacIntyre* (South Bend, Ind.: University of Notre Dame Press, 1994), 303.

446 Linda Colley, "Britishness in the 21st Century," 10 Downing Street, December 8, 1999, available at http://www.number-10.gov.uk/output/Page3049.asp/ (accessed July 12, 2008). See generally Christina Julios, *Contemporary British Identity* (Burlington, Vt.: Ashgate, 2008). Dr. Colley is currently a professor of history at Princeton.

447 Bhikhu Parekh, *The Future of Multi-Ethnic Britain: Report of the Commission on the Future of Multi-Ethnic Britain* (London: Profile Books, 2000) ("the Parekh Report").

448 Ibid. A decade later, speeches and symposia are examining the Report, e.g., London School of Economics, "Revisiting the Future of Multi-Ethnic Britain: the Parekh Report 10 Years On," November 23, 2010, at http://www2.lse.ac.uk /publicEvents/events/2010/20101123t1830vOT.aspx/. See also Christopher Allen, "The Death of Multiculturalism: Blaming and Shaming British Muslims, *Durham Anthropology Journal* 14, no. 1 (2007).

449 Cécile Laborde, "From Constitutional to Civic Patriotism," *British Journal of Political Science* 32, no. 4 (2002), 596.

450 Jamie Mayerfeld, "The Myth of Benign Group Identity: A Critique of Liberal Nationalism," *Polity* 30, no. 4 (1998), 576-577.

451 Ibid., 557.

452 Reference here is to those million or so Israeli-Palestinians who live on in what is considered Israel proper and who have no intention of joining a Palestinian state, not those on the West Bank and Gaza.

453 Bernard Avishai, *The Hebrew Republic: How Secular Democracy and Global Enterprise Will Bring Israel Peace at Last* (New York: Houghton Mifflin Harcourt, 2008).

454 This matter has still not been settled even today. For instance, citizens of a Catholic part of Brooklyn, New York, have lodged complaints against a flea market which is open in their neighborhood on Sundays. They suggested that it should be open on Saturday instead. Eric Konigsberg, "The Flea Market is a Success, and the Neighbors Are Furious," *New York Times*, July 26, 2008, Section B.

455 "Israel Marks Its 60th Anniversary," *BBC Online*, May 8, 2008, available at http://news.bbc.co.uk/2/hi/middle_east/7389140.stm/ (accessed November 21, 2010).

456 Courtland Milloy, "Different Beat for Today's Columbus Day," *Washington Post*, October 11, 2004, Metro section.

457 Reuters, "Language Riots Erupt in Madras," *Globe and Mail*, December 11, 1986; "Language Riots in Goa," *Washington Post*, December 22, 1986.

458 Samuel Huntington, *Who Are We? Challenges to America's National Identity* (New York: Simon and Schuster, 2004), 166-167.

459 Ibid., 176-177. See also Thomas F. Pettigrew, "Reactions Toward the New Minorities of Western Europe," *Annual Review of Sociology* 24 (1998), 77-103.

460 Pat Kane, "Brown's Britain: A Warning from History," *Sunday Times*, August 12, 2007, Features section; Tom Buerkle, "A Nation Asks: What Exactly Does It Mean to Be British?" *International Herald Tribune*, May 7, 1999, News section; Patrick Wintour, "Labour Tries to Reclaim the Flag; Ministers Launch Debate on Modern Britishness to Resolve Party's Problem and Put Pressure on Hague," *Guardian*, March 28, 2000, Home section.

461 Robert D. Putnam, "Health and Happiness," in *Bowling Alone: The Collapse and Revival of American Community* (New York: Simon and Schuster, 2000), 326-335; Francis Fukuyama, *The Great Disruption: Human Nature and the Reconstitution of Social Order* (New York: Touchstone, 1999); Robert N. Bellah, Richard Madsen, William M. Sullivan, Ann Swidler and Steven M. Tipton, *Habits of the Heart* (Berkeley: University of California Press, 1985);

462 E.g., Ferdinand Tönnies, *Community and Society*, trans. Charles P. Loomis (East Lansing, Mich.: Michigan State University Press, 1957); Tönnies, *Community and Association*, trans. Charles P. Loomis (London: Routledge & Kegan Paul, 1955); Emile Durkheim, *The Elementary Forms of the Religious Life* (1915; reprint, New York: Collier, 1961); Martin Buber, *I and Thou*, trans. Ronald Gregory Smith (New York: Charles Scribner and Sons, 1970); Martin Buber, *Paths in Utopia* (Boston, Mass.: Beacon Press, 1958).

463 Robert Putnam, *Bowling Alone*, 326, 329.

464 Ibid., 331-333.

465 Michael Sandel, *Liberalism and the Limits of Justice*, 2nd ed. (New York: Cambridge University Press, 1998), 179.

466 See Dennis H. Wrong, *The Problem of Order* (New York: Free Press, 1994).

467 As the solution this chapter proposes rests on the assumption that the basic rights of minority groups will be fully respected, those who live in constitutional democracies will more easily relate to it than people in theocracies, as noted at the outset. Regardless, this is a normative essay, and should apply to all peoples.

468 "Diversity Within Unity," Institute for Communitarian Policy Studies, George Washington University, available at http://communitariannetwork.org/diversity-within-unity/ (accessed December 24, 2010).

469 Samuel Huntington, *Who Are We? Challenges to America's National Identity* (2004), 173-177; Dennis L. Carlson, "Constructing the Margins: Of Multicultural Education and Curriculum Settlements," *Curriculum Inquiry* 25, no. 4 (1995), 407-431; Spike Gillespie, "A Battle Over Books in Texas," *Christian Science Monitor*, November 4, 2003, Features section; Susan Snyder, "Learning Curve for Philadelphia Schools," *Philadelphia Inquirer*, June 1, 2003, Sunday Review section.

470 I leave for another day the question of the difference between native minorities and immigrants; immigrants, not to be confused with asylum seekers, have fewer rights.

471 Jared Bloom and Amitai Etzioni, eds., *The Way We Celebrate* (New York: New York University Press, 2004), 18-19.

472 Ibid., 19-20.

473 *Church of Lukumi Babalu Aye v. City of Hialeah*, 508 U.S. 520 (1993).

474 "Diversity Within Unity," ICPS, George Washington University, http://communitariannetwork.org/diversity-within-unity; Amitai Etzioni, *Security First: For a Muscular Moral Foreign Policy* (New Haven, Conn.: Yale University Press, 2007), 186-192; Amitai Etzioni, "Should the United States Support Religious Education in the Islamic World?," *Journal of Church and State* (Spring 2006), 279-281.

475 See Francis Wilkinson, "Segregationist Dreamer," *New York Times Magazine*, December 31, 2006.

476 Samuel Huntington, *Who Are We? Challenges to America's National Identity* (2004). See also Carol Swain, *New White Nationalism in America: Its Challenge to Integration* (New York: Cambridge University Press, 2004); Carol Swain, *Debating Immigration* (New York: Cambridge University Press, 2007).

INDEX

A

Achieved relations, versus ascribed; *see* Civil society.

ACLU, 17, 19, 42, 62-63, 167, 233n.

Advertising, as changing preferences, 120-122; empirical studies of disclaimers in, 155.

Afghanistan, 6, 15, 51, 69, 133.

Air travel, safety fears about, 22; air traffic rates, 22-23.

Airport security; *see* TSA.

Al Qaeda, 54, 56; *see also* Sept. 11.

American Civil Liberties Union; *see* ACLU.

American Values, Institute for; *see* Institute for American Values.

An-Na'im, Abdullah, 77, 214n.

Axelrod, Robert, 123.

B

Becker, Gary, 120, 181-182, 221n, 222n.

Bellah, Robert, 84, 192, 215n, 224n, 237n.

Bentham, Jeremy, 158.

Berger, Peter, 132, 142, 224n.

Bhat, Radhika, 211n, 217n.

Bhutto, Benazir, assassination of, 54.

Bin Laden, Osama, 55-56; *see also* Sept. 11.

Block, Michael, 181.

Bowling alone; *see* Putnam, Robert; Civil Society.

Brandeis, Louis, origins of right to privacy, 100, 217n; on transparency, 149.

Brown, Gordon, administration's characterization of terrorists, 4.

Bush, George W., administration's characterization of terrorists, 4; immunity from for telephone and Internet companies, 43.

C

Campaign finance reform, 152-153.

Caning; *see* Shaming.

Carnivore, FBI program of intercepts, 40-43.

Carter, Jimmy, administration's position on corporate crime sentences, 175.

CCTV, use of for preventing crime and terrorism, 94; *see also* Surveillance.

Chemerinsky, Erwin, 167.

Chong, Dennis, 125-126.

Citizens, in civil society, 136-138; and national ethos, 187-198.

Civic Renewal, National Commission; *see* National Commission on Civic Renewal.

Civil liberties, loss of after Sept. 11 attacks, 17; how lost generally, 17-32; and law enforcement, 27-29; willingness to sacrifice for security, 24-27, 62, 68; balancing with security, 43-49, 61-62, 88; of minorities, 187; *see also* ACLU, Electronic Privacy Information Center; Privacy.

Civil society, generally, 129-148; defined, 130-132; distinguished from good society, 132, 148; philosophical foundations of, 133-135; role of the law, 135-136; virtues promoted by, 138-140; and voluntary associations, 141-143; achieved relations, versus ascribed, 144-146; rights and responsibilities in, 146-147.

Civilians, distinction from soldier defined, 6; casualties of, 15, 52, 56-57, 60; problem of insurgents mixing into, 51-52; loss of life from UAS, 56-57; antagonized by UAS, 58-59.

Cole, U.S.S., bombing of, 54.

Colley, Linda, 189, 192, 236n.

Communitarianism, defined, i-ii, 83-84; rights and responsibilities, ii-iii, 84, 146-147; view of privacy and security, 43-49, Fourth Amendment as reflection of, 43, 64, 85; and platform of the civil society, 129, 135; view of individual identity, 193; view of national ethos, 187-198.

Cooter, Robert, 115, 117-119, 123-125, 221n.

Crime rates, public perceptions, 29-31; recidivism, 102-104, effect of registering offenders, 103-104.

Criminal record; *see* Social forgiveness, Second chances.

Cultural differences, respect for; *see* National ethos.

D

Democracy, threats to, 17-32; definition of, 18; as enhanced by security measures, 31-32; as rationale for U.S. foreign policy, 67; as promoted by transparency, 152-153; and PACs, 157.

Diversity Within Unity (DUW), 194-198.

DNA, tests and databases, 83-97; preventive collections, 86, balancing interests, 88-91; uses for common good, 91-94; Hi/Hi profiles, 94, accountability, 95-97.

Drones, *see* Unmanned Aviation Systems (UAS).

E

Ehrenhalt, Alan, 84.

Electronic Communications Privacy Act (ECPA), 35-36, 38.

Electronic Privacy Information Center (EPIC), 41, 63.

Ellickson, Robert, 110-111, 117, 221n.

Elshtain, Jean Bethke, ii, 131, , 144-145, 224n, 226n.

Encryption, 37.

Enemy combatant, distinction from terrorist, 5.

Epstein, Richard, 109, 111, 219n.

Ethos, national; *see* National ethos.

Etzioni, Amitai, activity in insurgency, 51; participation in NPR debate, 165-166, 168, 232n; public position on corporate crime sentencing, 178-179; Diversity Within Unity movement, 194-198.

Eyewitness identifications, unreliability, 91, 216n.

Polls, on safety and civil liberties, 23-29; on air travel, 22-24.

Predator, 54; *see also* Unmanned Aviation Systems (UAS).

Prescriptive state, generally, 129-148; role of the law, 135-136; virtues promoted by, 140-141; and voluntary associations, 144; achieved relations, versus ascribed, 144-146; rights and responsibilities in, 146-147.

Privacy Rights Clearinghouse, 101.

Privacy, as enhanced by technologies, 33-37; balancing with security, 43-49, 61-64, 90; and TSA scanners, 61-62; and DNA tests and databanks, 83-90; of secret past, 99; origins of right to, 100; measures to protect reputations, 105.

Punishment, shaming, 165-173, alternate, 165-173, 181-185; corporate, 175-185.

Putnam, Robert, 132, 142, 144, 146, 192, 225-226n, 237-238n.

R

Rawls, John, 119, 133-134, 225n.

Recidivism, 102-104; *see also* Crime rates.

Regulation, era of deregulation, 150; mandatory disclosure as form of, 156-157.

Rehabilitation, corporate, 183; *see also* Recidivism.

Rights and responsibilities, as communitarian norms, ii-iii, 146-147; *see also* civil liberties.

Ripken, Susanna Kim, 152, 158, 161, 229n.

Rorty, Richard, 79, 214n.

Rosen, Jeffrey, 63, 215n, 218n.

Rosenblum, Nancy, 132.

S

Samaritan Acts; *see* Good Samaritans.

Sandel, Michael, ii, 84, 193, 238n.

Scanners, airport screening, 61-64.

T

Taylor, Charles , ii, 75, 84.

Technology, as enhancing privacy, 33-37; liberalizing, 35, scanners and privacy, 61-64; DNA banks, 83-97; social forgiveness, possibility in light of, 99-101.

Terrorists, status of, 3-15; defined, 5, 203-204n; distinguished from soldiers, 5-6; distinguished from criminals, 7-9; failure of criminal law to deter, 7, 55; rights owed to, 10; procedures for, 10-11; using civilian status , 52; prospective prevention of, 7, 55.

Tönnies, Ferdinand, i, 83, 237n.

Toqueville. Alexis de, 130, 132.

Transparency, 149-164.

TSA, airport screening, 61-64.

U

UAS, *see* Unmanned Aviation Systems (UAS).

Unmanned Aviation Systems (UAS), generally, 51-60; and civilian status of terrorists, 53-54; collateral damage to civilians, 56-57; legality of, 57-58; alienation of population, 58-59; argument they kill in cold blood, 59-60; moral turning point of use, 60.

USA PATRIOT ACT; *see* Patriot Act.

V

Voluntary associations; *see* Civil society.

W

Wall Street Journal, 150, 162, 179.

Walzer, Michael, 84, 134-135, 215n.

War, terrorism compared, 5-6; moral turning point of, 60; civilian casualties in, 15, 52, 56-57, 60.

Warren, Samuel, article on privacy with Brandeis, 100, 217n.

Webb, James, 101.

About the Author

After receiving his Ph.D. in Sociology from the University of California, Berkeley in 1958, Amitai Etzioni was a Professor of Sociology at Columbia University for 20 years, part of that time as the chair of the department. He was a guest scholar at the Brookings Institution in 1978 before serving as a Senior Advisor to the White House from 1979-1980. In 1980, Dr. Etzioni was named the first University Professor at The George Washington University, where he is the Director of the Institute for Communitarian Policy Studies. From 1987-1989, he was the Thomas Henry Carroll Ford Foundation Professor at the Harvard Business School.

Dr. Etzioni served as the president of the American Sociological Association in 1994-1995, and in 1989-1990 was the founding president of the international Society for the Advancement of Socio-Economics. In 1990, he founded the Communitarian Network, a not-for-profit, non-partisan organization dedicated to shoring up the moral, social and political foundations of society. He was the editor of *The Responsive Community: Rights and Responsibilities*, the organization's quarterly journal, from 1991-2004. In 1991, the press began referring to Dr. Etzioni as the "guru" of the communitarian movement.

Dr. Etzioni is the author of numerous books, including *The Monochrome Society* (Princeton University Press, 2001), *The Limits of Privacy* (Basic Books, 1999), *The New Golden Rule* (Basic Books, 1996), which received the Simon Wiesenthal Center's 1997 Tolerance Book Award, *The Spirit of Community* (Crown Books, 1993), and *The Moral Dimension: Toward a New Economics* (Free Press, 1988). His most recent books include *Security First: For a Muscular, Moral Foreign Policy* (Yale University Press, 2008), *My Brother's Keeper: A Memoir and a Message* (Rowman & Littlefield, 2003), and *From Empire to Community: A New Approach to International Relations* (Palgrave Macmillan, 2004).

Outside of academia, Dr. Etzioni's voice is frequently heard in the media. He has contributed numerous articles and columns to magazines and newspapers, as well as academic journals and law reviews. In 2001, he was named among the top 100 American intellectuals as measured by academic citations in Richard Posner's book, *Public Intellectuals: A Study of Decline.*

Also in 2001, Dr. Etzioni received the John P. McGovern Award in Behavioral Sciences, as well as the Officer's Cross of the Order of Merit of the Federal Republic of Germany. He was also the recipient of the Seventh James Wilbur Award for Extraordinary Contributions to the Appreciation and Advancement of Human Values by the Conference on Value Inquiry, as well as the Sociological Practice Association's Outstanding Contribution Award.

Dr. Etzioni lives in Washington, D.C.